THE CHANNEL ISLANDS
UNDER TUDOR GOVERNMENT
1485-1642

The Channel Islands under Tudor Government, 1485-1642

A STUDY IN ADMINISTRATIVE HISTORY

By

A. J. EAGLESTON, C.V.O.
Sometime Scholar of Balliol College.

CAMBRIDGE
Published for the Guernsey Society
AT THE UNIVERSITY PRESS
1949

PUBLISHED BY
THE SYNDICS OF THE CAMBRIDGE UNIVERSITY PRESS
London Office : Bentley House, N.W.1
American Branch : New York
Agents for Canada, India, and Pakistan : Macmillan

Printed by
The Guernsey Press Co., Ltd.,
at their Printing Works,
8, Smith Street and Le Marchant Street,
St. Peter Port, Guernsey Channel Islands

PREFACE

When he died, in January 1944, Arthur John Eagleston left in typescript a book on Tudor government in the Channel Islands. From 1913 until his retirement in 1932 he had been an Assistant Secretary in the Home Office, and for a part of that time he had been in charge of the Channel Islands business there. Eagleston was characteristic of the best products of the Oxford Greats school (he took a first both in Mods. and Greats and was a scholar of Balliol) ; his interests were wide and in many places they went deep ; he combined the qualities of a good administrator with the instincts and tastes of a scholar. His work at the Home Office frequently led him into the writing of reports and handbooks which required considerable historical research for their compilation ; and it is thus not surprising that this handling of the affairs of the Channel Islands, incomprehensible apart from their deep historical roots, should have interested him in their history at large. This book is one of the products of an active retirement.

His work here makes no claim to comprehensiveness, even in the limited period with which it is primarily concerned. It is a study of the principles and practice of government in an outpost of English rule during the century and a half when England was governed directly by the Sovereign and the Privy Council. The peculiar value of this work lies in the author's method of approach. He could understand the problems facing Elizabeth's Council and the captains and governors it sent out to manage the islands, because he himself had handled the twentieth-century successors of those problems ; better than most insular or academic historians he could put himself imaginatively in the shoes of Sir Thomas Leighton or Sir John Peyton, or the secretary of state for the time being, and feel as they felt when they were involved in a constitutional conflict with the islanders. He is, indeed, often putting what might be described as the " Whitehall " point of view in these controversies ; and it is most important that someone should have been found to do this, for the islanders' point of view has been put time and again by the island historians. But more than this, aided by publications which did not exist in Le Quesne's or Tupper's days, Eagleston had read more deeply in the State Papers and the records of the Council than any previous historian of the Channel Islands ; nor did he neglect the records kept in the islands themselves, those records which have been so rarely disturbed by the historian. But all this learning is worn very lightly ; the book is written easily and fluently, and the author is writing all the time of real people and real problems, not a set of abstractions.

The part of a literary executor is self-repression. In preparing this manuscript for the press I have tried to do no more than the revising and correcting which the author himself would have done, resisting all temptation to take up interesting or arguable points or to investigate questions raised by him ; for there is no finality in historical work. In checking his references, for example, I have merely seen to it that the reference printed is the reference he wished to give and that it is given in recognizable and consistent form. Save in a very few instances, I have not expanded or modified his apparatus. The only substantial alterations I have made are these : a passage in the first chapter describing current governmental practice in the Channel Islands has been cut out altogether, because the reforms of 1948 have largely destroyed the point of it ; the author's chapter XI, which was very long, has been divided into two, and the subsections rearranged so that the political controversies should go into chapter XI and the ecclesiastical difficulties into chapter XII ; and in the footnotes references to the State Papers have been translated into references to the corresponding entries in the printed *Calendars*, even where it is clear, as it often is, that the author was quoting directly from the original document—I have done this because the *Calendars* are more accessible to most people than the State Papers in the Public Record Office, they frequently contain all the information that is required, and it is in any case a perfectly simple matter to refer from the *Calendar* to the original where that may seem desirable.

This book owes its publication to the determination of Mrs. Eagleston, to the initiative and enterprise of the council of the Guernsey Society, to the generous co-operation of La Société Guernesiaise and to the most acceptable grants made by the Jersey Society in London, La Société Jersiaise and Balliol College, Oxford. Acknowledgment is also due to the Trustees of the National Maritime Museum, Greenwich, and to the Trustees of the British Museum, for permission to reproduce pictures in their collections. Mr. J. Hurstfield kindly helped me with the proofs, and made many useful suggestions. The index was compiled by Mrs. Eagleston and Miss Venetia Eagleston.

In a sense the book is a memorial to its author ; but he would no doubt have wished to dedicate it to the memory of his only son, John Nelson Eagleston who died, while a prisoner of war in Germany, in March, 1945.

JOHN LE PATOUREL.

CONTENTS

LIST OF ILLUSTRATIONS.

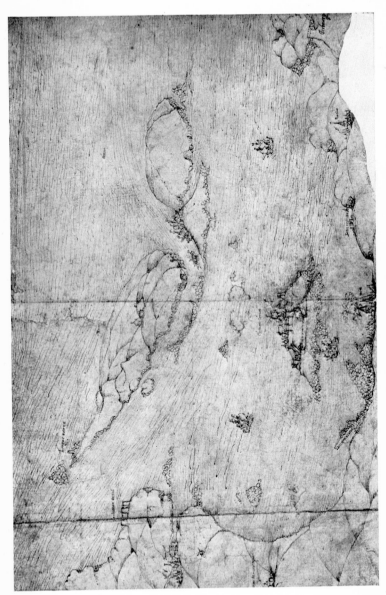

View of St. Peter Port Town, Castle Cornet and the Roadstead, Guernsey, in the Sixteenth Century.

Frontispiece

CHAPTER I

INTRODUCTORY

The purpose of this book is to give an account of some aspects of the history of the Channel Islands during the period when the Tudor system of government prevailed in the islands and England alike, that is from 1485 until the outbreak of the Civil War in 1642. It deals for the most part with constitutional questions ; the relations of the islanders and their institutions to the governors sent to them from England and to the King and his Council in London ; and it tends to regard island affairs as presenting a series of administrative problems which the three parties just mentioned had to solve between them. There is a general reason for this : these questions may well be regarded as the chief matters of interest in the history of the islands ; they were very little concerned in the national wars of Henry VIII, Mary, or Elizabeth, or in any of the great movements of the sixteenth century except to a limited extent in the Reformation. There is also a particular and personal reason : the writer's own interest in the subject is due to the fact that for some years he was in charge of the division of the Home Office which is responsible for dealing with Channel Island business and as such constantly had to do with the relations of the islands with the government of Great Britain. This is a most educative experience for any Englishman ; and nothing is better adapted to correct the insular frame of mind which disposes Englishmen to think that something like their own constitution and system of Parliamentary government is the only method by which a modern people can enjoy the blessings of freedom and self-government than a little practical experience of Channel Island affairs.

These islands, though ruled by kings of England since 1066, have developed in a way which has no exact parallel in England or in the British Empire. Having their own system of law, based on the customary law of Normandy, they have never been incorporated into the system of English local government, but have been treated as a miniature dominion of the crown, administered by a governor who, under different titles at different periods, represented the king and was responsible to him for their safe keeping and good government.

1

Partly because, as very small communities, they could not develop political institutions or aspirations as highly developed as those of the American Colonies in the eighteenth century or the Dominions in the nineteenth and twentieth centuries, and partly because English dominions on the continent of Europe since the sixteenth century have been of small extent in relation to the Empire as a whole, the Channel Islands have always preserved a particularly intimate relationship with the Sovereign and his Privy Council. Thus Channel Island legislation, to this day, takes the form of an Order-in-Council, though much of it originates in the islands themselves, and, when it originates in England, the islands are consulted. In the event of a difference between the islands and Whitehall, however, a peremptory order may constitutionally be issued ; and thus, so far as the forms of institutions go, it may be said that the Channel Islands can show an important relic of that conciliar government which was characteristic of English affairs in Tudor times.[1]

In the sixteenth century, however, and down to the outbreak of the Civil War in 1642, the government of England and the government of the Channel Islands were all of a piece. The Sovereign and his Privy Council were the working government of England, and they supervised, often minutely, the affairs of Jersey and Guernsey. The subject and the period here chosen have therefore a double interest : the historian who examines the facts of Channel Island history in the sixteenth and early seventeenth centuries is necessarily studying at close quarters the practical working of the Tudor system of government and the political history which underlay it ; at the same time he is studying the period in which many of the modern institutions of government in the Channel Islands took shape, often in a form which is recognizable still to this day. Our story begins with the first introduction of the system. In the Channel Islands no less than in England the accession of Henry VII marks the end of the Middle Ages and the beginning of modern history. The process of constitutional development which is still going on in the islands takes its beginning from the disputes between the people of Jersey and their Tudor governor ; and it was in consequence of one of these disputes that the king issued the Order-in-Council of 1495, which was intended to lay down the lines on which he meant his officers to govern Jersey, and which has in fact become a most important source of the constitutional law of the island.

The beginning of a new epoch is apparent in the historian's material as well as his subject matter : his sources become more abundant in quantity and more modern in form. In-

2

stead of the documents of the mediæval period, for the most part formal in character, such as charters, writs, and exchequer accounts, we now get petitions of grievances, reports of royal commissions of inquiry, and, from the accession of Elizabeth onwards, considerable quantities of documents of a kind which is familiar to administrators today—complaints and memorials on general questions, the observations of the governors, Council Office memoranda on the points raised in them, and the reports of royal commissions and committees of Council drawn up after hearing and considering the arguments of all parties to the dispute. These documents are not so abundant or continuous as they are in later times, but they do not differ substantially in kind from the original records on which the historian of the eighteenth or nineteenth century works.

In fact it is only with the Tudors that anything like continuous narrative history becomes possible at all. The material is still uneven and patchy : the extant records which supply our information come in jerks rather than in a steady stream, and it is a curious fact that the two islands appear in the light of history alternately and not together : they go in and out like the old man and woman in the old-fashioned toy barometers. For the first part of our period the light falls entirely on Jersey : in addition to the *Chroniques de Jersey* which are discussed below, there is a considerable body of important documents ; but until shortly before the accession of Elizabeth there are relatively few documents relating to Guernsey in the Record Office. From 1560 on the other hand until well on in the reign of James I there is an almost continuous stream of documents about the affairs of Guernsey, and only one or two isolated sets of papers dealing with Jersey. Under James I the position is reversed again ; we hear little of Guernsey and there is abundant material for Jersey giving full details of the two great controversies which were fought out in the island—the dispute between the bailiff and the governor as to their respective positions and powers, and the question whether the island church should be Presbyterian or Episcopal. From 1624 until the outbreak of the Civil War in 1642 both islands relapse into obscurity : between 1626 and 1630 the exigencies of Charles I's wars with France and Spain occasionally gave rise to disputes on constitutional points between the islanders and their English governors, but except for this we have very few documents for this period.

With the Tudors we get not only a body of records of the modern type but also a narrative history. The sixteenth century *Chroniques de Jersey*[2] is the first attempt at a continuous history of either island. It covers the period 1460-1580 ; for the later part it is contemporary, and what was not within the author's own knowledge unquestionably comes direct from people who played the leading part in the scenes described. The book is anonymous, but from internal evidence it was certainly written in or shortly after the year 1585 by a member of the de Carteret family, and describes the chief events in the history of the island and of the de Carteret family, which to the author's mind are practically the same thing. Mourant in his edition very aptly compares it to the family records of the Roman noble houses which were embodied in funeral orations pronounced over the illustrious dead. And certainly the *Laudatio* delivered over the ashes of a Fabius or Metellus in the days of Cicero must have been a history of the Republic as illustrated by the exploits of members of the family very much on the lines of the *Chroniques de Jersey*, though the latter ends with a wedding, not a funeral, in the family.[3] A first reading of the *Chroniques* is apt to awaken a feeling of mistrust. The family bias is so obvious, and the narrative is so full of picturesque details as to suggest that it is a romance. Further examination however restores confidence. The author was clearly a man of intelligence and education with a respectable knowledge of English as well as insular history ; he thoroughly understands the value of original documents, and makes good use of the island archives ; and wherever his history can be checked by contemporary records it is apparent that the family and local tradition he followed is singularly accurate in substance and detail. His family bias really affects his story very little ; his family feeling is so thorough-going and so naif that he hardly realises that what is good for the de Carterets may not be good for Jersey. He can say in one paragraph that the governor was a tyrant addicted to rape, violence, and extortion, and in the next that he was on the best of terms with the de Carteret family. This suggests that he was hardly likely to misrepresent the truth for the sake of the family. His prejudice has affected his narrative in quite a different way : he does not mis-state facts, but he quietly omits some things which he does not like.

We have therefore in the *Chroniques de Jersey* a valuable, and in the main a very accurate account of the island history during this period.

CHAPTER II.

JERSEY UNDER HENRY VII.

The accession of Henry VII marks an important change in the political position of the Channel Islands : it is the date of their final separation from continental Normandy. For nearly forty years after the reopening of the Hundred Years War by Henry V, the islands were situated, as they had been before 1204, in the middle of an Anglo-Norman dominion which bestrode the Channel. After the final loss of lower Normandy in 1450 they became once more, what they remained till the end of the nineteenth century, outposts and frontier fortresses of England against the continent and ports of refuge for shipping going up and down the Channel. Henry VII with his usual realistic and unsentimental outlook gave up any thought of re-conquering Normandy. The idea lingered for a time at the back of men's minds and occasionally made a shadowy re-appearance,[1] but it had ceased to be a serious object of policy and for all practical purposes it was dead.

But it must not be forgotten that the separation of the islands from Normandy was two-sided. The severed parts of the old province might have been reunited by a French occupation of the islands as well as by an English conquest of Normandy, and at certain points in the Wars of the Roses this seemed possible and even likely. It was always a temptation to the losing side to offer the islands to France in return for French help. Queen Margaret and the Lancastrian party drove a bargain of this kind in 1463, and a French force under the Comte de Maulevrier occupied Jersey and held it for seven years until, on the final restoration of Edward IV, an expedition from Guernsey, commanded by Richard Harliston, Vice-Admiral of England, drove out the French with the enthusiastic support of the people of Jersey.[2] Harliston was made governor of the islands ; and after the Lancastrian triumph at Bosworth he, being a strong Yorkist, took the part of Lambert Simnel and attempted to make himself lord of Jersey under the protection of the French and the Duchess of Burgundy (Margaret of York), but he was driven out by the inhabitants. After this the French made no more efforts to unite the islands to Normandy. They did indeed surprise Sark in 1549—it was uninhabited—and

5

occupied it with a garrison for several years ;[3] but this was merely the establishment of an outpost for privateering purposes and was not followed by any expedition against the other islands.

Any help that the French got in these attempts came solely from English partisans of York or Lancaster as the case might be : the islanders themselves remained throughout unshakeably loyal to the English connection. During the French occupation of Jersey a spy once reported to the governor that one Rawlin Payn had said to him that if an English force landed he would find five hundred men who would turn out with him in their harness to support them, and that there were in the island a thousand good men for the King of England and scarcely any one who loved the French.[4] At the subsequent enquiry by the French authorities Payn denied on oath that he had said anything of the kind ; but I have no doubt that he did say it, and in any case it accurately represented the general feeling of the islanders. At a later date the Jersey people told their governor, the Protector Somerset, in a formal petition, that they would " rather die English than live French " ;[5] and Edward IV's charter of 1469 contains a well deserved compliment to their continued loyalty, and in particular to their recent services in helping to recover the island and castle from the French.[6]

Henry VII at once confirmed the former charter of the islands[7] and continued Harliston,[8] the soldier who had recovered Jersey from the French, in the governorship. The tradition embodied in the *Chroniques* is entirely favourable to Harliston. Allowance must of course be made for the fact that his daughter and heiress married the eldest son of the Seigneur of St. Ouen and was later the heroine of an epic struggle between her husband and the English governor of the day ;[9] but there is no reason to doubt the chronicler's story that Harliston was courteous, liberal (this probably means that he was not too strict in exacting royal dues), and generally popular. It was especially remembered—this detail can hardly have been invented—that he was much bent on encouraging the use of the longbow in the island, as became an English soldier of the fifteenth century ; and that he did this by the simple and direct method of tipping any boy or young man whom he saw practising with the long bow. Naturally he found a good many archers in his way when he made his regular Saturday journey from Mont Orgueil to St. Helier and back.

He did not however retain his office long under the new dynasty : his sympathies were Yorkist, as was natural for a man

6

who had been brought up in the household of the Duke of York and had served Edward IV for many years ; and as soon as a Yorkist pretender appeared Harliston took his part. The Chronicler says that when Perkin Warbeck was set up by the Duchess of Burgundy, Harliston left his government and went to Flanders to support him. But the Chronicler though accurate in substance is often out in his dates ; and it appears from the *Rolls of Parliament* that Harliston was attainted for joining the Earl of Lincoln in Lambert Simnel's rising. He was pardoned in September 1486, when he is described as " late of the island of Jersey " ; but he was attainted again in 1494 as a supporter of Perkin Warbeck.[10] It appears that after 1485 he thought to make himself lord of the Isles under the protection of France and the Duchess of Burgundy, but was prevented by the inhabitants.[11]

After Harliston's treason the government of the islands was divided, and he was succeeded in Jersey by Matthew Baker,[12] esquire of the body to Henry VII, whom tradition represents as a " surly, malicious, and vindictive man who did wrong to and extorted money from many people ". This brought him into conflict with the Royal Court and particularly with the Seigneur of St. Ouen, who according to the *Chroniques*, was the leader of the islanders in resisting Baker's tyranny and earned his special hatred thereby. The story of the struggle between de Carteret and the oppressor is told with an abundance of picturesque detail which recalls Scott's mediæval romances. Baker—so the story runs—forged a letter in which de Carteret offered to betray the castle to the French ; arranged for one of his men to find it in the street, and asserted that de Carteret had dropped it there while lying in ambush to kill him. De Carteret was brought before the Royal Court ; the finder of the letter, a ruffian named Le Boutillier whom de Carteret had once saved from hanging, offered wager of battle. The bailiff, who was in the plot with Baker, refused to listen to de Carteret's plea that he ought not to be required to meet a man of Le Boutillier's low birth and criminal record, fixed a day for the judicial combat, and sent both parties to prison meanwhile.[13] The Chronicler adds that Le Boutillier was allowed to go where he liked about the castle and was well fed, but de Carteret was kept in close prison and very hardly treated ; also that Baker took the additional precaution, when the lists were got ready for the combat, of having ditches and holes dug and covered over so as to trap de Carteret.[14] The governor then went to London to put his side of the case before the King and Council, and to provide against opposition gave orders that no vessel should leave the island without special permission, and persuaded his colleague in Guernsey to do the same.

But all his schemes were brought to nothing by the courage of a woman. Margaret de Carteret, the wife of the seigneur of St. Ouen and daughter of Harliston, had been confined just before Baker left the island ; but seeing that her husband and children were threatened with ruin, she took a boat to Guernsey only five days after her child was born and persuaded a friend there to take her to England. She overtook Baker at Poole, and only escaped him by a special providence. Baker was waiting on the quay when her boat came in, wishing to hear the news from Guernsey, but at that moment there came such a hailstorm that he and all his people took shelter in a house, and Margaret de Carteret landed without his knowing. Next day at dawn she started for London and went straight to Bishop Fox, who laid her case before the king and got her an order under the Great Seal for her husband to be released and the case to be heard before the Privy Council. She was just in time, for as she came out of the Presence Chamber after her audience she met Baker coming in. Margaret rode hard for Southampton with the royal order, and by great good fortune found a boat on the point of sailing for Jersey ; so that she got home and set her husband free the very evening before the date fixed for the combat.

De Carteret went to London himself, armed with testimonials to his loyalty and general character from the Royal Court and the leading men of the island, and won a complete victory over Baker. The Chronicler says that at the moment Baker was merely censured for his conduct, and the Council reconciled him with de Carteret, but that not long after on fuller information he was dismissed.

Exactly how far the details of this picturesque story can be accepted must remain doubtful. Some of the touches, e.g. about the unfair arrangements for the combat, suggest that the Chronicler had been reading romances of chivalry. But Margaret's journey to London must surely be true in the main : it seems an unlikely story to be invented out of nothing, and it is just such as would have been carefully preserved by family tradition. And the main point of the whole thing—that there were serious complaints of misgovernment by Baker—is certainly true. Henry VII issued two orders dealing at length with the government of Jersey, the powers of the captain, and the rights of the inhabitants. He certainly would never have troubled to do this unless difficulties had arisen ; and in fact the earlier of the two orders expressly sets out that " many and divers grievances doleances and complaints " have been made

8

by the inhabitants of Jersey against Matthew Baker and that it is made for the purpose " of ending and obliterating the said complaints and controversies . . . . . . to provide for the tranquility and repose of our said subjects and between our captain and them to place and nourish perfect amity ". The terms of the orders make it clear that the complaints against Baker related mainly to arbitrary arrests and imprisonments, and his levying of taxes and dues, and also that there had been some friction between the Governor and the Royal Court as to their respective powers and jurisdiction.

It is remarkable that two orders should have been issued within a few months to deal with the same subject, and the differences between them are no less remarkable, the first, dated 3rd Nov. 1494, is a writ of Privy Seal :[15] it refers to the island complaints as actually pending before Council, describes Baker as governor, and speaks of reconciling him with the Jersey people. Its subject matter is limited to four or five clauses, all directed to restricting the powers of the governor and protecting the people from oppression by him. The second, dated 17th June, 1495,[16] is an Order in Council, mentions no governor by name, and contains a long series of regulations for the government of the island, dealing not only with the conduct of the governor, but with the duties of other local authorities, and the defence of the island generally. It seems odd that the King and his Council should have made two bites at the cherry like this : and the only reasonable inference is that the story in the *Chroniques* is substantially correct : when the matter first came before the king he thought that Baker and the islanders might be reconciled, and issued instructions intended to deal with the complaints of oppression ; but when the case was thoroughly examined in Council it was realised that Baker's misgovernment was more serious than had been supposed at first ; and he was dismissed and a formal Order in Council drawn up laying down a complete code of regulations for the administration of the Island. The king had of course good reason to desire that the islanders should be well-governed and contented : it was only a generation since a French governor and garrison had held the castle and the island for some years, and Henry's recent experience with Harliston had pointed the moral.

Henry VII's ordinances are of great importance in the history of the islands. Some of his regulations came to be, and still remain, fundamental rules of the constitution, though in all probability he had no intention of legislating on constitutional matters, or indeed of doing any more than issuing instructions for the administration of the government, or at most defining existing customary rights and duties. The Orders relate in terms to Jersey only, but they are in fact a statement of the system of government which the Tudors applied to both islands, and they form a carefully devised code for the control of outlying possessions which were also frontier fortresses, corresponding in that day to Malta and Gibraltar at a later time. The object is clearly to provide for the safety of the fortresses, and to give the governor all necessary powers for that purpose, to protect the people from arbitrary misuse of authority or infringement of their ancient rights and liberties, and to provide against misconduct by the local authorities or infringements of the King's rights by the inhabitants.

Under the head of defence there is a series of regulations directed to the safe-keeping of the castle : only natives of England and Wales of approved loyalty are to be employed in the garrison (2 and 29) ; a market is to be held weekly near the castle so that the garrison need not go about the island to buy food (8) ; the garrison are to be paid their wages in the castle (27) ; and the customary inspection of the castle by the local authorities on St. George's day to be carefully controlled (3). With this we should perhaps class the regulation (11) which forbids any of the islanders to cause any assemblage of people except it be for the defence of the island.

Under the second head we find that the captain is to be sworn on entering office and find surety for his conduct (1) : he is expressly forbidden to imprison any islander on his own authority except in case of treason, or to interfere in any way in any judicial procedure : all law cases are to be tried by the Royal Court (4 and 5) ; the soldiers of the garrison are to be answerable under the ordinary law for any injury done to the inhabitants (2) ; the governor is to help the Royal Court to enforce their decisions in case of disobedience (6) ; he is forbidden to require any licence for journeys between the island and the king's other dominions but he is to be notified before anyone goes out of the dominions (13 and Order of 1494).

Certain regulations are apparently intended to control both the governor and the local authorities. Thus the nomination of the bailiff, dean, vicomte, and procureur is to be made by the king, and neither the governor nor the jurats to interfere (17) ; neither governor nor jurats are to levy any taxes " except it be done at the good grace of the king for the common weal and defence of the island " (15). And any dispute between the governor and the jurats is to come before the Council for decision. (28)

Regulations are also laid down for the conduct of the local officials of the island. Jurats of the Royal Court are forbidden to keep taverns, bakeries, or breweries (22) ; they are to take an oath on entering office (18), to keep a signed record of the acts of the Court (19) : and the island seal is only to be used in the presence of seven jurats (26) : when any jurat is found in fault and censured for not well and loyally executing his office, he is to be expelled from office and never again received therein or in any other office in the island (20).

Provision is also made for conducting the election of the constables of the parishes (24), and there are regulations safeguarding the king's right to levy customs (14), to require a day's work a year from every inhabitant on the fortifications of the castle (12), and to call on his tenants in chief to help in the defence of the island (10).

As I have already suggested, it is very unlikely that the king when issuing these ordinances had any idea of introducing constitutional reforms or passing legislation affecting the constitution of the islands in any way. The only passage in either document which refers to any constitutional question is the clause of the first Order, which directs that the ancient laws and privileges shall be maintained, and annuls any acts of any governor which might hinder the execution of those ancient laws. It is clear that the Orders were not intended to modify the existing fundamental law of the island in any way, but to lay down a series of executive rules regulating the conduct of the governor and the king's other officers in the island, defining their duties and their relations to each other, and providing for the settlement by the Council of any differences between them. They also included some regulations as to the duties of the Islanders generally in regard to taxation and defence. Some clauses of the Orders, e.g. those forbidding the levying of any tax without the king's consent and imprisonment or interference with the course of justice by the governor, have proved to be of great importance from the point of view of constitutional law, but they were evidently regarded at the time as statements and definitions of the existing law or custom, not as embodying any new principle. The preamble to the Order of 1495 clearly sets out the purposes of its authors, viz. the safeguarding of the king's castle, the due administration of justice to his subjects, and the peace of the inhabitants. The Orders are executive and not legislative in their character ; and it is quite in keeping with this strictly practical object that they take for granted the existence in the island of a system of government and a set of officials of various kinds : they refer to the governor or captain, the bailiff, jurats, etc., without attempting to describe their origin, nature, or the constitutional position of their various offices.

It is desirable therefore to give a brief account of the working constitution of the Channel Islands under the Tudors, and the chief organs of government.

At the head of the administration of each island was the governor, who at this period was frequently called captain. He was appointed directly by the king and exercised vice-regal powers. It was a post of high rank and great responsibility : in view of recent experience the Tudor kings naturally looked on Jersey and Guernsey as fortresses and outposts of first-rate military and political importance, and took corresponding care in choosing the men they sent to govern them. Throughout this period the governors of both islands were usually men of good but not unduly high social rank—the Tudors preferred not to employ great lords for serious administrative work—and competent administrators with military or diplomatic experience. The only exception was Edward Seymour, Earl of Hertford, who was appointed in 1546 and continued to hold office after he became Duke of Somerset and Protector. He necessarily had to govern by means of lieutenants. The two Paulets, who governed Jersey from 1571 to 1600, were also out of the island on other service during most if not all of their term of office, but this was not an ordinary case of an absentee governor. Each of them had served as his father's lieutenant for many years before being appointed governor, and was therefore able to supervise the government even from a distance with good knowledge of local conditions and personalities.

The post was not altogether an easy one. The governor's first duty was to protect the islands from invasion, and to furnish the home government with intelligence—the records are full of reports from the governors about the position in France ; but the islands were not mere fortresses which could be ruled by a soldier with no regard to anything but military considerations. The governor was also responsible to Council for the civil administration of the island, which meant that he was expected to get in the king's revenues and pay the ordinary expenses of government out of them, and to keep the islanders reasonably quiet and contented. There was a small permanent force of at most forty or fifty English and Welsh soldiers in each island : this was enough to provide a nucleus garrison for the castle, and to deal with local disturbances on a small scale ; but any serious danger of war or of general disorder in the islands would require strong reinforcements from England, and the islands could only be permanently secured against a foreign invasion by the willing support of the great body of the inhabitants. The people, as has been said above, were entirely loyal to the English connection, but they regarded themselves as part of the Duchy of Normandy not an English county ; they were intensely attached to their ancient institutions and their Norman customary law, and, as they very soon showed, they had far too much spirit to submit to anything like military tyranny. It was the protest of the people of Jersey against an overbearing governor that laid the foundations of modern constitutional developments in the islands.

The chief organ of administration in the islands, and the medium through which the governor chiefly had to work in his dealings with the inhabitants, was the Royal Court. This consisted of the bailiff, as president, and twelve jurats, and was traditionally believed to have been instituted by King John after the loss of continental Normandy. The bailiff was appointed theoretically by the king, but in practice by the governor, and was, with very rare exceptions, a member of one of the leading island families. An Englishman in this office would have been of very little use to the governor or to anyone else : as Sir P. de Carteret told the Secretary of State in 1621 an Englishman " would find many great difficulties in the execution of the office, who can be but ill acquainted with the common country language of the isle, the terms of our laws, customs, and style of proceedings, *hardly known to ourselves* ".[17] The jurats were elected for life by the islanders, but they could be dismissed by the king in case of misconduct, and throughout this period this meant in practice that the Council could dismiss jurats or compel them to resign if it were seriously dissatisfied with their conduct on political or any other grounds. The jurats were always islanders, for the obvious reasons that no Englishman, even if he could speak the language, would want to hold this laborious and unpaid office. It is an important point in the constitution and work of the Royal Court that the whole body of jurats were judges both of fact and law : the bailiff presided over the Court but had no power to rule on points of law, and no authority to direct its decisions in any way except such as he might derive from his personal character and attainments.

The primary duty of the Royal Court was to administer justice according to the ancient customary Norman law of the island. It was in fact the only court of law in each island. Originally Norman and later English judges had come on assize at regular intervals ; but in the fourteenth century these visits came to an end, and thus the decision of the Royal Court was now final except for an appeal to the King in Council. This was inconvenient in practice, being costly for the islanders and troublesome for the Council who found themselves loaded with a mass of appeals, often very trivial—the islanders being litigious by nature—which they could not devolve on any inferior court ; but it was of course a valuable safeguard for island liberties. The Royal Court also possessed and exercised somewhat vaguely defined powers of making and enforcing regulations in the nature of local by-laws on minor matters of police and good government such as the prevention of nuisances, regulation of shop hours and arrangements, fixing the prices of necessary foodstuffs, etc.

In addition to the Royal Court there was in each island a body called the States which was regarded as being in some sense representative of the island as a whole and is sometimes referred to as " the generality ". There can be no doubt that this grew up gradually as the Royal Court formed the habit of calling to its assistance in cases of special difficulty notables and representative men of the Island. The early records of the States of Jersey describe them as being summoned " pour conseiller la justice ",[18] and their original constitution was not very clearly defined : the Royal Court evidently called together such leading men as it thought might be useful for the occasion. By the end of the sixteenth century the States in each island had settled down to a fixed establishment consisting of the bailiff, who presided, the twelve jurats, the rectors of the parishes, and the constables of the parishes, who were the heads of the local administration of the parish elected by the chief householders. But as late as 1542 the Royal Court of Jersey summoned certain of the " principaux " of each parish to the States " pour assister et donner conseille ensemble avec les dits connetables ".[19]

The functions of the States, like their constitution, were also somewhat vague to begin with, and in the early stages it is not always easy to distinguish between acts of the Royal Court and acts of the States. The same subjects (e.g. fixing prices and controlling trade) were sometimes dealt with by the Court and sometimes by the States, and there is no apparent reason for the difference of treatment. Gradually however it seems to have become recognised that the States were the proper body to deal with more important matters : this was natural as the States were in essence the Royal Court reinforced by important persons from outside, and also because the States were regarded as representing the island as a community. Thus it was the States which passed ordinances intended to meet any sudden emergency or public danger, such as forbidding the export of grain in time of scarcity or directing precautions against bringing the plague from Southampton. The States also came to represent the islands in any exceptional dealing with the English government : ordinary commands from the king went

14

to the Royal Court to register and put in force ; but the States were summoned to receive royal letters of a general nature addressed to the island as a whole, and it was the States which undertook the defence of the insular liberties whenever they seemed to be threatened, as for example by attempts of the Admiralty Court[20] or English ecclesiastical courts[21] to exercise jurisdiction in the islands.

Further there was one very important power which the Royal Court never shared with the States. Any general tax on the inhabitants was imposed by the States and the States alone. Direct taxation was rare in this period : there are a few instances in which the States levied money for purposes of defence, such as the purchase of gunpowder or the repair of cannons ; and after the establishment of Presbyterianism they taxed the island to pay the expenses of students for the ministry who were sent to the French Protestant colleges. But the great majority of levies were for the cost of sending delegates to London to represent the views or wishes of the islanders before the Council. Of course the position of the States as the representative body of the island was greatly strengthened by the fact that the very costly business of laying island grievances before the Council could only be undertaken formally and efficiently if the States were prepared to vote the money. Naturally also when the States levied the tax they appointed the officers who received and spent the money and the delegates who went to London on behalf of the island.[22]

A principal duty of the States in modern times is legislation. There is very little trace of any activity of this kind in the sixteenth century or the seventeenth. We are apt to think that it is a necessity of civilised life to have a legislature continuously occupied in revising political and social arrangements to bring them into line with changing conditions. The Tudor ideal was stability : an orderly community ought to be regulated by a body of ancient laws, customs and liberties, by which government and people were alike bound; and legislation was a far less frequent element of government than it became in later centuries. It is not surprising therefore that there was little legislation in the Tudor period and most of that was not passed by the States. Henry VII's reforms in Jersey were effected by an Order-in-Council issued *proprio motu* : in other cases royal commissioners sent to inquire into insular complaints embodied their findings in a series of ordinances which were then formally approved by Council : in a few cases only do we find an anticipation of the modern system under which a legislative measure is passed by the States and confirmed by Order in Council. Thus in 1581 the States of Guernsey on the instruc-

15

tions of the Government prepared a code of insular law which was approved by the Queen in Council :[23] and a year earlier, on representations being received from ministers and people alike that owing to inadequate pay the island livings could not be properly filled, Council gave orders that the matter " should be referred by the governor, bailiff and jurats to the generality, and what they should in their assembly conclude should be confirmed by Her Majesty ".[24] This last was a question of taxation and therefore on any showing a matter for the States, but these two are instances of legislation in the full technical sense and they are interesting as showing the beginnings of the legislative powers and duties of the States.[25]

It is notable that throughout this period the Royal Court and the States invariably acted in complete harmony. There were often of course acute personal and family quarrels between individual members of these bodies, but I have not found any instance in which the States as an assembly differed seriously from or overruled the majority of the Royal Court. The reason is that the government of both islands was in the hands of a relatively small group of long-established families of landowners and merchants. The jurats and the constables of the parishes, whose office was a regular stepping-stone to the higher one of jurat, were elected from them alone ; and their control over the people was complete and unquestioned.

It follows from this that the practical problem of government, as it presented itself to the king's representative in the island was simply that of dealing with the local aristocracy. This was not always easy. Chief-Justice Coke showed towards the end of this period how the English Common Law could be used by a professional lawyer to thwart the designs of the Government. The jurats of Jersey and Guernsey found their ancient customary Norman Law a still more powerful weapon to defeat anything which they considered to be an attack on their liberties. They were not professional lawyers, and they were accustomed then, as they have been in later centuries, to use great freedom in interpreting the law according to what they considered to be the requirements of the particular case before them ; and they had a body of high-spirited and tenacious local gentry behind them. The fact that the bailiff, who was the king's representative in the Royal Court, and appointed direct by the Sovereign, was merely *primus inter pares* and had no authority over the jurats[26] did not make the Governor's position any easier. In these circumstances to keep order, raise the King's revenue, and carry out the requirements of the English government in time of war or other emergency, required a combination of tact and firmness that not every governor possessed.

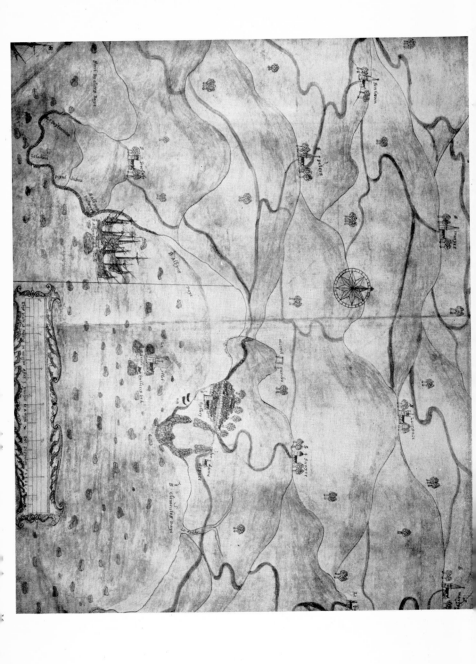

CHAPTER III.

JERSEY UNDER HENRY VIII and EDWARD VI.

Baker's successor in the governorship of Jersey was Thomas Overy or Auvery.[1] As he was a leading citizen of Southampton and had several times been mayor of the town, he was well known to the islanders. Tradition depicts him as a most successful governor who fostered the trade of the island and was popular with everyone. The report of the Royal Commission of 1515[2] indicates one at any rate of the reasons for his popularity. The jurors who were sworn by the commissioners to make inquiries presented five cases in which domain land had been held for a number of years at a rent much below its real value (in one case without rent at all) to the loss of the king's revenue, and all but one of these cases date back to Overy's governorship. It seems clear that he had been consistently lenient with people who wanted to rent royal domain, and so he was naturally popular.

His successor, Sir Hugh Vaughan,[3] was of a very different type. He appears in the tradition as the arch-oppressor of the islands and, at any rate in the later part of his career, as the arch-enemy of the de Carterets. As the Chronicler describes him he is a picturesque figure ; a young Welshman of no birth, originally a tailor by trade, but handsome, brave, and high-spirited. He attracted the attention of Henry VII while he was still the Earl of Richmond, and rose with the fortunes of the Tudors. The records show that he was gentleman usher by 1491 ; was knighted in 1503 when Henry VIII was created Prince of Wales, and was made High Bailiff of Westminster and Captain of Jersey (1502). He had caused something of a sensation by killing his opponent in a tournament at Richmond, and a certain amount of legend gathered about this exploit.[4]

Vaughan was not a satisfactory or popular governor. " He forgot himself," says the Chronicler, " and abandoning himself to his own pleasure, and giving way to a licentious and dissolute way of life, he became so debauched as to commit rapes freely so that girls dared not go on the roads alone for fear of him. Further if he claimed any man's lands he used to send a soldier of the garrison to fetch him to show his title deeds, and as soon as he got sight of them he would break the seal

17

and tear them to pieces. He beat and struck various people so that often they were in great danger of death ".[5]

These charges are fully confirmed by contemporary documents. At an inquiry into Vaughan's conduct held in 1531, the jurors found as follows :—" Touching the 17th article where it speaks of the ravishing certain girls, according to common rumour it is duly proved, but that of themselves they did not see the acts committed. But it is received beyond doubt as true ". The same jurors found that Vaughan had beaten and maimed Edmond Le Gallais and others to compel them to supply fuel to the castle, and that three other men (named) had died after being ill-treated by Vaughan. The curious story about the destruction of title-deeds is borne out by a petition presented to the Council in 1529. The parishioners of St. Martin's complained that for twenty years they had been deprived of an endowment given to found a weekly mass, whereby 1040 masses had been " destourbés " to the prejudice both of the living and the dead. They said that Vaughan had sent for their chaplain, imprisoned him till he gave up the letter of foundation, and then torn the letter to pieces.

It is not surprising that representations were made to the King in Council about Vaughan's conduct, or that a Royal Commission was sent to inquire into the business. What is astonishing is to find the Chronicler in the same paragraph in which he describes Vaughan's atrocities going on to say that he was throughout on the best of terms with the de Carteret family, and drew the connection closer when he saw trouble brewing, by deposing the bailiff, Lemprière, who had been to England to complain of him, and putting Helier de Carteret in his place, besides taking two more of the de Carteret brothers into his service. He adds that when the Royal Commission came, " by the means of the Seigneur of St. Ouen and his brothers everything was quieted for a time ". The devastating candour of this account staggers the reader : it is so obvious that the Chronicler thinks that tyranny and misgovernment are minor matters so long as the tyrant does not annoy the de Carterets.

There is no doubt about Vaughan's connection with the de Carterets at this time. On the 30th April, 1513, Vaughan sent Helier de Carteret to London with a letter and presents for Wolsey. He describes de Carteret as his servant, reports that he has given him the office of bailiff, and begs that the gift may be confirmed for life by the king.[6]

A Royal Commission was appointed in 1515 and sat at Jersey on 18th and 19th September to inquire by means of sworn jurors into Vaughan's conduct : the commissioners were two English lawyers, George Treneton and Reginald Meinours. The text of the Commission and the findings of the jurors have been preserved. It is notable that the terms of reference are quite general : the Commissioners are directed to inquire (a) into manors and other property or rights belonging to the king and withheld from him, and (b) into " all revolts, disturbances, transgressions, misprisions, corrupt practices, and extortions, as well of our officers as of others our tenants, subjects, and jurats, and of other persons whatsoever ". Obviously this document was carefully drawn so as to avoid any suggestion that it was due primarily to complaints against Vaughan, and to enable him to meet charges of extortion by alleging that rents due to the King were withheld, and to reply with charges of misconduct on his opponents.

The report shows that Vaughan took full advantage of the situation. The jurors found several cases of misconduct by Lemprière, the bailiff whom Vaughan had recently deposed— he had kept a tavern while jurat; he had levied fees for himself as bailiff ; he had occupied certain mills without any known title ; and while acting lieutenant-governor he had illegally compelled the inhabitants to pay for repairs at the castle. Two jurats (doubtless supporters of Lemprière) were found guilty of keeping taverns and of misconduct in court ; and several people were found to have occupied the king's land for many years at an improperly low rent to the loss of the king's revenues.

The findings against Vaughan are very mild when compared with the Chronicler's account of his behaviour and with the findings of the 1531 jurors. There is not a word about rape and the only act of violence mentioned is a single case of assault. The jurors found that he had continued to levy the export tax on wheat instituted by the French ; that he had taken bribes from foreign merchants, and monopolised export business for his own profit ; and that he had leased a mill without any right to do so and continued to enforce payment of the rent after the Royal Court had decided against him.

It so happens that two cases which were heard in 1515 crop up again in 1529-31, and a comparison between the two sets of documents shows clearly the spirit in which the earlier was conducted. In 1529 the Prior of L'Islet complained that Vaughan had interrupted his possession of the Priory by putting in two priests, whereby he had lost £30 in revenue, of which Vaughan received 25 nobles. The jurors of 1515 found that two men (one being the man named in the 1519 petition) had forcibly entered the garden of the priory and had gathered fruit and broken down trees to the value of 20 gold angels. It will be noted that the 1515 jurors put the whole blame on the two priests and say nothing of Vaughan in the background. The second case is still more illuminating. The jurors of 1531 found that a certain mill had been leased to one Guillaume Trachy, who improved it so as to increase its value by 10 qrs. a year, and that Vaughan dispossessed him and put in another tenant. The petitions of 1529 add some further particulars of Trachy's wrongs : he had been compelled by fear of death to pay 10 nobles and a fat ox worth 4 nobles ; and when he appealed to the Privy Council and his son came back with a royal order for the case to be heard Vaughan beat and imprisoned the son. The findings of the 1515 jurors on this case was that the mill had been leased to Trachy for 20 crowns a year whereas it was worth 40 crowns, and the king had been robbed of 20 crowns a year for 16 years.

It is plain that the inquiry of 1515 was a skilful piece of whitewashing. When Vaughan realised that some inquiry was inevitable, he used his influence with Wolsey to get the reference to the Commission drawn in terms that enabled him as far as possible to avoid the issue of his own misconduct : two English commissioners were appointed (in 1531 there were two English and two Jerseymen) who, even if they were not bribed by Vaughan as a later petition says, could know nothing of local circumstances, and could be easily hoodwinked by the king's officers : then with the help of a sympathetic bailiff and all the family influence of the de Carterets, Vaughan got a set of findings which threw as much odium as possible on his opponents, provided him with excuses for screwing up the king's revenue, and only went against himself in a few comparatively unimportant cases. When the islanders plucked up courage to make representations to the Privy Council again (in 1529) the petitioners said that on a previous complaint to the Council Wolsey sent to the island two lawyers who were in the pay of the captain, who showed their partiality by recording such things only as made for the captain, and the complainants were imprisoned and ruined. At the inquiry of 1531 this was fully borne out. The sworn jurors found (Article 20) that the commissioners of 1515 " did much harm. Contrary to the truth of what they themselves had found, they would not hear any pleas except about such things as they thought would be to the advantage of Vaughan to colour his misdeeds. Whereby many irreparable evils followed both in the death of worthy people and the destruction of their goods, because the Cardinal favouring and supporting Vaughan and giving credit to the commissioners would not do execution on his misdeeds ".

The result of the inquiry was a complete triumph for Vaughan who was left the unquestioned master of the island.

The Chronicler's way of putting it is that " by the means of the Seigneur of St. Ouen and his brothers everything was quieted for the time " (appaisé). He adds that " by their good means and counsel Vaughan became far more moderate than he had been before, and thereby the Island was in peace for some time ".[7] It is very doubtful whether this is much more than a conventional tribute to respectability. Vaughan may have taken warning by his escape and moderated his high-handed behaviour for a time ; but if so it did not last very long. Within four years a furious quarrel broke out between Vaughan and Helier de Carteret,[8] the bailiff, which lasted for some twelve years. It began, says the Chronicler, with a law-suit in which the governor claimed that the fief of La Trinité was forfeited to the Crown on the ground that the late owner, Thomas de St. Martin, had traitorously plotted to betray the castle to the French. The defence was a flat denial that St. Martin had ever been accused or convicted of treason. Vaughan, seeing that the members of the Court were favourable to the defendant, began to bully and threaten them and said to the bailiff, laying his hand on his sword, that if he did not find for the Crown he would run him through. The bailiff leapt up and ordered the doors to be opened (the court was sitting in a private house because the plague was in St. Heliers). He drew his sword clear of the scabbard and gripped Vaughan's wrist, telling him that if he moved he was a dead man, no matter how many of his men were at hand, for he would run him through whatever came of it. Then the people poured in, and the jurats in open court decided against Vaughan's claim. He threatened to depose the bailiff from his office, and after a further exchange of high words they parted.

This is the story in the *Chronicle*, and the curious thing about it is that the defence was an audacious falsehood, and everyone in the Court must have known it. De St. Martin had notoriously sided with the French during their occupation of the island, and had been attainted of treason and his estates forfeited. He had however got a pardon from Edward IV and recovered his seignory. Why then instead of simply pleading the pardon, did the defence put forward, and the Court accept, the flagrant untruth that no treason had ever been committed at all ? Doubtless because during the French occupation many landowners had committed technical treason by adhering to the *de facto* government, and few of them had pardons. It was better therefore to put forward a defence which would cover everybody rather than one which was personal to the Seigneur of La Trinité, and the jurats would realise this as well as anyone else. Vaughan could never

21

bring witnesses from England to swear to acts of treason fifty years old, and he could not depend on island witnesses.

It is no wonder that this direct attempt to confiscate one of the chief manors in the island led to a breach between de Carteret and Vaughan. If the governor was going to rake up what people had done during the French occupation of 1460-8, no one's estate would be safe. And the attack on Trinity Manor touched the de Carteret brothers personally, for the seigneur was their sister's son.

Soon after this de Carteret went to London to complain to the King and Council. Whether he was intended to act as a representative of the islanders generally is not clear, but his main object certainly was to protect himself against Vaughan's threat to depose him from his office of bailiff ; and however it began the affair certainly settled down into a single combat between de Carteret and Vaughan over de Carteret's personal interests which lasted for years.

In the first stage de Carteret had the better of it. In May 1519, Vaughan wrote to Wolsey saying that de Carteret had summoned him to appear before the Council, and asking permission to wait till Michælmas term, because de Carteret had also got a writ ordering the bailiff and lieutenant-governor to appear in Chancery at the same time, and they could not all be out of the island together. Whether Vaughan actually came in the autumn does not appear ; but if he did, de Carteret still continued to have the best of it for in December 1521, a patent was issued granting him the office of bailiff as from 10 June ; and in March 1522, he received a grant of the Manor of St. Germain. At this point Vaughan evidently realised, if he had not done so before, that the situation was getting serious. The grant of St. Germain diverted the revenues of the fief from the governor's pocket to de Carteret's. The *Chronicle* says that he found means through his friends and by gifts and bribes to get Cardinal Wolsey on his side, and Wolsey helped him to spin out the proceedings for 12 years.

This is fully borne out by the documents. In or before 1 July, 1522, Vaughan took proceedings in Chancery to set aside both the grant of the manor and that of the office of bailiff. It is not easy to see on what grounds a direct gift by the king out of the royal domain could be legally questioned, and it would be a daring proceeding for anyone who had not strong backing. But Wolsey was chancellor and all business passed through his hands, and Vaughan was Wolsey's man. On 13 July, 1522, Vaughan wrote to Wolsey asking him to send an order that de Carteret should meddle no further with the fief of St. Germain till he (Vaughan) had tried his patent

22

with him. De Carteret's agents, he said, receive the rents daily by reason of an order which he has obtained from the king.

A further letter of 3 November, shows that the suit related both to the manor and to the post of bailiff, and that Vaughan was appearing by attorney in answer to a *sub pœna*. He also counter-attacked by organising a petition against de Carteret : in a letter of Nov. 1522, he told Wolsey that the Jersey people had complained that de Carteret did not administer justice and had broken commands sent him at divers times by the king.[9] The petition is dated June 4, 1524, and purports to be from " the jurats, dean, rectors, constables, and all the inhabitants of the island having authority therein, as well as the whole community ". Actually it is signed by eight jurats only, and sealed with the seal of the dean's court (de Carteret had apparently taken the seal of the island away with him). After setting out some other grievances the petitioners say that they are greatly troubled because de Carteret has obtained by the grace of the king an order under Privy Seal requiring them under a penalty of 100 marks to obey and help him at all times in all matters that he may wish to do. " We.... have always obeyed and helped him whilst he held the office of bailiff and carried on the administration of the bailiwick in these parts and whilst he observed the laws and customs confirmed to us, but when he ceased to follow them and against the oath taken by him strictly to observe them sought to overthrow them, we dismissed him from office and do not assist him ; and in his absence the Honourable Sir Hugh Vaughan....has by virtue of his patent, the office being vacant, provided for the appointment of another bailiff ".[10] Vaughan's appointment was duly confirmed. On 21 August, 1524, Letters Patent were issued appointing the dean, Richard Mabon, and John Lemprière to act as joint bailiffs (the dean as a priest being forbidden to act in criminal cases) during the controversy between Vaughan and de Carteret, and also sequestrating the rents and revenues of St. Germain.[11]

De Carteret now found himself in a hopeless position. He had lost his official income and the revenues of his manor, and being one of twenty brothers his private estate was probably not large ; and he was kept waiting interminably in London because Vaughan had got an order from the Cardinal requiring him not to leave London without permission and to attend every meeting of the Council. After four or five years of this he had spent all his money and the Cardinal still would not hear his case ; and when the last day of term had come, he took the desperate resolution of braving the Cardinal and the Star

Chamber, and insisting at whatever risk on being heard. The Chronicle[12] describes the scene with minute and vivid detail: either it is the authentic narrative of someone who was present or the work of a historical novelist of the first rank, which the Chronicler certainly was not. I have no doubt it faithfully reproduces Helier de Carteret's own account : the day when he successfully outfaced the dreaded Cardinal and the hardly less dreaded Star Chamber was the greatest moment in his own career, and one of the highlights of the whole family history ; and de Carteret no doubt repeated his story to his children and grandchildren till they knew it all by heart, and every detail was firmly embedded in the family tradition. It is worth repeating as a living picture of the Star Chamber at work.

" Now after de Carteret's counsel had opened his case and the Cardinal in his usual way refused to hear him but began to deal with some other business, the bailiff took courage to speak himself to the Cardinal, all the Council being seated in full session in the Star Chamber, and recommending himself to God and imploring the Divine help he began to cry so loudly that everyone could hear, " Sir, I beg and entreat you to give me justice ! " The Cardinal heard him well enough, but in his usual way acted the deaf man and pretended not to hear, and gave orders to go on with another case and had himself begun afresh to open it. The bailiff began again to cry at the top of his voice, " Sir, I entreat you for justice, or at least some show of justice ". The Cardinal could not act deafness any longer as the other lords were there, and the bailiff cried so loud for justice ; so he said " Dost thou ask for justice ? If thou hadst justice and thy deserts, thou shouldst be punished as an example to others for brawling in Court (comme un homme faisant procès extraordinaire) and for doing much mischief in thine own country ". The bailiff plucked up heart and answered, " Sir, if I were what you say, I should indeed deserve to be punished ; but you do me wrong, Sir to bring a charge against me which you cannot make good ". Then the Cardinal rose in a great rage saying to the lords of the Council who were there, " Did you ever see so froward a man ? He must talk and act masterfully in his own country seeing he is so malapert here ". And thereupon he called for the keeper of the Fleet, which is a very costly prison where they send gentlemen who give any offence to the Council, and the ordinary charge for every meal is an angel. And as the Cardinal wanted to send the bailiff there everyone said to him that he must look to himself or he was in the way to be ruined. But the bailiff answered boldly, " Sir, I had rather go to prison in the Fleet than lose my livelihood, but before you send me there I

24

beg and entreat you Sir, to tell me the reason why you send me there ; if it is for demanding justice of you for upholding the rightness of my cause. If it is for anything else, Sir, I pray you to name it at once and before all. Sir, you have made me wait in this city for three years and more by your express order, and all this time I have not been able to get a hearing. You have kept me out of my livelihood by sequestration ; all my money is spent ; I am a poor gentleman burdened with a wife and children and I cannot help them in any way whatever ; consider then, Sir, if I have reason to speak or not ". All the people were amazed to hear the bailiff speak so boldly. Then the Cardinal answered, " I tell thee thou art a brawler and unfit to hold any place or charge or rule in the island ". The bailiff said, " Sir, you cannot make that good ". The Cardinal answered, that he would show it to him under seal of the island,[13] and the bailiff said, " Sir, you cannot show that, for I have the keeping of the island seal myself, and therefore, Sir, I entreat you for justice ".

The Cardinal did not know how to answer, so he broke up the Court in a rage, saying, " Thou shalt have no more for the present ".

The Chronicler says that the Council sympathised with de Carteret, and that Wolsey's enemies, Norfolk and Compton, sent for him secretly, told him that he was a true man and offered him any money he needed. De Carteret then went to meet the Cardinal after dinner and while attending him to his lodging said, " Sir, I entreat you for justice," and the Cardinal answered very kindly, " You[14] must wait till the time comes, but the first day of next term I promise you I will settle your business, for in truth I think you have been wronged ".

And on the first day of the next term an order was made restoring de Carteret to his office and manor, his opponents to pay his costs and account for his revenues during the period of sequestration ; and soon afterwards the Cardinal effected a reconciliation between him and Vaughan. The *Chronicle* dates all this rather vaguely as not long before the fall of the Cardinal (October 1529) ; and there is a memorandum extant dated sometime in 1529, noting that the Court had ordered that unless before Saturday next they showed cause why de Carteret had been sequestrated, the injunction should be dissolved and de Carteret restored to possession. If however the *Chronicle* is right in introducing Compton—and there seems no reason why this detail should have been invented—the scene in the Star Chamber must have happened in the first half of 1528, because Compton died of the plague in that summer.

Vaughan seems to have become dissatisfied with Mabon

25

and Lemprière as acting Bailiffs, we do not know why, and before the end of the controversy appointed a certain Jasper Pen (or Payn) in their place. There is a confirmation, dated December 10th, 1527, of a deed of November 12th, granting Pen the office of bailiff during Vaughan's governorship.[15] Pen is described in the *Chronicle* as a poor adventurer who had not much to live on. He was apparently a merchant, and there can be little doubt that the Jasper Pen who, on 1 December, was granted a licence to export 300 tons of salt to the Channel Islands and export merchandise thence to France is the same man. Probably he is the Jasper Pen who appears in 1524 as captain of the " Michæl Flower " of the West Country ; the Jasper Pen who went to Calais in March 1522 in the retinue of Lord Berners, Deputy of Calais (and was taken prisoner, for his wife received a licence to beg alms for his ransom), and the Pen who served in the wars as captain of the " Harry Tothill " may or may not be the same.

It is admitted that Pen did no credit to the office. At Southampton on his way to Jersey he fell in with some Spanish shipmen, and sold them £40 worth of corn, getting payment in advance on the strength of his rank as bailiff. When he got to Jersey Pen did not deliver the corn and stayed inside the castle ; whereupon the Spaniards, being resourceful men and quite indifferent to excommunication, kidnapped the dean one night and extracted the £40 from him under threat of taking him to Spain. He got no repayment from Pen and no sympathy from the governor.[16] One of the complaints against Vaughan was that he had given the office of bailiff to Jasper Pen, " who does not know the laws and customs of the island or understand the language, and justice is abused because he and the jurats and the officers of the Court cannot understand each other ' ; and at the inquiry of 1531 the jurors found on oath that Pen was not a man fit for the exercise of the office. He was dead before then, but there is a letter of Vaughan's dated March 2nd, 1529 in which he appointed Helier de la Rocque bailiff " until the King has decided between me and Helier de Carteret ", Pen having voluntarily resigned.[17] This suggests that by that time Vaughan was beginning to feel uncertain of his ultimate success.

It is not surprising that the islanders disapproved of Vaughan's changes of bailiff ; in 1529 they complained to the king that great desolation and damage exists because Vaughan has appointed four bailiffs (i.e. Mabon and Lemprière, Pen and de la Rocque) to the hindrance of justice, and asked for a decision as to which of them is to exercise the office. This grievance was removed by the reinstatement of de Carteret, which the Chronicler with his strong family bias regards as the end of the story, merely adding that Vaughan fell out of favour with the King who grew weary of continual complaints against him. The islanders however had many other grievances which were not removed by the reconciliation between Vaughan and the de Carterets ; and when it became clear that Wolsey was on the point of falling and that Vaughan could no longer reckon on his support, they made organised representations to the King and Council. Fortunately the records contain both these petitions (or a substantial number of them) and the report of the Commission of Inquiry which was appointed ; and by comparing these with each other and with the report of the earlier Commission of 1515 it is possible to form a fairly clear idea of the charges brought against Vaughan and how far they were justified.[18]

The petitions reached the Council at the end of October, 1529, i.e. shortly after Wolsey's fall from power ; some of them may have been drawn up earlier, as they appear to have been addressed to the Royal Court and forwarded by that body to the Council. The Commission was appointed on 17 August, 1531 ; the commissioners were two Englishmen and two Jersey-men, John Lemprière, seigneur of Rozel, Robert Kirke, John Dumaresq, seigneur of Bagot, and Richard Foster, Yeoman of the Chamber. They sat in September 1531, and conducted their inquiry like the Commission of 1515 by means of juries of twelve men selected from a panel of 48, 4 from each parish, furnished by the Royal Court. Their report is in two parts— (1) as to an inspection of the castle, its garrison, stores, etc., (2) the findings of the juries on 20 articles submitted to them (the articles are not preserved, but they are summarised in each case).

It is at once apparent that this inquiry was quite different from the one in 1515. Every article deals with charges directly levied against Vaughan or his servants : he was given no opening for counter-attacks upon the complainants. And when the inquiry was completed the commissioners took the curious step of asking the jurors publicly in the presence of the Royal Court if they had observed any partiality, affection, or fault in them (the commissioners). The jurors replied that the commissioners had conducted themselves honestly, impartially, and discreetly, and the Royal Court bore witness to the same effect. The reason for this precaution is obvious : it was stated in a petition, and the jurors had found it to be true, that the commissioners of 1515 had refused to hear any pleas except such as they thought would be to the advantage of Vaughan : and these Commissioners meant to leave no loophole for any such charge against themselves.

27

The jurors seem to have done their work conscientiously. In their findings on the various articles they are careful to distinguish : one is proved " by the report of the complainants, by the 12 sworn men, and by the common fame of the inhabitants " : another is proved " by the report of the majority of the jury " ; another " is duly proved according to common rumour but of themselves they have not seen the acts committed ".

The tale of Vaughan's misdeeds as found by the jurors (and accepted by the commissioners) is a long one. Some of the old grievances of 1515, the tax on the export of wheat started during the French occupation, and exactions from foreign residents, reappear. In the latter case Vaughan displayed a cynical humour of his own. Giving out that additional fortifications were needed, he ordered the foreigners to bring their ploughs to the castle and set them to plough up the rabbit-warren. He kept them at this work until they paid him 100 marks, after which no more was heard of the fortifications. Vaughan had played tricks with the currency—not an uncommon practice of 16th century governments—taking current money at a rate fixed by himself and paying it out at the regular rate, and taking English angels at six shillings and eightpence after the king had ordered them to be current at seven and sixpence. A careful inquiry into affairs at the castle revealed grave administrative scandals : the permanent garrison should have been at least 40—it had been 40 in Overy's time and 60 in Baker's, and Vaughan's own list contained 40 names—but only 18 men were actually there. Although the stores of provisions were not inadequate at the time of the commissioner's visit there was plenty of evidence to show that they had been got in after the commissioners landed and sent away again when the inspection was over.

As to individual wrongs there is a formidable list of cases of violence. The jurors found that the article touching the murders done by Vaughan's servants at his counsel and commandment is duly and fully proved ; and that another article, as to ravishing certain girls, is duly proved according to common report " but of themselves they have not seen the acts committed ". No names are given in either case, but the jurors name three men who were beaten and mishandled by Vaughan so that they died shortly afterwards.

The petitions sent to the Council also contain a number of cases in which Vaughan violently extorted money or otherwise interfered with the rights of property owners, Only one of these can be identified in the findings of 1531 ; but several others are confirmed by other documents. The unfortunate tenants of the manor of St. Germain paid their rents to de

Carteret on sight, as they said, of a document under the Great Seal : Vaughan however said that if de Carteret brought as many such commands as would fill the chapel (of the castle) he would make no more of them than a calf-skin, and imprisoned them till they paid over again. Several people were imprisoned and forced to pay money which the petitioners felt was not legally due.

With the material available it is possible to form some estimate of Vaughan's conduct as governor. So far as the king's service was concerned the complaints were probably not taken as seriously as they would be to-day. Levying taxes of doubtful legality and playing tricks with the currency were things which most governments did when they could, and in any case only affected the islanders. A certain amount of speculation with stores would surprise no one, though the state of things revealed by the Commission of 1531 probably went too far to be satisfactory to the home authorities. The primary duty of the governor of an outlying possession was to keep order and this Vaughan certainly did. It is clear that from the unsuccessful complaints of 1515 until the Commission of 1531 Vaughan was completely master of the island. He appointed and deposed bailiffs at pleasure and apparently controlled the majority of the jurats. Appeals to the Privy Council did not trouble him as a rule ; a powerful churchman like the Prior of L'Islet (who had formerly been king's chaplain) might get his property restored by an appeal, but when ordinary people like the Trachys went to England and came back with an order for their case to be heard he simply disregarded the order and imprisoned the appellant. In the same way he refused to carry out decisions of the Royal Court which were against his interests.

It is clear that de Carteret's campaign did nothing to shake Vaughan's position as long as Wolsey was there to back him up. It was not until Wolsey was drawing near to his fall that de Carteret made his dramatic appeal before the Star Chamber and succeeded. And though de Carteret may have begun as a champion of the insular liberties, he very soon lost sight of the general question and devoted his energies to fighting for his post as bailiff and his manor of St. Germain. His ultimate victory was only of value to the common cause in so far as it was a shock to Vaughan's power and an indication that he was not invincible before the Council. The petitions of 1529 bear eloquent witness to the terror which Vaughan inspired. One of them ends with a prayer to the king that it may be taken " as a denunciation and advertisement and not as an accusation, for they neither dare nor wish to accuse or take proceedings against Vaughan for fear of the things aforesaid ".

Even after an inquiry had been decided on, the fear still remained. A petition sent to the Royal Court on behalf of the poor commons of the island sets out that after the king's messenger had made proclamation that the inhabitants should live in quiet and have redress of their grievances, Vaughan caused the procureur to publish that anyone who wished to complain must go to England and sue, " which many dare not do because they are poor and he rich and befriended at Court ".

The evidence leaves no doubt that the islanders had good cause to complain of Vaughan's conduct and to be afraid of him. He was both avaricious and tyrannical in his dealings with the people. Under the system in force then and for long after, the governor received the royal revenues, paid the expenses of government, and pocketed the balance : he had therefore every motive for keeping the receipts high as possible, and he made the most of every claim which could be put forward on behalf of the Crown, even raking up treasons of 60 years before, as in the case of La Trinité.

It is not to be supposed that his claims were always groundless. We have particulars of one case in which he was certainly in the right. In the course of the long struggle between de Carteret and Vaughan over the bailiffship and the manor of St. Germain, de Carteret, being driven to extremity by the delay of his hearing and want of money, got an order from the Court of Requests on the strength of which he collected several years' arrears from the tenants and so managed to carry on for some time longer. Vaughan then imprisoned the tenants till they were forced to pay over again, and told them that " if Carteret brought as many commands as would fill the chapel (of the castle) he would make no more of them than a calf-skin ". Legally and constitutionally Vaughan was quite right : no order of the Court of Requests had any legal effect in Jersey, and 40 years later de Carteret's nephew went to London with complaints about English courts of law interfering in insular suits contrary to the privileges of the island and obtained an Order in Council forbidding the Court of Requests or any English Court to grant any process against an inhabitant of Jersey.[19]

The case of Doray is perhaps more illuminating because more typical. He complained that after the Court had awarded him possession of a disputed mill, the governor and the vicomte in concert refused to execute the order. Vaughan replied that the judgment of the Royal Court was void because the matter related to the royal domain : if he had allowed the jurats to determine the king's inheritance the king would have lost the mill and other lands to the value of £300 a year.[20]

An instructive parallel can be found in a letter from the governor of Guernsey to the Council in 1596.[21] The Royal Court had found against the Crown on a question of royal dues, and on appeal the Council had ordered the governor to " make choice of other jurats such as should be indifferent, and so the matter to be again fully and deliberately heard ". The governor reported that it was impossible to find a quorum of jurats who were not partial : they were mostly in the same position as the defendant and believed that by finding in his favour they would also be able to appropriate similar royal dues on their own estates. The bailiff seeing that " these partial fellows would neither hear nor weigh anything that could be produced for the confirmation of Her Majesty's right.... hath stayed to pronounce a sentence so corrupt and prejudicial to her royal prerogative until your Lordships be thereof advertised ".

This goes to the root of the difficulty which Vaughan and all governors of the islands constantly had to face. In all matters affecting Crown rights and dues the jurats being mostly seigneurs and landowners themselves could not be trusted to deal impartially with the Crown. The independence of the judiciary was not a principle in favour with Tudor governments : in England the Crown might have taken drastic measures with any court that decided a suit relating to royal domain, with any bias against the king. In the islands at this time the governor was expected—as many Privy Council Office documents show—to exercise some sort of control over the local courts, especially in cases where some of the jurats were suspected of partiality. Scrupulous governors like Leighton appealed to the Council as required by Henry VII's ordinance. Vaughan, being a rough and high-handed person, short-circuited the correct legal procedure and ignored the local courts when it suited him. He had the soldiers of the garrison (all English or Welsh) under his orders and the castle prison conveniently at his disposal ; and he preferred to assert his claims directly and by the strong hand rather than wait for the tedious and uncertain proceedings of civil justice.

It is possible that Vaughan justified his action, so far as Crown tenants were concerned, by the ordinances issued by the Comte de Maulevrier during the French occupation of the island. They purported to be based on insular custom, and they contain a clause to the effect that Crown debtors may be summarily imprisoned in the castle without legal process.[22] Vaughan was quite ready to use French precedents when they suited him : he continued to levy the export duty on wheat instituted by the French governor.

It is not surprising therefore that a high-spirited people tenacious of their constitution and their liberties, did their best to curb him and get redress. They had no success until his patron Wolsey had fallen, but as soon as the Cardinal's position was seen to be insecure a formidable list of complaints, as we have seen, poured into the Council, and the Commission of Inquiry reported strongly against Vaughan. Shortly after this report he ceased to be governor of Jersey. The Chronicler says that he retired, much against his will, in 1532, and was given a pension of £200 a year. The fact that the reversion of the governorship had been granted some years before to Sir Antony Ughtred whose wife was a cousin of Anne Boleyn probably helped to procure his dismissal. He cannot however have fallen entirely out of favour, for in October and November 1532 he appears as very active in his office of bailiff of Westminster, where the plague was then raging. A letter to Cromwell says :—" The death is swaged, and there is good rule kept, for Sir Hugh takes pains in his office, like an honest gentleman. I pray you be good master unto him ".[23] He can hardly have been under 70 at the time, as he had served Henry VII before the battle of Bosworth. The Chronicler says that before he left Jersey he told Helier de Carteret with tears in his eyes that he had been badly served by the people (naming them) who had given him such ill advice against the bailiff. This is no doubt true : it must have struck Vaughan forcibly that the earlier inquiry when he had the bailiff and the de Carteret influence on his side had ended very differently from the later one.

After Vaughan's disappearance from the scene things quieted down in Jersey, and the next few years were uneventful. Sir Antony Ughtred[24] died after 2 years in office, and his successor, Sir Arthur Darcy,[25] sold his post after a short time to Lord Vaux[26] who in turn sold it to the Earl of Hertford (afterwards Duke of Somerset and Protector).[27] So great a man did not of course exercise his office in person, and the Jersey people had some trouble with his lieutenants. The first of these was a certain Robert Raymond, who is described by the *Chronicle* as an ex-gunner of the Tower of London, a man of low birth and rough manners, and overbearing disposition ; the islanders formally complained to Hertford of his tyrannical ways (" prétendant d'avoir sa volonté en toutes choses, fut à tort ou à droit "), and Hertford dismissed him and appointed Henry Cornish.[28] There was trouble with Cornish also—in May 1546, the Council wrote to Hertford saying that Edward Perrin, seigneur of Rozel, complained of injuries done to him by Cornish, and that he should be replaced by another lieu-

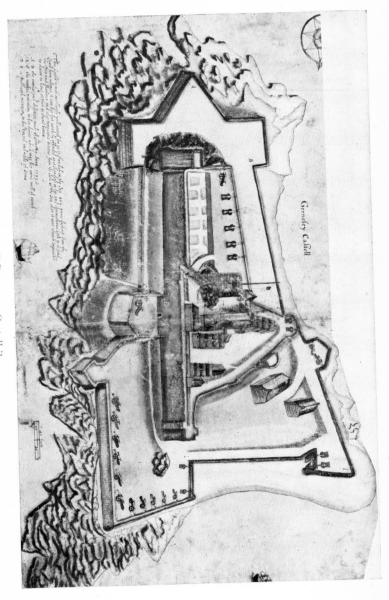

"Gernesey Castell."

To face page 32

tenant till the matter was heard and determined. Hertford asked them to postpone the matter till winter " being in the king's service and having no one but his steward to whom he could entrust so important a matter at a time when the enemy might annoy that isle " : or if the business could not wait to send a commissioner to make inquiries on the spot. The Council insisted however (June 1546) on Hertford's appointing another lieutenant and sending up Cornish to answer the complaints. The final decision was in Cornish's favour : Perrin was sent to the Fleet and ordered to apologise to Cornish publicly in the Royal Court.[29]

This seems to have been a personal matter turning on boundaries and seigneurial rights disputed between the Seigneur of Rozel and the royal domain. There were more general grounds of complaint arising out of the abuse of purveyance. The *Chronicle* says that a certain Thomas Cook, whom Cornish had made purveyor for the castle, pushed his requisition so far that he nearly created a famine in the island and the butchers were afraid to send their meat to market without Cook's licence. Having enforced supplies by beating and imprisoning objectors, he sold them for his own profit and shared the proceeds with Cornish.[30] There is obviously some exaggeration here, but no doubt the story is substantially true. The right of the governor to requisition supplies for the garrison at a rate fixed by himself was a source of disputes all through this period ; and Thomas Cook was not the man to exercise it fairly or honestly. A few years later he headed a party of soldiers from the garrision who robbed the bailiff and another well-to-do man of all their money and valuables, after getting into their houses by a trick ; and fled to Normandy with the proceeds.

These however appear to have been the last movements of a dying storm. Hertford's lieutenants might misconduct themselves to some extent when they thought their master was too busy to watch them, but these were small matters compared with Vaughan's 30 years of high-handed oppression, and the English government was ready to listen to complaints. Evidently the resolute way in which the islanders had finally stood up to Vaughan had not been lost on the authorities.

There seems to have been trouble in Jersey in 1546, but it was due not to anything done by the governor's lieutenant but to neglect or misconduct of the jurats. On 1 December, the Council addressed a severe letter to them, saying that there had been far too many appeals from the decisions of the Royal Court, owing partly to partiality in the jurats and partly to their neglecting to attend the Court or to give their opinion when asked ; and commanding them " as you will answer for the contrary at your peril," when summoned by the bailiff, " to show themselves diligent and attendant upon him as well in aiding helping and assisting him for and toward the good preservation and commonwealth of the said isle but also for the due administration of justice sincerely and equally to be ministered to all parties ".[31]

Hertford's governorship was marked by one unique incident. On 23 December, 1541 he wrote to the States[32] directing them to send 2 members to the Parliament then about to be elected. The letter was read in the States on 16 January, and ordered to be notified to the various parishes. No more seems to have been heard of it, and no member for Jersey appears in the return of members to the Parliament of 1542. Evidently the States were afraid to disobey a formal order from their governor, but argued that if they passed it on nothing would happen as the parishes would not have the slightest idea how to set about electing an M.P. It is strange that such a letter should have been sent at all. It can hardly have been a mistake on the part of the Chancery or Council Office staff, as they must have been familiar with the process of issuing writs. It may have been due to the fact that Hertford having had a good deal to do with Calais about this time,[33] and knowing that Calais was represented in Parliament jumped to the conclusion that the other outposts on the other side of the Channel were or ought to be represented too.

Hertford was succeeded by Sir Hugh Paulet,[34] and for 50 years the Governorship of Jersey was in the hands of successive members of this powerful family, and we hear nothing of any trouble between the islanders and their governor.

CHAPTER IV

THE REFORMATION IN THE CHANNEL ISLANDS

The period covered by the preceding chapter is the time of
the Reformation in England : the first effective step, the Submission of the Clergy, took place in 1532, the year of Vaughan's
retirement. This had no application to the Channel Islands
which were not represented in the Convocation of Canterbury
since they were *de facto* (though not *de jure*) part of the diocese of
Coutances. But the series of Acts of Parliament which formed
the legal framework of the Reformation were all drawn so as to
apply to the islands and were enforced there as a matter of
course.[1] As far as our records show, the changes seem to have
been accepted quite calmly : there is no sign at this stage of any
particular feeling for or against it. This is not surprising : no
one was likely to object to being relieved of Peter's pence[2] and
other payments to Rome or to grieve for the loss of the right of
appeal to the Pope, which was a luxury beyond the means of
two small and poor islands ; and at that distance they were
probably unmoved by the wrongs of Katherine of Aragon and
indifferent as to the succession.

Even the dissolution of the monasteries appears to have
caused no excitement. We have a letter dated 20 September,
1536 from the lieutenant governor of Guernsey to Cromwell
reporting that he had carried out instructions by calling together all the foreign friars (observants) in the island.[3] He
told them they must be sworn to the king (i.e. take the oath
prescribed in the Succession Acts) or else abide the rigour of
the laws. They then asked leave to return to Normandy,
saying that they had before taken an oath which they would not
change, but rather forsake the convent. The lieutenant
governor accordingly provided them with a passage to their
next convent in Normandy, and took possession of their property for the king.

It was quite natural that the uprooting of the monasteries
in the islands should not cause any such wrench as it did in
England. The idea of the king taking possession of monastic
land was familiar to all the islanders, and aroused no such
feeling of sacrilegious horror as it did in the peasants who rose
in the Pilgrimage of Grace. When Henry V had seized the

alien priories 120 years before it amounted to comparatively little in England, but in the islands it affected a large part of the total amount of ecclesiastical land. The idea of the king taking over church land was therefore not new or surprising in itself. The report just quoted suggests that most of the religious in the islands were foreigners drawn from the French houses of their order, which would naturally diminish popular sympathy for them. Further the dissolution of the monasteries would make no difference to the social or economic life of the islands. In England the seizure of church land intensified an agricultural revolution (the change from arable to pasture) which was already causing some distress. Nothing of the kind was happening in Jersey and Guernsey ; and it did not matter to the people whether the land belonged to a convent or to the royal domain ; it was used in the same way in either case.

When the Reformation went from questions of ecclesiastical policy and endowments, which passed over the heads of the people, to matters of doctrine and church services, which touched their daily life and habits, the changes made by authority were received with much the same general acquiescence. They made little more objection to the Protestantism of Edward VI than to Henry VIII's Catholicism without the Pope. The Act of 1547 for the confiscation of obits, chantries, etc., and the Act of Uniformity of 1549 applied like the earlier acts to Jersey and Guernsey, and were duly enforced there. In 1548 the rectors were ordered to bring their books and rent rolls to the Castle for the governor's inspection.[4] This served the double purpose of furnishing particulars of the endowments, and showing which rectors would and which would not submit. All but one or two did submit. In 1549 the Royal Court of Jersey ordered the arrest and imprisonment of " all brawlers and disturbers of the peace and maintainers of the superstitions of the Bishop of Rome ", and made husbands responsible for their wives and masters for their servants. This was no empty threat : in 1552 a farmer was sent to prison because his wife had taken a rosary to church, and various people were convicted of privately attending mass. In April 1550 the Council wrote to the people of Jersey that the governor had reported their " imbracing of his Majestes lawes and procedinges in thorder of the Devyne Service, wherin if any scruple should arise amonges them to referre it to the Counsail ".[5]

In April 1550 a commission was addressed to the governor and some other gentlemen of Jersey to take possession of all obits and masses, superstitions, sacraments, and all church bells except one in each parish, sell them and use the proceeds for fortifications, after providing pensions for the priests who were dependent on the chantry endowments.[6] The church bells in Guernsey escaped, it does not appear why.

Under Queen Mary the Roman Catholic religion was re-established in the islands as it was in England, but there were unmistakeable signs that Protestantism had begun to take independent root and was no longer merely imposed from above. Obviously the influx of Protestant refugees from France and the Walloon provinces, who could carry on propaganda among the islanders in their own language, had had its effect. The *Chroniques de Jersey* record that many leading Jerseymen were convinced Protestants and refused to attend mass, preferring to go over to Normandy and take the sacrament in the Reformed Churches at St. Lo and elsewhere.[7] No Catholic in the islands had given his life for his religion under Henry VIII or Edward VI, but in 1556 three Guernsey women were found to be heretics on examination by the dean and curates and condemned by the Royal Court to be burned. The horrible story which Foxe tells of this martyrdom—that one of the woman gave birth to a child at the stake which was burned with its mother—is unhappily true. Foxe's narrative is based upon and closely follows official documents, as can be seen by reference to the petition, attributed to December 1558, from Matthew Causey, or Cauchés, brother of one and uncle of the other two women.[8] This was written within two and a half years of the actual burning, when the same governor and bailiff were in office, and when the facts must have been well known to everyone in Guernsey : and in 1565, when the jurats who tried the case were charged before the Privy Council with burning the child along with the mother, they admitted it.[9]

From Jersey there comes a case of a different kind, which shows that there also the spirit of the Reformation had taken hold.[10] In 1555 a priest named Richard Laverty was condemned to death by the Royal Court for infanticide—he had killed the child of his maid-servant of which he was the father. The dean, who was present in the Court, claimed that Laverty ought to be handed over to his Ordinary (the Bishop of Coutances), and strongly pressed the Royal Court to do so. But the Court firmly refused to alter their decision ; the governor and the bailiff backed them up and the priest was duly hanged. This incident, happening as it did under a catholic sovereign, shows how much progress the reaction against clerical claims to independence of the civil power had made even in so remote a place as the Channel Islands.

With the accession of Elizabeth Protestant discipline and worship were restored in Jersey and Guernsey. The Injunctions of 1559 and the Acts of Supremacy and Uniformity of the same year, which broadly speaking put things back where they had been at the death of Edward VI, applied in terms to all Her Majesty's dominions and therefore to the islands. In point of fact Jersey and Guernsey soon began to take a very decided line of their own and went considerably further than the Church in England, as will be shown in detail later.

Matters did not take the same course in both islands. Jersey settled down quietly to a Protestant regime : the governor, Hugh Paulet, belonged to a family with strong Puritan sympathies, and many of the leading families (de Carterets, Lemprières, etc.,) were convinced Protestants who had refused to conform under Mary. The instructions of the English government were vigorously carried out ; any inclination to Catholic beliefs and practices was firmly suppressed.

After the first years of the reign we hear little of Catholics in Jersey. Already in 1559 the Council was thanking the bailiff and inhabitants for their conformity to religion and to the Queen's other orders and their obedience to their captain;[11] in 1562 a royal warrant addressed to Guernsey holds up " our other isle of Jersey " as an example of a place where " one uniform rule is limited to all our subjects .... by the wisdom of our Captain ".[12]

In Guernsey things did not go so well at first. There were some Protestants among the leading families : William de Beauvoir, afterwards bailiff, had been a friend of Calvin and a deacon of the English Church at Geneva. But the bailiff and jurats who had burned Catherine Cauchés and her daughters were still in office ; they and other notables were entirely Catholic in their sympathies, and a large part of the population so far sympathised with them as to entertain a strong dislike for Protestantism and Protestants even if they were not zealous for the Catholic religion.

A long and interesting letter[13] sent to Cecil in 1565 by Adrian de Saravia, a refugee scholar who was a minister and schoolmaster in Guernsey, gives a picturesque account in Ciceronian Latin of the demoralisation in the island.

" The people are made of fraud : you cannot believe a word they say and they have no scruple about perjuring themselves ; they would utter a thousand perjuries rather than injure a friend. . . . Their contempt for God and hatred of the Gospel is sufficiently shown by the vicious life led openly by evil-doers and by the paltry number of godly men. If three or four at most were removed from the island by death or otherwise the ministry of God's word would come to an end among us. If a minister goes into the country to preach they greet him with laughter and jeers and sometimes the congregation make such a noise that he is obliged to stop in his sermon, and worse than this, they fill the pulpit with filth as well. They only keep their hands from actual violence from fear of the Queen's authority : if they were left to their own devices we should find them more barbarous than any Turks. And all this is done with the knowledge and connivance of the magistrates, and is worse in the places where they live. For we are treated with more respect in parishes where there is no resident jurat. When religion is despised and neglected you cannot wonder that every sort of wickedness flourishes ! Here the innocent are wronged and robberies and murders committed with impunity. I cannot say that the laws are broken, for they have no laws. They boast about their ancestral customs, but they are changed from day to day at the will of inexpert judges. And yet this little island has all kinds of different law-courts and everything is full of law-suits : I do not believe there is a man who has not a case pending in one court or another. But everything is so confused that I do not believe it possible for a case to be fairly decided even if the judges tried to do so. It astonishes me that the common people, downtrodden as they are, do not complain of this state of things, but in some strange way they actually like it : they have grown so hardened to their sufferings that they have lost any feeling of them. And so the jurats lord it over them like so many dumb cattle. . ."

" In the war time when an invasion was expected and they had to take arms, I saw everything full of confusion and disorder and the men quite untrained. The Governor held the castle, but the captains of parishes had no idea how to command their men : some refused to move a step outside their own houses for fear of seditious disturbances ; others strayed about in a disorderly way uttering threats against the Huguenots whom they blamed for all the evil which they feared, so that we had more cause to be afraid of them than of a successful invasion. They were just the same when the danger was over. In the midst of the general rejoicing, on the day when peace was proclaimed a drunken and seditious gathering led by one of the jurats went about cursing the Huguenots and were ready to turn their arms against their own countrymen if any of the professors of the Gospel had come in their way."

If this stood alone it would require to be taken with a good many grains of salt. Preachers and especially preachers in exile usually make the most of their contemporaries' vices and short-comings. But there is confirmation from other sources for Saravia's unflattering picture. As early after the Reformation as 1543, when a French landing was threatened, the lieutenant of Guernsey reported to his chief that the islanders were faint-hearted and discontented and not to be trusted to defend the island without English backing. "If ye knew how 'fraid the knaves are ye would hang some of them. Sir, I think there was never men that hath the trouble as the bailiff and I have with them, both night and day, and never rest to bring them in some readiness ; and all will not serve ".[14]

Again in 1562 the governor told Cecil that " the generality here mislike the late alterations in England, so as the Queen has few faithful favourers, and there is little hope that the temporal justices will answer their trust ".[15] And in 1566 the dean (John After), a strong Calvinist, reported to Cecil in the same terms as Saravia, viz :—" The people of Guernsey. . . . be as they have always been and rather worse than now, for murderers, thieves whoremongers that daily fly out of Normandy for these and such like offences, which by custom and covenage be harboured here, whereof groweth such mixture of evil and loose life as is horrible to rehearse. They all like well the privileges of England, but the bulls from Rome be in such singular recommendation that no laws of the realm can yet pull back the unbridled sort from Rome nor the French favourers of the same. And as they be unarmed for their own defence, so be they void of good-will, wisdom, manhood, or other good means to front any foreign invasion, and therewith very easy to be intreated to Romish superstition. Some there be notwithstanding whose hearts be governed in the fear of God and of faithful obedience to their natural prince, which though they be the fewest in number yet their honest credit and countenance astoundeth all the rest. The government, committed by ancient usage to the inhabitants, has been greatly abused so that no good laws passed in England are esteemed here, and by that means looseness of life and wicked manners hath won such power among these people as by their common election there is no man thought sufficient to execute the romth of a jurat other than such as can most craftily cover and continue vice and hereby scorn the favourers of honesty and virtue ".[16]

A curious proof that these moralists were not merely railing at large but were writing about actual facts has come to light. Saravia's story about the insular dislike of Huguenots and the attack on them when peace was proclaimed with France (April 1564) is confirmed by the " Articles touching the Jurats of Guernsey " laid before the Privy Council in 1565. One paragraph runs as follows :—

" The same Jurats, namely John Marchant and Richard de Vic, being drunken as commonly they fail not to be, leading dances in the street at St. Peter's Port, Nicholas Martin, Jurat, furnished as his fellow jurats aforesaid, came unto them crying for aid against Huguenots. They forthwith leaving the dance assembled company, joining themselves in aid with the said Martin, who with some blows given drove one very honest man into his house, and so passed raging and crying along the streets ' Where be these Huguenots? We will have their hearts upon the points of our swords!' The honest sort nevertheless considering their estate and the might at hand, keeping their houses, avoided the daring of their seditious rage at that time ".[17]

The Government were naturally not satisfied with the state of things. In 1562 a warrant was addressed to the " Commissioners Ecclesiastical for reforming religion in Guernsey " (presumably the Commissioners appointed in 1561 to inquire into church property in Guernsey)[18] setting out that " our subjects in our isle for lack of stabilising of ecclesiastical order be at discord and variance amongst themselves .... and are like daily to grow to more inconvenience if remedy be not provided ", and instructed them to consider the complaints (of religious discord) and " to direct order to our captain or his lieutenant and to the dean and certain of the jurats .... for the good order of the ecclesiastical government according to the laws and usages of our realm of England ".[19] In the same year (1562) the bailiff, Helier Gosselin, was dismissed, whether as a result of this commission or of the petition of the martyred women's relatives, but no permanent effect was produced. Gosselin was re-elected a jurat, and, as we have already seen, down to 1565 leading Protestants in the island were reporting very unfavourably of the state of religion in Guernsey, putting the blame for it on the Catholic sympathies of the jurats. The Council had other reasons for dissatisfaction with the jurats, and at last their patience gave way and they decided that drastic action was necessary. In July 1565 a number of the jurats were summoned to London to answer for their conduct and in August seven of them were dismissed from office.[20]

This was the final and decisive step in the Reformation in Guernsey. The Huguenot refugee Nicholas Baudouin had already set up a Presbyterian organisation in the Town Church of St. Peter Port ; and in 1563 he got the governor's permission for the election of elders and deacons and the formation of a consistory. This was sanctioned, so far as St. Peter Port was concerned, by the Order in Council of 7 August, 1565. At this time the Council evidently had before it the question of religion in the islands and decided that Protestantism—if necessary Protestantism of the French Calvinistic type—must be securely established there. The dismissal of the obstructive and reactionary jurats removed the only serious obstacle to this policy in Guernsey. Their successors were evidently good Protestants ready to cooperate vigorously in enforcing Calvinistic religion and morality on the people. The Chief Pleas of 1566 were signalised by a crop of godly ordinances, making attendance at divine service compulsory and forbidding games during service time, dissolute dances and songs, profane swearing and blasphemy at any time.[21] In a few years a Presbyterian Church was established throughout the island.

CHAPTER V

NEUTRALITY

It is clear that the early years of the Reformation were a period of real disorganisation. This was not due entirely to religious causes. The mass of the people apparently gave no sign of deep or general attachment to Catholic doctrine and practice, to the expelled monks or to the cause of the Pope. But on the other hand there was not much Protestant feeling either : consequently there was nothing to compensate for the disorganisation caused by the change or to take the place of the old religion that was uprooted ; and as the majority of the jurats were strongly Catholic in sympathies, the people followed their accustomed leaders in this as in other matters. And they had a very strong practical reason for disliking the Reformation—they feared that it would do serious harm to their trade.

The position is well summed up in a report of 1562 :—
" Formerly the state of the isles depended on the Pope's bulls and patents of France as well as privileges of England, therefore they think they should be friends of all rather than subjects of any, and the generality here mislike the late alterations in England ".[1]

This goes to the root of the matter : such resentment as Guernseymen felt against the Reformation and the Protestant ministers was mainly on commercial grounds : they were afraid that their cherished privilege of neutrality would be lost when Papal authority was cast off. This was an arrangement by which the islands and the sea round them as far as the eye could reach were treated as neutral in time of war, and enemies' ships and goods were immune from capture within those limits. The origin of the practice is unknown, but in 1483 Edward IV obtained a bull from the Pope[2] forbidding, on penalty of excommunication and interdict, any attack on ships, persons, or goods in the islands or on the sea surrounding them whether in time of peace or war. The bull was accepted with enthusiasm both in the islands and in France. Charles VIII of France and the Duke of Brittany caused it to be proclaimed in the port towns of their dominions : and the privilege of neutrality was recognised and enforced by the courts both of France and of the islands.[3] A very striking instance of respect

43

for the privilege happened during the Protector Somerset's war with France in 1549-50. The story in the *Chroniques* is that an English captain, trusting to numerical superiority, wished to attack some French ships that were in harbour ; but Somerset's lieutenant called out the islanders and protected the French ships and their goods against the English by armed force.[4]   It was undoubtedly transgressed on occasion ; but few, if any, laws or treaties were uniformly and automatically observed in the 16th century, and the arrangement was so obviously convenient and profitable for the people on both sides that no one wanted to do away with it.   The central Government did not always find it equally convenient : a local neutrality in time of war presented awkward diplomatic problems even to the imperfect international law of that period. In 1544, when England and the Emperor were making war together against France, some Flemish ships cut out two French prizes from Guernsey Harbour.   The castle fired on them and the English Government demanded restitution of the prizes on the ground of the neutrality of the island.   The Regent of the Netherlands protested indignantly—and very naturally— to Chapuys, the Imperial ambassador in London, that it was monstrous that the English should claim to protect enemy ships in the islands when the Emperor was expressly bound by treaty to go to war with France if England *or the Channel Islands* were invaded.[5]   It was equally unreasonable that the English while claiming complete freedom of trade between France and the islands should refuse to recognise the Emperor's licences to Flemish merchants to trade with the enemy and should detain ships carrying goods under such licences.

As the neutrality of the islands did not depend on any agreement between governments, but was a privilege granted by the Pope and enforced by ecclesiastical sanctions only, the repudiation of Papal supremacy in England naturally created a delicate situation : it was henceforth high treason for the islanders to appeal to the Pope's authority or to refer to a Papal bull.   In actual fact the neutrality seems to have been observed by all parties in the same way as before, but the islanders felt that without some formal undertaking to take the place of the bull the position was precarious, and they had neglected their defences on the strength of their neutrality : as Dean After said :—" they have long been preserved from invasion by privileges from England, patents from France and bulls from Rome, so that they have had no thought of danger".[6]

The English government could of course, if it chose, allow enemy vessels to trade with the islands in time of war, and the question was whether the French government would recipro-cate. As early as 1528 we find the French ambassador reporting to his government that the King and Wolsey would like a confirmation by France of the privileges of the isle of Guernsey, " a sort of neutrality which they obtained long ago from the Pope " ;[7] and in 1543 the people of Jersey petitioned their governor, Lord Hertford, and the king that they might be allowed to trade with the French as in former wars.[8]

Elizabeth's general charters both to Guernsey (1560)[9] and to Jersey (1562)[10] expressly authorised trading with all persons, even the enemy, in time of war, and described the practice as a custom going back beyond the memory of man. In regard to Guernsey, however, which had a greater overseas trade than Jersey, difficulties arose almost at once. In 1578 the Royal Court of Guernsey formally petitioned that in times of hostility no French might have privilege and protection in the island unless they brought like privilege and protection for the islanders from France, as is customary ; and they hoped to get this from the French King if it were granted in Guernsey. They added—obviously as a hint to the Council of the advantages of neutrality—a request that if they had to trust only to the safeguard of England the island might be garrisoned and fortified.[11] The authorities seem to have been in favour of the proposal : a memorandum of this period, entitled " Notes for the consideration of the Council," says :—" as to the confirmation of their privileges, they must be renewed at every change of prince, the Pope's name and authority being annihilated "; and goes on to suggest that the extent of neutral waters, whether within view of the isle or only within cannon shot, should be settled, and a penalty laid down for infringement.[12]

No formal decision seems to have been given at this time but a few years later the question arose in such a form that the Council found it advisable to give a ruling on the general issue.

In February, 1586 the governor of Guernsey seized four French ships and their cargoes, believing them to have Spanish goods on board.[13] The Frenchmen appealed to the Royal Court, which declared the seizure invalid on the ground of the neutrality of the island. The governor, who was acting under orders to seize Spanish goods, declined to release ships or goods without order from the Council, and the Royal Court then appealed to the Council. On this particular case the Council, after consulting the law officers, ruled that the goods, although of Spanish origin, were French owned and not liable to seizure. They therefore upheld the decision of the Royal Court, but found that the Governor was not to blame as he had reasonable grounds for thinking the goods to be Spanish. They went on to consider the general question of neutrality, taking the precaution of consulting Sir Amias Paulet, the governor of Jersey, as a person of long experience of the islands, and there is a very interesting memorandum of June 1587 setting out the practical arguments for and against neutrality. The advantages were : the protection of the islands from invasion (an important matter considering their weakness as against Normandy and Brittany) the profits of the trade, the revenue derived from customs, the provision of work for English merchants and sailors, and the value of the intelligence to be obtained from intercourse in time of war. It was admitted that this cut both ways as the enemy also obtained intelligence, but the conclusion was that on the balance England gained ; and there is the significant remark that the enemy got much more intelligence from London by way of Flanders than they ever would from the Channel Islands. The disadvantages were that the French also profited in trade and customs revenue, and that on the whole the balance of trade—as then understood—was against England.[14]

The decision of the Council was clear in favour of neutrality. They informed the governor in a letter of 11th June, 1587 that they were satisfied that the privilege had in fact existed, " and touching the expediency, for that the public benefit that both the crowns of England and France did receive in time of hostility or unkindness by continuing the said islands in a kind of neutrality to serve for a common vent is sufficiently known, it seemeth very convenient and necessary, the matter of such reasons and considerations continuing still, that their privileges grounded on the same should likewise be still maintained and continue ". The governor was therefore instructed that no such arrest should be made in future to the prejudice of the island privileges and liberties : strangers trading or coming to the island in time of restraint or hostility were to get the governor's licence, notice being given to the foreigners affected " upon like restraint or other cause of onkindnesse ".[15]

It does not appear that the position was ever regularised by any formal diplomatic instrument, and the theory of local neutrality when the nations were at war, though naturally popular with the islanders and their neighbours in Normandy and Brittany, was not likely to commend itself to the new monarchy in France as administered by Richelieu.[16] It is true that in 1614 the Parlement of Brittany formally recognised the neutrality of the Islands in a decision on the seizure of Jersey ships, and as late as 1671 a book published at Rouen and entitled *Us et Coutumes de la Mer*[17] lays it down that a prize is not good if it is made in a place of security or refuge like Jersey or Guernsey. But this was in time of peace between the two countries : when war broke out in 1626 the French government disregarded the traditional neutrality of the islands and issued proclamations forbidding all trade with them.[18] This was largely ignored by the Norman and Breton merchants. Falle, writing about 1690, has preserved a tradition that " in the greatest heat of the war about Rochelle the hosiers of Paris and Rouen had free access to these islands and carried off many bales of stockings ";[19] and contemporary records show that there is a great deal of truth in this if it is understood of trade forbidden by the king but recognised more or less openly by local port authorities. A letter of Sir Philip Carteret shows that two Norman gentlemen were carrying on an organised smuggling business on a large scale,[20] and a memorandum from the Jersey authorities states that " St. Malo and other places" continued to trade with the islands in spite of the orders of their government.[21]

This memorandum (July 1627) was a formal proposal to the Council that the neutrality of the islands should still be recognised by England whatever the French government might do. The Jersey people were satisfied that if this were done the French merchants would evade the prohibitions of their own government, and, being rich and influential, would either prevent any invasion of the islands, or would enable it to be defeated by delaying it or sending secret information. The arguments advanced in favour of neutrality are on precisely the same lines as those of the Council memorandum of 1587, the argument from protection being expanded into a direct statement that if neutrality is recognised a small garrison will be sufficient ; if not, a strong permanent garrison is the only way of preventing sudden invasion, and this will be very costly.

It was no doubt on account of the flagrant disregard of his previous proclamation that somewhere about Christmas 1627 the king of France " sent commissioners to the ports and sea towns next adjoining these islands forbidding all his subjects upon pain of death " to have any dealings with the islands.[22] Whether this would have been effectual must remain uncertain, as at this point the British Navy took a hand. A guardship for Jersey was sent over from Portsmouth, and the captain at once proceeded to seize a French ship lying in the harbour with £200 in money and £1300 worth of canvas on board. This effectively put a stop to the contraband trade ; as Carteret said, " having had commission to protect the Islands he hath almost undone us ".[23] The Council considered but apparently took no action on the request of the islanders for the recognition of their neutrality. Probably by 1627 the idea that it was possible for the islands to remain officially neutral while the king was at war had begun to seem irrational and impracticable ; possibly also the Council did not feel confident that with the imperfect naval discipline of the day they could make the captains of king's ships distinguish between French vessels which were good prize and those which were exempt as trading with the islands.

After Buckingham's expedition to La Rochelle there was no war with France until the end of the 17th century, and the question of neutrality was therefore not raised in practice. It was finally swept away by William III in 1689.[24] Obviously this relic of the mediæval chaos of local franchises and privileges could not continue to survive the establishment of a more orderly system of international law ; and the islanders found privateering against the French so profitable and the protection of the British navy so efficient that they soon ceased to regret their neutrality.

Plan of Elizabeth Castle, Jersey, c. 1600

To face page 48

CHAPTER VI

THE CHANNEL ISLANDS AND THE DIOCESE OF
COUTANCES.

One effect of the Reformation in the Islands was to bring home to everyone that the longstanding arrangement by which these English possessions formed part of the French diocese of Coutances was as inconvenient politically as it was natural geographically. The anomaly seems to have struck Henry VII when the dream of recovering continental Normandy was finally given up, for he obtained bulls from the Pope transferring the Channel Islands first to the diocese of Salisbury (28th October, 1496), and then to that of Winchester (20th January, 1499). He wrote to the bishop on 26th October of the same year notifying the change and instructing him to take spiritual charge of the islands,[1] and early in the next year the bishop presented a vicar to one of the island parishes.[2] But the transfer seems to have been ignored almost at once ; after 1500 no case can be found in which Winchester exercised any jurisdiction, whereas Coutances continued to do so without intermission until the end of Mary's reign and after.

It is easy to see how this came about : the islands were near Coutances and easily reached from there, whereas communication with Winchester was difficult and uncertain : the Bishop of Coutances did not act personally but through the dean of each island, who held the offices of chancellor and archdeacon and for all practical purposes discharged the duties of a bishop. The islanders of course found it much easier to deal with their dean and their French neighbours than with unknown English-speaking officials from overseas. The Bishop of Winchester and his officials evidently did not consider these small and poor additions to the diocese which were only to be reached by a difficult sea-voyage worth any trouble to retain ; while his brother of Coutances was naturally unwilling to give up his accustomed jurisdiction and revenues.

It came, however, as something of a surprise to Henry VIII when, in May 1542, he was informed by his officers in Jersey and Guernsey that the Bishop of Coutances " who claymeth ... ordynary jurisdiction within the saide Isles as parte of his dioces .... hathe of late not onlie attempted sondry things there by his mynisters concerning his saide ecclesiasticall jurisdiction in the name of the Busshop . . . . . but also . . . . intendeth within brief tyme to repayre hymself to the saide Isles ".[3] Paget, the ambassador at Paris, was instructed to tell the French authorities that the great matters now in treaty might be hindered by this attempt of the bishop in derogation of the king's proceedings against the bishop of Rome, and to require them to direct the bishop not to exercise such juris- diction unless by the king's consent as other bishops of the realm do, in which case out of love for the King of France the king would suffer him to use jurisdiction and take the profits incident to it. Paget executed his instructions promptly and found the admiral of France very willing to oblige (the French were on bad terms with the Emperor just then, and angling busily for English support) but unable to understand why he should be brought into the business at all. He said he would send the bishop instructions to exercise jurisdiction in the king's isles as other bishops did if Paget would give him a draft of the letter but asked why there was any need to say anything to the bishop, since if he offended the laws Henry could deprive him. Paget answered that the laws extended to the death of such as main- tained the usurped power of Rome, and as this was a French prelate Henry would be loth to have occasion to use that ex- tremity, and furnished the desired draft letter to the bishop, cautiously writing it in Latin not French " so as they should have none advantage of me in their tongue ".[4] A month later the Council, either less alive than Paget to the pitfalls of the French language or loftily indifferent to foreign idioms, them- selves " devised " a letter in French to the bishop's vicar- general.[5]

Whether or not the bishop complied strictly with Paget's draft instructions—that he should not exercise jurisdiction in the name " of the Bishop of Rome whom some call Pope ", but in that of the King of England according to the laws there—he evidently found some formula which satisfied both his own conscience and the susceptibilities of the English government, for he continued in the exercise of his jurisdiction until some years after Elizabeth came to the throne. It is strange that the arrangement should have gone on undisturbed through the religious changes of Edward VI and Elizabeth ; but it is cer- tain that an order in Council was issued in April 1550 directing that the bishop should continue to have ecclesiastical juris- diction in all things not repugnant or contrary to the King's laws, orders, and proceedings. And in 1565 the bishop took advantage of his being sent on a diplomatic mission to Lon- don to complain that he was deprived of his accustomed dues, and got an Order in Council instructing the insular officials to take order that all such dues and sums of money as have been heretofore usually and ought of right to be paid may henceforth be paid to him or his officers.[6]

This success however proved to be a snare to the bishop. He followed it up so vigorously with the result that he lost everything. He took proceedings by his proctors in the Royal Court of Guernsey against the dean, claiming possession of the deanery and the dean's benefices on the ground that he had not been canonically instituted by the bishop or paid his fees. The dean, who belonged to the most advanced section of the Reformers, replied that he had sworn to renounce all foreign jurisdiction, and had been duly instituted by the episcopal authority of the realm ; and he refused to recognise the bishop's authority unless his proctor on his behalf would take the oath of allegiance to the queen, and would renounce Papal authority according to the ecclesiastical laws of England or according to the reformed churches in the diocese of Coutances. This offer was naturally not accepted, and the matter went back to the Privy Council. The bishop's attempt to interfere with the queen's ecclesiastical appointments naturally threw a new light on his claims ; and at this stage the Council seem to have become aware of the bull and royal letter of 1499 ; and after some consideration they decided to take advantage of them. In a letter of June 1568 they notified Guernsey that the Bishop of Winchester was now " in charge to govern and direct our ecclesiastical estate " in the islands, and his officers must be obeyed accordingly.[7] " If henceforth any further pretence or demand be made from Coutances you may with good speech advise them to repair unto our Council for order to be taken as the case shall best require ". This was followed by an Order in Council (11 March, 1569) directing that Henry VII's letter as to the separation of the islands from Coutances and their union with Winchester is not from henceforth to be brought into any question but to be followed and executed. The order contains a provision that no islander is to be compelled to go to England for any ecclesiastical cause, but the same to be determined in the island by commission unless by the assent of both parties according to the ancient usages of the isle.[8]

The Bishop appears to have brooded over his losses, for in October 1580, when a small Papal force was occupying an Irish fortress, news came to Jersey that a Papal delegate from Italy had held a secret synod at Coutances at which it was agreed that the clergy of Lower Normandy should pay the cost of an expedition to be sent against the Channel Islands in the

Pope's name. " The Bishop of Coutances was the greatest doer, and protested he would never be satisfied until he was possessor of the Islands, for they had refused to pay his dues. He hopes that the King will favour him underhand, and the clergy say that the Pope's army being in Ireland, now is the time to go forward ". The lieutenant-governor of Jersey sent the bearer of this news to his father (Sir Amias Paulet) the governor and warned Guernsey ; and Sir Amias reported to the Council. The letter suggests that he was not much alarmed (" that enterprise doth require a captain of better calling than the Bishop of Coutances and his clergy, and cannot be put in execution without the authority of the King of France ") ; but he evidently did not wish to make too light of the news because it gave him an opportunity—of which he took full advantage— of pressing the Council to send him supplies and ammunition for the Castle.[9] The projected expedition never got beyond the stage of talk : a few weeks later the invading force in Ireland was forced to surrender, and having no commission from any belligerent sovereign they were all executed as pirates. This naturally was not encouraging to the Bishop of Coutances and his clergy.

The Order in Council of 1569 finally severed the last formal link which connected the islands with the diocese of Coutances. The surprising thing is that it should have lasted so long. Of course a bishop's court was in those days an essential part of the everyday machinery of government : quite apart from the control of the subordinate clergy or of purely ecclesiastical matters, it dealt with all causes relating to wills and marriages, punished offences such as blasphemy, perjury, and sabbath-breaking, and regulated dealings with the fabric of the churches (e.g. burials in church, family pews, etc.) and the funds set apart for church maintenance and poor relief. All these things could have been done by an official of the Bishop of Winchester. Yet the English Government showed an extraordinary reluctance to sacrifice the formal connection of the islands with the foreign diocese of Coutances, and even adopted for the purpose of maintaining it the curious theory that the island churches formed part of the diocese and were related to the Bishop in the same way as the Huguenot churches in the continental part of the see—a view which both the bishop and the Huguenots would certainly have repudiated.

If this theory had only appeared in the dean's pleadings before the Royal Court, we should have concluded that it was meant simply to annoy the bishop. No doubt the island Protestants gladly recognised that it did serve that useful purpose, but it clearly rested on more serious grounds than that, as it was the official position of the Englishmen. The explanation undoubtedly is that there was a feeling abroad that a formal separation of the islands from the diocese of Coutances might impair the title of the Crown to the duchy of Normandy. It is extraordinary that any value should still have been attached to the maintenance of a legal claim to Normandy, but it certainly was.[10] Early in the next century Coke laid it down that " the possessions of these Islands being parcel of the Dutchy of Normandy are a good seizin for the King of England of the whole Dutchy ".[11]

It was universally admitted that the islands being part of Normandy must be governed by Norman law and custom, and this was held to apply to ecclesiastical as well as temporal matters. This view is clearly stated in a petition submitted to Council about this time : the authors are not named but it obviously comes from the Protestant party in Guernsey and from internal evidence appears to be connected with the dismissal of the Catholic jurats. Its official tone suggests that it may be a formal recommendation from the dean and his friends supported by the governor. " As long as the Queen holds the isles *governed by the laws of Normandy spiritual and temporal*, Her Majesty is not out of possession of the Duchy, but may by the laws, usages, and customs of Normandy maintain just claim and title to the Duchy ". The petitioners went on to make the strange suggestion that " the bishop of Winchester may have superintendence of the spiritual regiment, saving always to the bishop of Coutances such rights and duties as by any payment appertaineth to that see, or at least such rights and duties as the reformed churches in that diocese yield there for the consequence that dependeth thereon ".[12]

The Protestants in the islands and the Government in London were accordingly faced with a delicate problem—how to combine continuance in the diocese of Coutances and observance of the ecclesiastical law of Normandy with the establishment of the Protestant religion and some connection with the Church of England. It was solved by the argument that the Huguenots were *de facto* the established church in Coutances, and that their doctrine was identical with that of the Church of England. The Guernsey petitioners told the Council :—" Spiritual government in Normandy in the diocese of Coutances is reformed, and therefore it may be considered whether that order of reformation may with the reformed order of the realm be tolerated in the said isle, part of the same diocese. This reformation differs nothing in doctrine from this realm and agreeth best in rites and ceremonies with the reformation of life manners and language of the islands ".

This view was formally accepted by the English government. The Order in Council of August 1565 echoes the actual words of the petition :—" Whereas the Queen's most excellent Majesty understandeth that the Isles of Jersey and Guernezey have anciently depended in the Diocese of Constance, and that there be certain churches in the same Diocese well reformed, agreeably throughout in doctrine as it is set forth in this Realm", the Geneva order of preaching and administration may be used in the two town churches of St. Helier and St. Peter Port, " provided always that the Residue of the Parishes . . . . . shall diligently put apart all Superstitions used in the said Diocese, and so continue there the Order of Service ordained and set forth within this Realm ".[13]

The suggestion that the Bishop of Winchester should have episcopal charge of the Islands while they still remained nominally with the diocese of Coutances was obviously impracticable ; but we have seen it was not until 1569 that the Government took the apparently simple and obvious step of separating the Islands by a clean cut from a foreign and Papal diocese.

CHAPTER VII

THE ESTABLISHMENT OF PRESBYTERIANISM

The original intention of the English government was to enforce uniformity with the Church of England. Paulet in Jersey thought at first (January 1560) that " most of the inhabitants much misliked these devices in matters of religion set forth after the private fantasies of a few, chiefly Frenchmen ", and was disposed to suspect that the Huguenot refugees were " spies and practisers for the French ".[1] But it soon appeared that this was a mistake, and that in the islands the effective choice was between Catholicism and the Presbyterianism of Geneva and the French Huguenots. The Anglican compromise never got any hold on Jersey or Guernsey. The people spoke the same language as the French Protestants : an influx of refugees had begun under Edward VI and it increased in the early years of Elizabeth when the wars of religion broke out in France. Among these were many ministers, some of them men of ability and distinction who had been pastors of important churches in France.[2] Their influence was of course overwhelming, and there was nothing on the Reformed side to oppose to it. The Catholic rectors, who had conformed to keep their benefices, could be no great spiritual force ; there were few or no natives of the islands suitable and willing to enter the ministry, and when all services were held in the language of the people and the sermon had taken the place of the Latin mass as the central feature of the service, English ministers who could not preach in French were useless. The complete Presbyterian system of the French Reformed Churches soon established itself in the islands. Two leading French ministers, Nicholas Baudouin of Rouen, and Guillaume Morise, Sieur de la Ripaudière, of Anjou, set up churches on the Presbyterian model with elders, deacons, and a consistory, in the towns of St. Peter Port and St. Helier. Their example was followed throughout the islands, and in 1564 the first Synod of the two islands met in Guernsey.[3]

This movement seems to have had the full support and sympathy of the civil authorities in the islands. The lieutenant-governor of Jersey, Amias Paulet, took part in the solemn Communion Service " administrée selon la pureté de l'Evangile " which inaugurated M. de la Ripaudière's reformed church at St. Helier ;[4] and the governors or their lieutenants habitually presided at colloques and synods. This was no doubt party policy : they must have seen that their real dependence was on Protestant enthusiasm if they wished to keep the islands orderly, contented, and safe from invasion. But it was not merely policy : the Paulets, who governed Jersey throughout these years, and Thomas Leighton, governor of Guernsey from 1570 to 1610, were entirely in sympathy with the Puritans.

Elizabeth and her Council supported the governors when the matter came before them. About 1565 several things combined to call for a decision about the ecclesiastical establishment of the islands. The Bishop of Coutances, as we have seen, was pressing his claims in person : shortly before, in 1564, some Catholic sympathisers in Guernsey sent up a formal remonstrance against the proceedings of Nicholas Baudouin and Dean After (the latter was accused of forbidding kneeling in church, fasting, and ringing the bells at services and funerals, of administering the sacrament without surplice or cope to seated communicants, and of burying without prayers or religious service);[5] and the people of Jersey sent up a deputation headed by the Seigneur of St. Ouen to represent to the Council that if the islands were not allowed to follow the organisation and doctrine of the French Reformed Churches the French ministers would leave them, and they would have no one who could preach the Gospel to them in their own language which " leur serait un grand distourbier et retardement a travailler a la gloire de Dieu et au salut des pauvres ames ".[6]

This was a plain hint to the English Government that if they wanted the islands to be Protestant they must allow them to be Protestant in their own way, and it was accepted. Whatever the Council thought of the religious aspect of the question, they agreed with the two governors as to the political aspect ; and in August 1565, as we have seen, an Order in Council was issued allowing the two churches of St. Helier and St. Peter Port to follow the Geneva order provided the rest of the parishes used the Anglican service.[7]

This was a triumph for Presbyterianism in the islands and was treated accordingly. The limitation to the two town parishes was frankly disregarded, as was a series of injunctions issued by the Bishop of Winchester, requiring all but the two parishes to use the Anglican Prayer Book, and to have sermons six times a year setting forth the Queen's supremacy in ecclesiastical matters.[8] A complete Presbyterian system of church government covering both islands was set up, and in 1569 the Synod drew up a set of articles entitled " Police et Discipline

Ecclésiastique ", and resolved that it should be presented to the Bishop of Winchester. It was never formally sanctioned by any English authority, but in June 1576 it was officially adopted by a full Synod of the islands at which both governors were present, and was henceforth the regular system of church government in the islands—in fact part of the insular constitution—recognised formally by the local civil authorities and at least tacitly by the English Government.[9]

It is strange to modern ideas that Elizabeth's government, which attached great importance to religious uniformity and vigorously suppressed Presbyterianism in England, should have allowed it to establish itself unchecked in the islands. But there were, as we have seen, strong political reasons for this. The islands were of great importance as outposts and ports of shipping, and it was essential to keep them loyal and contented. Further, in those days the importance attached to religious uniformity decreased rapidly with distance. In the next century Charles I and Charles II did not object to the existence of Puritan or Roman Catholic communities on the other side of the Atlantic : at that distance there was little danger of infecting the carefully guarded flock in the mother country, and the government could not interfere effectually without much more trouble and expense than they could spare from their business at home.[10] In the same spirit Elizabeth and her Council were prepared to tolerate a Presbyterian Church in the islands, where by reason of difference of language and bad communications, it could have little influence on the Church of England, provided the people wanted it and her governors wished or thought it necessary to let them have their way ; and the curious theory (explained above) that the queen's title to Normandy depended on the islands being governed by Norman law worked in the same direction.

And it must be remembered that at that time the Anglican Church settlement had not yet hardened into its final shape : it was still fluid, and it was by no means certain how far it would go in compromising with Presbyterianism. There was a strong Presbyterian movement within the Church of England. In 1577 the Archbishop of Canterbury himself (Grindal) was suspended by the Council for his reluctance to act against the Presbyterians, and several times between 1570 and 1590 bills for establishing Presbyterian forms of discipline and worship in the Church of England were introduced into Parliament and found powerful support, and were only prevented from going forward by the arbitrary action of the queen.

The church system of the islands therefore would not in itself necessarily cut them off from the Church of England, and in fact the responsible Anglican authorities did nothing to combat the reform movement in Jersey and Guernsey or to enforce uniformity with England. This should have been the duty on the ecclesiastical side of the dean and the bishop, but they no more carried it out than the governors did on the temporal side. Dean After was himself a strong Calvinist, and, as we have seen, actively introduced the practices of Geneva into the islands : he never took any steps to assert his spiritual authority as dean, but sat in the Synod on an equality with the other rectors. The Bishop of Winchester (Robert Horne) who was the ordinary since the queen's orders of 1569, was an advanced reformer who disliked vestments and was zealous in destroying "superstitious objects", (i.e. stained glass, statues, religious pictures, etc.,) in all churches within his jurisdiction, and had made no attempt to interfere with the establishment of Presbyterianism in the islands.

The island churches, for the time at any rate, did not formally repudiate his authority : in fact they were ready to recognise him as a nominal superior provided he did not try to interfere in practice. The synods of 1567 and 1568 sent polite greetings to the bishop, and in 1569 they instructed the dean to present their Book of Discipline to him. Up to 1575 rectors were instituted by the bishop after taking the oath of canonical obedience and supremacy.[11] But this ceases after the *Discipline* was formally voted by the synod of 1576 ; under this the appointment of a minister is a matter for the governor, the consistory and the people of the parish, and no authority above the colloque of the island is recognised.

The most remarkable light on the relations between the insular churches and the bishop comes from the year 1575, when the Colloque of Guernsey, driven to despair by the defiant obstinacy of a person of Catholic sympathies (Elie Bonamy, son of one of the Catholic jurats of Mary's time), who refused to take the Sacrament, to recognise the authority of the Synod, or to obey their order to make a public confession of his fault, appealed to the bishop to use his authority and to speak for them if the case came up to the Queen. So far from taking any advantage of so splendid an opportunity for asserting his episcopal authority, the bishop wrote in the most friendly way to his dear brothers in Christ, entirely approving of their proceedings, offering to help them to the best of his power, and saying that he had explained his views on what ought to be done to "our common friend and brother in Christ" the governor (Leighton). This was in January 1576 : in June, Leighton and his colleague of Jersey took part in the synod which enacted the *Discipline*.[12] Clearly the bishop of Winchester was quite content to leave the islands to enjoy the Presbyterian system which they preferred.

It will be convenient to sketch briefly the nature of this system, and the way it worked in practice.

The system was based on the absolute equality of each minister and each congregation with every other. The Presbyterian Church in the islands was an equal federation of parish churches, and any approach to the hierarchical arrangement of the Anglican or Catholic Churches was an abomination in their eyes. Each parish was governed for ecclesiastical purposes by a consistory composed of the minister as president and a suitable number of elders and deacons, which met every Sunday. Above this was the colloque representing all the parishes of the island : it met at least once a quarter (in practice more frequently), the governor or his lieutenant presided, and each parish was represented by its minister and one elder (other elders could attend if they chose, but only one from each parish could vote). The colloques of the two islands met in synod once a year, later every other year, and the parishes were represented, as in the colloques, by their minister and one elder apiece.

A curious clause in the *Discipline* of 1576 which was dropped in the revision of 1597 requires the synod to elect one minister from each island to attend the General Synod of the French Reformed Churches " a fin de nourrir le consentement et union tant en doctrine qu'en police ". There was a cautious proviso " et cela selon le bon avis de MM les gouverneurs "; and it does not appear that any minister from the islands did in fact ever attend a French General Synod. The practice was not likely to commend itself to Queen Elizabeth's representatives.

The method of appointing ministers was elaborate. According to the *Discipline* of 1576 the right of nomination belonged to the governor. His nominee came before the colloque, who satisfied themselvrs as to his life and doctrine, heard him preach two or three times, then formally received him into the company of faithful ministers and nominated him to the vacant church. The people then go through the same process of satisfying themselves as to his life and doctrine and hearing him preach, and either accept or refuse the candidate. In any case of difference the matter is decided by the governor and the colloque after hearing the parties.

The revised *Discipline* of 1597 showed a notable encroachment upon the powers of the governor : it laid down that candidates were to be presented to the governor *after* their approval by the colloque and their names had been submitted to the church—i.e. the governor's right of nomination was reduced to a mere veto on the choice of the colloque.

In actual practice however this elaborate procedure cannot during this period have been of much importance in either form. The island churches were almost entirely dependent for their pastors on French refugees : these, having previously held charges—often large and important ones—in France, of course easily satisfied the requirements as to preaching capacity and evidence of character ; and as there were frequently not enough of them available to go round all the parishes, there was little room for differences between the various parties concerned in the appointment.

Elders and deacons were selected by the consistory,[13] who were required to call to their help two or three jurats who are themselves church officers, submitted to the governor for approval, and then brought before the church for election, or if there are sufficient grounds, for rejection. The duty of the elders was to enforce church discipline on the members. The deacons were financial officers charged with collecting contributions for the relief of the poor and distributing them under the instructions of the consistory.

Church discipline was a formidable affair in those days. The positive duty of attendance at public worship was rigidly enforced ; everyone was expected to attend church twice on Sunday, and there was a catechism for children in the afternoon. (A kindly proviso in the *Discipline* allows crying babies to be taken out.) There were week-day services, once a week in the country and twice in the town parishes, at which one person from every household " able to hear and understand " the service was required to be present, and the head of the house was responsible for seeing that his children and servants did their duty. Communion services were held once a quarter, and there also attendance was compulsory. Members were catechized before their first Communion and once a year afterwards, and failure to reach a proper standard of Christian knowledge and conduct meant exclusion from the sacrament (and possibly civil penalties).[14]

Every step was taken to ensure that the pure doctrine was poured into vessels worthy to receive it. A woman who contradicted the preacher in the pulpit, and a man who came to church drunk and went to sleep during the evening sermon to the scandal of the whole congregation (did he snore ?) both incurred ecclesiastical penalties. And naturally Sabbath-breaking (e.g. fishers setting nets on Sunday), attendance at Mass in France as well as in the islands, the possession of Popish books and witchcraft were severely dealt with. But church discipline was far from confining itself to purely ecclesiastical matters ; any conduct which might be considered unworthy of a Christian and a Protestant was equally the concern of the church authorities. Quarrels between husband and wife or between neighbours, drunkenness, profane swearing, dancing on May Day, led to citation before the consistory and spiritual censures.

The Church concerned itself not only with marriages but with betrothals, which were required to take place in the presence of a minister or elder, and once entered into could not be broken off without the consent of the consistory or colloque. A young lady who wanted to break her engagement because her betrothed had not taken the Sacrament (apparently he had failed at the catechising) and " did not seem to her able to instruct her in the fear of God " was firmly refused by the colloque, who evidently suspected other motives.[15]

The enforcement of discipline was in the hands of the elders, whose duty it was " to watch over the life and morals of the flock, to reprove slight failings by the Word of God, and to report more serious ones to the consistory ". For this purpose they had full inquisitorial powers : the *Discipline* expressly says that they are to visit every family, and to inquire *from their servants and the neighbours* as to their life and character—if they live in the fear of God, if they go to service regularly, if they have family prayers morning and evening, and say grace before and after meals. Any occasion of scandal, whether it was observed by the elders themselves or was mere hearsay, should be reported to the consistory.

At the Sunday meeting of the consistory all " scandals in the Church " reported by the elders were considered, and if it seemed desirable the person responsible was summoned before the consistory and heard in his own defence. The penalties at the disposal of the church courts were (in ascending scale) private admonition, public admonition, temporary exclusion from the Sacrament, and full excommunication. This last could not be inflicted by the consistory but was reserved for the colloque, and there was always an appeal from the consistory to the colloque, and from the colloque to the synod.

If the accused admitted his fault he was often required to make a public confession or the minister was directed to read his confession from the pulpit : this was in effect a form of public admonition.[16]

The church courts showed themselves no respecters of persons. An elder who had sworn " Sang Dieu " was deposed from office and ordered to make public confession of his fault, but as he was not an habitual swearer the consistory was authorised to "user de quelque modération". A minister whose treatment of his wife had caused scandal was ordered by the colloque to confess his fault " as a minister and as a husband " from the pulpit : he was given an appropriate text (I Timothy, III, vv. 1-3) to preach from and directed to make an abject apology in words dictated by the colloque " speaking in the singular number ".

At the same time the courts were genuinely reluctant to proceed to extreme measures as long as there was any hope of repentance. De Schickler gives many instances of delay in carrying out a sentence of excommunication.[17] An interesting report to the Council in 1618 says that the usual practice has been merely to suspend contumacious persons from the Sacrament and only to excommunicate in case of obstinacy, and that excommunication being rarely inflicted is " of great terror and respect " among the people.[18]

It is obvious that with an ecclesiastical system of this kind, which sets up a net-work of church courts covering the whole territory in their geographical extent, and the whole range of human life in their subject matter, serious questions are bound sooner or later to arise about the relations of the spiritual and the secular power. This did not happen at once in the islands. The Presbyterian system was established with the full approval and active help of the governors and the leading families, and for a time Church and State worked in harmony to produce a pious commonwealth after the model of Calvin's Geneva. Church and State were coextensive and interrelated in the islands as in England, although it was a different kind of Church.

This is assumed in the *Discipline* : the Church is said to be divided into three orders or estates, the magistrate, the pastors, and the people. The governor is recognised as having the right of nominating pastors and approving other church officers ; and it is expressly laid down that it is the duty of pastors and elders to live and cause their flocks to live in obedience to the queen and her officers. More significant perhaps, because it comes in incidentally, is the assumption that all or most of the jurats will also be elders of the Church. This appears in the directions for the election of elders and in the formal request of the colloques that the Royal Court should not sit when a colloque or synod is sitting in order that the jurats may not be prevented from attending to their ecclesiastical duties.

Throughout this period the Church confidently relied on the support of the Civil Power in enforcing its discipline and moral code. As the *Discipline* puts it, the magistrate bears the sword to compel the observance of the first as well as the second Table of the Law. In secular language the colloques of the islands called upon the civil authorities to put down Sabbath-breaking, to punish and if necessary to expel from the island people who neglected to go to church or take the Sacrament, to suppress dances and other disorderly amusements, and to seize erroneous and abusive books on religion. They had no hesitation in complying : the States passed ordinances making such things offences and the Royal Courts punished offenders who were brought before them.

Church and State therefore worked in harmony to ensure that the islands should be, as the Chronicler puts it, " well governed and regulated in the fear of God ". But the Presbyterian system contained within itself serious political implications, and it was apt to be an awkward bed-fellow for the civil government. It was not, as is sometimes said, a democratic system, at any rate in the 16th and 17th centuries. The ordinary mass of church members were firmly supervised by the consistory, and in practice the system of appointments to the consistory was one of cooptation worked by the parish notables not one of popular election. The people had merely the right of saying yes or no to the selected candidate and it would have taken a very daring small-holder or artisan to raise objections to the man chosen and recommended to him by his hereditary masters.[19]

There was a germ latent here which in more favourable circumstances might develop into a real measure of democracy; but in the islands and in the social conditions of the 16th century the right of election by the church assembly probably amounted to little more than the rights of the people of Venice when the new Doge, chosen by the Great Council, was presented to them with the customary formula—" This is your Doge, *if it shall please you* ". Presbyterianism at that time and place was an aristocratic, not a democratic system : a small group of ministers and leading laymen controlled the machinery of church government, and supplied the zeal and conviction which gave it life. As such it constituted a potential threat to the working of the Tudor political system. From the days of the Greek city states downwards aristocracies have been the strongest opponents of monarchies. The essence of the Tudor system was that all power in Church and State alike derived from the Sovereign, and all offices depended on him. The bishops governed the church and the king governed the bishops: in civil matters the king appointed to all executive posts, and chose his counsellors and called parliaments when he chose. But the Presbyterian Church confronted the State as a rival and self-sown organisation, not created by the king or dependent on his will ; and it was equipped in virtue of its own structure with a complete machinery for administration, deliberation, and the trial and punishment of offences against its rules. Queen Elizabeth had only one parliament to consider ; but her representatives in Jersey and Guernsey had to deal with two, the States and the Colloque. They consisted largely of the same people, but the Colloque claimed to derive its authority from a higher source and the leadership in it rested with the ministers rather than with the queen's officers.

The Church recognised as a matter of doctrine that the civil power had its own distinct sphere, and we have seen that the *Discipline* shows on the face of it abundant loyalty, and a very proper determination to render to Caesar the things that are Caesar's. It shows also a complete confidence that the civil authorities are working harmoniously with the Church towards the same end. In Guernsey an official definition of the relations between the two powers was issued. In 1589 Leighton, the governor, called a meeting of the Royal Court, ministers, and elders, and caused the ministers to deliver an address on the limit of the two jurisdictions, which was summarised in four articles and formally accepted by the assembly and the governor. It recognised the right of the Church to exercise its discipline, and the duty of the individual to submit to it : this discipline was limited to scandals and public faults in the Church ; and all crimes deserving of corporal punishment, fine or judicial censure were stated to be matters for civil justice.[20] But there were already signs that the two powers might not always be in harmony with each other. The address distinguishes carefully between the office and the person of the magistrate, and lays down that the magistrate as an individual is subject to ecclesiastical jurisdiction, with ominous references to Nathan reproving David and St. Ambrose excommunicating the Emperor Theodosius. And the colloques sometimes show a strong disposition to criticise or even dictate to the civil authority. It was natural that they should request the Royal Court to see that its godly ordinances were effectively carried out ; but it was going a step further when the Colloque complained that the Court was not doing its duty in punishing offenders, and threatened the constables with denunciation to the Court or exclusion from the Sacrament if they were not more zealous in putting down " insolences et desbordements " and enforcing church attendance.[21]

When the Church authorities laid it down that members who took their quarrels to the civil courts before referring them to the consistory should be excluded from the Sacrament, they

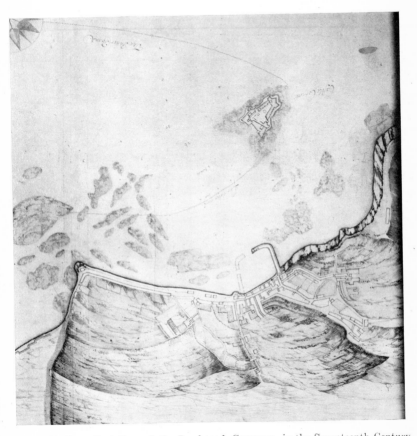

Map of St. Peter Port Town & the Roadstead, Guernsey, in the Seventeenth Century.

To face page 64

were no doubt deliberately following the Gospel injunction (Matthew xviii, 15-17), and probably this did more good than harm in so litigious a place as the islands then were ; but it contained obvious possibilities of encroachment on the sphere of secular authority. The articles of 1589 provided that offenders who had been punished by a magistrate might also be brought before the consistory " à ce qu'ils fassent leur profit du chatiment qu'ils auront reçu "; but it was a flagrant encroachment on the rights of the civil magistrate when the colloque ordered that accused persons who had been dismissed without punishment or acquitted by the civil court or even pardoned by the queen should still be brought before the consistory and subjected to ecclesiastical censures, and deposed from office an elder who protested that they were trespassing on the jurisdiction of the civil courts.

Still more remarkable is the case of Nicholas Carey who was excommunicated by his minister and in consequence suspended from his office as jurat. He obtained letters of absolution from the Archbishop of Canterbury, but in view of the opposition of the ministers the Royal Court put off readmitting him to his civil functions until the governor came back. Leighton, who had quarrelled with the excommunicating minister, Baudouin, called together the Royal Court with the ministers and some elders and summoned both him and Carey for their case to be heard. The Court found that Carey had done nothing very bad and that his excommunication had been frivolous, contrary to justice and to the Church discipline to which Baudouin had subscribed, and reinstated him in his office as jurat.[22] It is an amazing testimony to the interrelation of religious and secular jurisdiction in those days that on the one hand excommunication by a parish minister should operate to suspend a judge from his judicial functions, and on the other that the Civil Court, even with ecclesiastical assessors, should review and override a spiritual judgment.

CHAPTER VIII

GUERNSEY UNDER ELIZABETH.

It is necessary to turn back from the religious to the civil affairs of the islands. We hear very little of Jersey during Elizabeth's reign, for reasons to be discussed later, but there is a considerable body of documents relating to Guernsey.

All through the first years of the reign the defence of Guernsey gives rise to a good deal of anxiety. This was very natural as it was only a year or two since the French had ceased to occupy Sark, and from 1562-4 Elizabeth was at war with the French government in support of the Huguenot insurgents. Something like a panic was produced in 1564 by the expectation—unfounded as it happened—of a French landing,[1] and it is certain that the state of the islands defence was unsatisfactory and indeed alarming. From 1557 onwards the governor kept on reporting that the people were too weak to defend themselves and that " the Quene's estate depended mainly on her castle ", which was " not in repair to repulse an army ".[2]

The question of refortification was therefore urgent. The governor had been accustomed to get a certain amount of work done to the castle by the labour of the inhabitants ; but this customary *corvee* of a day or two's work or cartage of materials in a year, though possibly sufficient for minor current repairs, was of no use for any extensive rebuilding, and the island revenues could not produce the money required. In England the expense of Henry VIII's extensive fortifications had been met out of the sale of church lands, and something of the kind was the obvious resource in Guernsey. There the monastic lands had been taken over by Henry V when he went to war with France, and therefore already formed part of the royal domain. But the Government remembered that under Edward VI's act the Crown was entitled to all chantries, obits, and other minor religious foundations of this kind ; and in 1561 a Commission[3] was issued to the captains of Jersey and Guernsey and the bailiff and jurats of Guernsey directing them to inquire into all ecclesiastical property belonging to the Crown under the acts of Henry and Edward, and report their findings, in order that the proceeds might be appropriated to defence and the provision of schools.

The Commission got to work promptly and raised what money they could by selling and leasing the property which came to the Crown under the acts, but the results were unsatisfactory. In 1564 the governor reported that " the sales made by the late Commission being insufficient by one thousand pounds at the least, the weakest and most decayed part shall be first taken in hand and repaired as far as their present furniture will serve ".4 As usual at this period, any attempt to clear up doubts or disputes as to the extent of Crown property was immediately followed by a crop of fresh disputes and lawsuits. as to the correctness of the findings in individual cases. Also it was one thing to get in money and quite another to make certain that it was spent on the intended objects. In the present case this was specially difficult since, as we have seen the majority of the jurats were Catholics, and as such naturally disliked the diversion of chantry funds and the like to secular purposes, and were generally ill-disposed towards the policy of the Government. They showed themselves obstructive and openly hostile to it until finally the Council decided that it was impossible to carry on without a complete change in the local government of Guernsey ; and in July 1565 the bailiff and jurats were summoned to London to answer for their conduct and seven jurats were dismissed.

The Council's reasons for taking this drastic step are contained in a document in the Salisbury MSS. " Articles especially touching the dispositions of the Jurats of Guernsey whose names and dispositions follow ".5 This is a summary of the charges against the jurats : it was evidently prepared for and used at a meeting of the Council or the Star Chamber, as it contains marginal notes of the answers made by the accused to the various points. The charges are a curious medley. Only a few of them related directly to religious matters ; these were the burning of the martyrs, the raising of a fray in the streets against Protestants on the occasion of the rejoicings over the peace of 1564, and—in the case of one jurat—excessive and suspicious familiarity with the governor of Brittany. These however seem to have been the least part of their offences : it was evidently considered much more important that nine of the jurats " be the only impeachers and disturbers of the common quietness in the said isle, moving the people of the same to all insolent disorders and disobediences against God, the Queen's Majesty, and good surety of the isle, which people of themselves desire love and quietness were it not for the wicked persuasion of the said Jurats which move and stir them to the contrary ".

Later articles develop the charge in more detail : it appears that the jurats had collected the arrears due for the chantries, obits, etc., and had spent the money in proceedings against the governor : they then made the people believe that they would have to pay the money over again to the governor, and made use of the discontent which was naturally caused by this for the purpose of a political agitation against the governor, holding meetings (privy " conventicles " as the article calls them), and inducing people to sign " procurations in blank . . . . . such as no Governor dare in effect allow or approve ".

Naturally the Government was dissatisfied. The proceeds of the church lands on which they had reckoned for the necessary work of fortification had fallen far short of the sum required ; and they attributed this to the conduct of the jurats, who had spent the money which they had collected on lawsuits against the governor (presumably as to the rights of the Crown in particular cases) and used the Government's requirements as a means of exciting discontent and agitation. In addition to all this the jurats were unsound on the religious question and could not be depended on to keep the peace. The Council determined to show them " how displeasant it is to our prince to hear and understand of such proceedings where trust is reposed " by fining them £1000 to be spent on the fortifications, and dismissing seven of them.

Whether they ever paid the £1000 does not appear. Probably they paid something, as they got a pardon covering among other things all trespasses on the queen's lands and all dues, rents, arrears, etc., (with special reference to chantry lands), committed up to the date of Elizabeth's accession, as well all riots, routs, unlawful assemblies, and conventicles to the disturbance of the queen's peace.[6]

This sharp lesson produced its effect, for the time at any rate. In August 1566, the Governor reported " We could not proceed further through hindrances of the late deprived jurats. There is better hope from the last placed jurats, who are labouring, on receipt of the queen's letters, to reduce the rents to certainty ".[7] A few months later (January 1567) he again acknowledged the help of the bailiff and jurats by which " sundry concealments (will) be discovered and doubtful rents made certain ".[8]

The Government was evidently still unsatisfied as to the safety of the island, as in 1567 a Royal Commission was appointed to go into the whole question of defence. Their instructions were to examine the condition of the castle and the safety of the island generally, to inquire into the number of foreigners in the island with a view to guarding against danger from the presence of too many foreigners, and to discover how much money had been received in fines for the sale of chantry lands etc., and what had been done with it. Their report[9] was uncompromising : the fortifications had been neglected because of the islanders' obstinate belief that their neutrality was a sufficient defence—" they trustid altogethere to the Popes Bulls and other placetts obtayned of the French ". Consequently the only defence of the island lay in the strength and security of Castle Cornet, and this was in a state of such complete ruin and decay that " no gentleman that maketh account of his lyfe or credytt will take charge of this castle in the state yt ys yn, yn tyme of warre " ; and the principal inhabitants appealed to the Commissioners to call the attention of the Queen and Council to their position " being in utter despaire of their goods and lyves " if war should arise. Neutrality had had a bad effect on the spirit of the people as well as on the fortifications : the Commissioners found that they were imperfectly armed, quite untrained, and " not to be trustid unto for their harts and courages yn tyme of nede ". In any case their available force was small : in 1570 the new governor, an experienced soldier, reported that the muster of the island gave a total levy of eight hundred men of whom not more than three hundred were really fit for service, and in his opinion two hundred soldiers could overthrow the whole island.[10] The only financial expedient which the Commissioners could suggest was to sell the church bells, reserving the largest in each parish. This had already been done in Jersey, and they estimated that it would bring in £250 for fortifications.[11]

Sir Francis Chamberlain set to work actively to refortify the castle ; this necessarily led to strictness in enforcing royal dues, and we next hear of him (October 1568) as involved in a furious quarrel with the bailiff and jurats. Whether this was directly connected with the expenses of fortification is not clear, but it is significant that, although it speedily developed into a constitutional dispute as to the respective rights of the governor and the Royal Court, it began over a lawsuit brought by the farmers of the revenue against the dean for encroaching on the Crown rights. There may also have been other than financial reasons behind the quarrel. The bailiff and jurats told the Council[12] that Chamberlain was intriguing with the dismissed Catholic jurats, and inciting the people against the appointment of the Bishop of Winchester as ordinary. He may have done this to retaliate on the dean for appropriating Crown dues, but more likely religious differences came in also. The dean and the bishop both belonged to the extreme left wing of the Reformers : Chamberlain, who had been governor under Mary and had at least acquiesced in the burning of the martyrs,

cannot have been a very enthusiastic Protestant : probably also
he thought that the Bishop of Winchester was more likely to
interfere in island business than the foreign bishop of Coutances
who was only concerned to collect his dues (it is significant that
in this case we find the Bishop of Winchester making representations to the Secretary of State in favour of the bailiff and
jurats)[13] and did not want a rival authority in his government.

In any case, when the procureur took proceedings against
the dean on behalf of the farmers of the revenue, the Royal
Court sided definitely and (if the governor is to be believed)
very unfairly with the dean.[14] The procureur rested his case
on an ancient precedent signed by the bailiff and jurats : the
Court asked for the original in order to furnish the defence with
a copy, and then refused to restore it, thus enabling the dean to
proceed by verbal evidence (which it is implied would certainly be in his favour whatever the rights of the case might be).
The procureur refused to go on unless his document was
admitted in evidence and left the Court, thereby preventing
sentence being given as the presence of the queen's officers was
necessary to enable the Court to act : it is alleged that he was
also insolent to the Bench. The Court then sentenced him to
imprisonment for contempt, and followed this up by claiming
that this vacated the office and refusing to sit until another
procureur was appointed. They appointed representatives to
lay their case before Council, but two of the three selected were
members of the commission for the fortification of the island
and the governor forbade them to leave the island until the
queen's work was done, and when they insisted on taking
passage for England imprisoned them till the Council's pleasure
should be known " for neglect of the Queen's service and contempt of the Governor's command ".

What had begun as an ordinary lawsuit had now got on to
high constitutional grounds relating to the rights of the islands
and the powers of the governor. The deadlock between the
governor and the Royal Court was complete : they refused to
sit, on the ground that there was legally no procureur, and he
insisted that they must recognise the existing procureur and
discharge their duties. Obviously it would be an impossible
position for the governor if the Royal Court could at any time
compel him to dismiss his procureur by the simple expedient of
convicting him of contempt of court. The whole island was in
a turmoil : the jurats complained loudly that they were deprived of their right of access to Council : the people were
annoyed and inconvenienced because the Royal Court did not
sit : and the bailiff reported that " there are troubles in the
Island as I have not known for 48 years ". Chamberlain in

despair begged the Council to appoint a commission of " indifferent men chosen within the realm, who may understand all griefs in the government and reduce it to its ancient use or have it settled by your discretion and necessary rules left for posterity ".

Council appointed a small committee (the Bishop of London and the solicitor general) to hear the parties and on their report made an order (11th March, 1569) intended to settle the dispute.[15]   It is somewhat vague and platitudinous— Elizabeth's Council liked if possible to settle controversies by persuading or even coercing disputants into coming to an agreement among themselves rather than by a ruling imposed from above—and begins with an exhortation to the parties to forget all private and public quarrels and reconcile themselves and join together in all good friendship and concord.   In the same spirit the order wherever possible simply takes the line of declaring that existing rights and privileges should be observed without attempting to define them.   Thus the order directs that the governor on the one hand and the bailiff and jurats on the other should be regarded, obeyed and esteemed in such degree as belongs to their office and calling ; that all grants and confirmations of privileges from the queen and her progenitors should be observed and maintained with a special mention of the right of the Royal Court to make and enforce ordinances according to law and ancient custom.

Sometimes this confirmation of existing arrangements is accompanied by a qualification which is evidently intended as a set-off to placate the other side of the controversy.   The bailiff and jurats are to keep their ancient privilege of visiting and inspecting the castle, but they are " by all gentill meanes to exhorte, advise and perswade " the people to go on with the work of carting stone and other necessaries for the fortification of the castle ; it is expressly ordered that the union of the island to the diocese of Winchester shall not be called in question, provided that no more fees than before are to be taken in the Dean's Court and no one is to be required to go out of the island in any ecclesiastical cause.

Certain of the points in controversy are ended by a definite ruling designed as far as possible to remove the grounds of future trouble.   The procureur is directed to resign " voluntarely ", and the governor to appoint a new one, but there is an express order that the Royal Court " shall not omitt upon any cause the administracion of justice accordinge to the auncyente laws and customes ".   Clearly the Council did not mean to have another judicial strike in Guernsey.   Finally two general regulations of great importance for the future government of the island are laid down. The imprisonment of the dean and jurats by the governor is to be passed over, each side paying their own costs ; but it is ordered that the governor " shall not hereafter ymprison anie person of the said Isle withoute the order of justice, unles it be for martiall matters and farmes (i.e. revenue cases), in which cases the captayne hathe bene accustomed to ymproyson offendours as the custom in that parte permitteth ". And a special procedure is arranged for settling future disputes between the governor and the bailiff and jurats : any such controversy is to be considered in conference between them at a time and place appointed by the governor : if within 40 days it cannot be settled in this way then any one who wishes may appeal to the Council for redress " without anie lett or restrainte ".

Not long after this Chamberlain died, and the Government showed by their choice of his successor that they regarded Guernsey as an important and difficult governorship. The new governor was Thomas Leighton, of an old Shropshire family and married to a cousin of the queen : he had served with great distinction in the French war of 1562-4, and was clearly regarded by the authorities as one of the leading soldiers and diplomatists of the day, as he was several times called away from his government for special service. He was twice sent on embassies to France ; at the time of the Armada he was one of the commissioners appointed to supervise the local defence arrangements, and was one of Leicester's chief staff officers at Tilbury ; and when Essex was sent to Normandy in 1591 in command of the English forces co-operating with Henry IV, Leighton was his chief of staff. He belonged to the most advanced section of the Puritans which wished to introduce the ritual and government of Geneva into the English Church.

Leighton landed in Guernsey to take up his command in May 1570, and got to work at once with characteristic energy to take stock of the military position.[16] On 2 June he reported to Council that the fortifications of the castle were very unsatisfactory : Chamberlain's work had been badly done, and was quite insufficient to make the castle safe ; the local defence force was quite inadequate, and there were far too many Normans and other foreigners in the island. He began at once to repair the fortifications and mount guns, and at the end of August he reported that he had spent £100 on this work and pressed for more to be done.

The question of defence led at once to the question of finance, and Leighton plunged into this with the same energy and efficiency, and showed himself a strict guardian of the queen's revenues. In the same letter of 24 August he reported that " Her Majesty's and your Honours' name has by some been very much abused . . . for there have been many sums of money made of Her Majesty's lands and church goods by a Commission, the which was appointed for repairing of the Castle, but the money is shared out and gone and no penny bestowed as was appointed ".

In November he was on the track of a sum of £600 which had been issued to his predecessor, Sir F. Chamberlain, for work on the castle. £50 of this was found in the hands of Nicholas Carey and Thomas Effard who were to pay the workmen with it ; they showed warrants for part of the balance but said that Chamberlain had received the rest of the money in England and they had never had it.[17] Leighton therefore wanted the Council to extract the balance from Chamberlain's executors. He continued to pursue the Commissioners until in July 1571 he got authority to re-enter on land taken away " under colour of a commission but contrary to its meaning ", and to command the possessors to go to England to answer for their title.

At the same time he got a Royal Warrant authorising him to levy custom duty on all goods imported into the island in foreign vessels whether foreign owned or not. It appears that Guernsey sailors complained of great loss of work and of ships lying idle because English and insular merchants preferred to ship their goods in foreign vessels, and it was to meet this that he got the order that English goods imported in foreign ships should be treated for customs purposes as foreign. This naturally produced an outcry from the merchants, and the order was suspended for a time. In a report of December 1571 Leighton reflects mournfully :—" our English merchants are strange men to deal with, for in France they are content to pay two sundry customs and here grudge at one. Yet I take not but for goods conveyed in strange bottoms, and they are not content with that but seek to excuse the stranger ". He represented that if he were not allowed to take this custom the queen would have to pay the garrison, for the revenues of the island would not do it. This was a powerful argument, and evidently Leighton prevailed over the merchants, for nine years later as will be seen from the controversies of 1579-81, he was certainly levying customs on English goods imported in foreign ships, and the Council upheld it as " an ordinance thought meet for the maintenance of the navy ".

Not long after the settlement of the religious establishment secular troubles broke out in the island, which led to an acrimonius dispute between the governor on one side and the bailiff and some of the jurats on the other. It began, somewhat curiously, by an application to the Council from the bailiff and jurats dated sometime in 1578. They raised the old question of neutrality and the cost of fortifications, and go on to say that for lack of Justices of Assize out of England there has been loose government filling the isles with many evil customs, as keeping too many taverns and admitting runagates and exiles. They suggest that the bailiff and jurats should be ordered to abide by their ancient laws and that a Commission should be appointed " to bring the people to better obedience and reform abuses, which otherwise will not be so quietly compassed ". This is a remarkable application to come from the bailiff and jurats, and it suggests that the island was out of hand and they realised it. Certainly at some time between the sending of this petition and July 1579 there was a popular disturbance of some sort which led to the bailiff and jurats taking refuge in the castle. Exactly what happened is not clear : we only know of the outbreak from a reference in a semi-official letter, and the writer (Hamond, the legal member of the Commission) was at odds with the governor and disposed to take the people's side. He thinks that the disturbance was much exaggerated—" in truth there was no such matter (i.e. as a dangerous rebellion), saving that the jurats might pretend fear to make people odious, who hated them for injustice and for not defending them from injury ".

Either before or after this outbreak some Guernsey people appeared before the Council complaining of " divers and sundry grievances wherein they find themselves greatly wronged as well touching their liberties as the Administration of Justice ;" the bailiff and some of the jurats were ordered to answer, and in July 1579 a Royal Commission was appointed consisting of Leighton, the governor, John Hamond, D.C.L., Thos. Fleming, Geo. Paulet, lieut.-governor of Jersey, Edmund Yorke, and Hilary de Carteret, Seigneur of St. Ouen.[18]

Their terms of reference were to inquire :—

(1) whether by custom of the isle the Royal Court were bound by the laws and customs of Normandy, except as expressed in the book of extent and precepts (i.e. the Extente of 1331 and the Precepte d'Assize).

(2) whether and in what cases there is an appeal from the Royal Court to the Council.

(3) as to lands, rents, etc., concealed from Her Majesty and held by the inhabitants.

(4) to deal with certain individual cases.

(5) a question as to the law of stolen goods.

(6) to inquire of all abuses, misdemeanours, and

defects touching the jurisdiction of the bailiff and jurats, and of all protonotaries, registers, attorneys following, serving, and attending in any of their courts, and by what means and remedies the same may be both holpen and remedied.

It is plain that up to this stage it was the conduct of the bailiff and jurats that was in question, and there was no charge against Leighton. He points out in his petition that though he was in London at the time he was not called before the Council to answer any complaint, and that he was appointed to the Commission of Inquiry instead of being made a defendant. But when the Commissioners went over to the island and took evidence (September 1579)—Leighton apparently being still absent in London—a curious change in the situation took place. The bailiff and jurats on the one side and the complainants on the other got together, and agreed to turn their attack on the governor and put the blame for everything on him. As Leighton says :—" they played their parts in a play against me and the rights of Her Majesty, and . . . . in their complaint have not so much charged the bailiff and jurats as with suffering me to do injustice, and on the other side the bailiff and jurats in their answers have faintly defended and not answered for Her Majesty's right and authority, but covenously confessed the complaint and enforced the charge against me ". The inducement held out to the complainants was obviously that a concerted attack on the governor might lead to the reduction of the taxes and dues which he levied.

The immediate result of the Commissioners' inquiry was to increase the confusion and disorder in the island. They were there in September 1579, and in October and November the bailiff and jurats were complaining that " the people have been seduced to think ill of us as the only causes of the costs to be sustained for defrayment of the charges of the Commissioners and of us three, who were sent up to give attendance " ; and Leighton was indignantly reporting that the Commissioners " have set the country in such agog that, if they had might to their malice, the Queen would have neither wreck nor loyalty nor anything else, and her officers to stand for cyphers . . . . Such encouragements have grown by the manner of dealing and specially by the hard speeches and usage to Her Majesty's servants there, and by popular words and demeanour of one of the said Commissioners[19] that the humbleness of the people's obedience is much abated, and both they and the bailiff and jurats grown to more insolence than is convenient ".

Leighton had a good deal of justification for his complaints. After the Commissioners left, the bailiff and jurats gave out that

Council had found the charges against the governor proved and had granted the islanders' petition. This was quite untrue, as the whole case was still under consideration; and it is not surprising that Leighton asked the Council " to direct their letters and order for some good means that their insolence may have some abasement and some more respect be had of Her Majesty and her officers ". The Council responded by sending a sharp letter (3 December, 1579) to the bailiff and jurats saying that their Lordships " cannot but disallow " such proceedings, and commanding them in the queen's name to look to it " that they nor the inhabitants do in any wise intermeddle in anything touching Her Majesty's rights, revenues or privileges otherwise than they lawfully may do, and in late years have done, by the allowance of Her Majesty and her Governor, but therein wholly to suspend their proceedings " until they receive the Council's decision.

This was embodied in two Orders in Council of August and October 1580[20] which evidently represent an attempt to settle the matters in dispute at the present and to remove causes of controversy for the future. They were very far from producing the desired result. By the end of October Leighton was indignantly reporting :—" The disposition of the people hath been very disordered, and that in appearance by the practice and intermeddling of sundry popular and seditious persons, pretending the rights and privileges of the isle, but in truth seeking the overthrow of Her Majesty's prerogatives and revenues, which disorders have been encouraged and set forward by the connivance and secret furtherance of the bailiff and jurats ".[21]

In particular he said that the orders sent down by the Council as to the queen's rents and the customs on foreign goods had been strained and perverted by the Royal Court, who had imprisoned the farmers of the revenue for paying over the proceeds to the queen's receiver instead of to the people, had maintained (falsely) that no customs were paid on strangers goods in the time of the late governor, and had put the queen's law officers to silence. " They do the like in all cases touching Her Majesty, for they are become both judges and parties, and they have sent the Queen's Procureur out of Court, saying he hath not to do in these causes. Many refuse to pay the Queen's rent unless proved due by Guernsey witnesses, and they perjure themsleves to acquit one another ". Further, they had illegitimately increased the Douzaine of St. Peter Port to 22 by the addition of 10 of their own partisans, and had insisted on paying the expenses of a delegation from St. Peter Port by a general tax on the whole island contrary to Council's order that they should be met by a voluntary subscription from the persons who had actually benefitted by the Council's decision.

Leighton's view was that the bailiff, William de Beauvoir, with his brother and Nicholas Martin, another jurat, were the chief instigators of these disorders, and " unless they were removed from the seat of jurisdiction and sharply punished, no Englishman can govern there unless Her Majesty keep 300 soldiers to repress these mutinies ".[22] In April 1581 these three were arrested by a queen's messenger, and on 5 June they appeared to answer the complaints against them.[23] They were detained for a time, and on 30 July the Council gave its decision. It was embodied in an order addressed to the governor, bailiff and jurats which they were required to see observed " for the better maintenance of good order and quietness in the isle ". As this order records the " voluntary " resignation of the bailiff and jurats, it is clear that the struggle ended in a decisive victory for Leighton.[24]

It is possible from the surviving material to form a fairly good opinion on the nature and merits of the controversy between Leighton and the islanders. The complaints were comprised in 34 articles, 28 originally submitted and 6 more added when the Commissioners began their inquiry. They are not preserved, but their substance is plain from Leighton's detailed reply and from a report of the law officers which summarised in 3 parallel columns the articles and the answers of the Royal Court and the governor respectively.

It is at once apparent that the articles against Leighton were compiled on the simple principle of taking everything which anyone regarded as a grievance and blaming the governor for it, without any regard to consistency or even to the facts of the case. It was absurd to combine in the same article Puritan complaints of the closing of churches and consequent lack of sermons with anti-Puritan lamentations over the prohibition of dancing at weddings, and all the more because neither of them was any doing of Leighton's. Dancing at weddings had been forbidden by an ordinance of the Royal Court before Leighton set foot in the island ; and he had no difficulty in showing that all the churches were open when he came to London, but since then some had been closed because the people would not pay the ministers. A little later the Royal Court themselves asked for permission to levy contributions for the support of the ministry, explaining that in former times the parsons' livings consisted mainly of fees for acts done " after the superstitious order which they called the rites of the church, for which each household paid a good sum yearly ; they are greatly diminished now that we have godly preachers, so that three benefices can scarcely maintain one minister ". At least 9 of these articles relate to matters of this kind, for which Leighton was not responsible ; most of them were matters within the sphere of the Royal Court, as e.g. fees taken from jurats, and ordinances restricting export of certain goods and forbidding the sale of fish out of market ; others related to the appropriation of church property by Act of Parliament or the neglect of the parish treasurer of St. Peter Port to furnish any accounts.

The greater part of the remaining articles—some 14 in all—had to do with questions of taxation and royal dues. Leighton was accused of increasing customs and export duties beyond the legitimate amount and of impressing horses for official use and demanding supplies for the castle at less than market price. There had also been recent disputes over the Crown's rights to wrecks. Leighton met all complaints of this kind by maintaining that he had taken no more than he was entitled to by law and ancient custom, except in the one case of English-owned goods imported in foreign ship. He had been expressly authorised by an Order in Council of 1571 to levy strangers' customs on all goods brought in strangers' ships, and this was now upheld by the Council as " an ordinance thought meet for the maintenance of the navy ".

Council appeared to have been satisfied with Leighton's explanations : they certainly did not censure him for misconduct or extortion, but they made an attempt to prevent disputes on these points in the future by ordering that the rate of customs should be the same as under recent governors, and that the books of customs which were in the hands of the queen's officers should be shown to the Royal Court in order that they might make an abstract of the usual payments in those times, and give one copy to the governor and the other to the Council.

So far the points at issue were matters of financial detail and no political question was involved. Leighton had obviously been strict and careful in getting in the queen's revenue ; the question was merely whether in certain cases his view of what was legally due or the islanders' was the right one. This could be settled by the courts and in the last resort by the Privy Council, and there is no suggestion that Leighton attempted to interfere with the ordinary course of justice in such matters. On the contrary when he claimed campart from the tenants of Fief-St.-Michel, he took the case to the Royal Court in the regular way ; and when the decision was in his favour made no difficulty about the tenants appealing to Council. But there remain a certain number of articles in which Leighton is charged with actual misgovernment and tyranny. He was accused of imprisoning men without order of court and other violent acts ; of making levies and exactions of money ; of compelling the people to take ship against pirates ; of forbidding people to go on board foreign ships without licence, and seizing foreign merchants' goods. As to imprisonment Leighton said—correctly as appears from the law officer's notes—that the charges were general and therefore he could only meet them with a general denial. Only one specific case was mentioned, that of certain young men who were imprisoned for sedition and rebellion (by the lieutenant-governor in Leighton's absence). He said that this has always been lawful and usual : the law officers agreed that the governor had the power of imprisonment " in martial matters and farms " ; they explained this latter by saying that it had been usual for the queen's receiver to imprison for unpaid rents ; " but considering that the receiver is a man of little stay of living, and guided by the porter of the castle whose commodity it is to have many prisoners ", they suggest that this should only be done by order of the Court " provided the custom be satisfied with due expedition ". As to the other violent acts, Leighton said that he himself never struck anyone, and he never let his servants or soldiers do so without punishment if complaint were made to him.

The complaint about service against pirates was apparently based on the clause of the Précepte d'Assize exempting Guernsey-men from service out of the island.[25] Leighton's reply was that he never compelled anyone to serve, but allowed them to do so with their own consent when the pirates were in the roads within a mile of the island. He added rather pointedly that they had received no damage from this unless they had been prevented from trading with pirates. One cannot help suspecting that there was a good deal in this. If the Guernsey people preferred to see pirate ships lying in sight of their harbour rather than go out to drive them off, they certainly interpreted their privilege of neutrality and their exemption from service out of the island liberally ; and one cannot help suspecting that they had an understanding with the pirates and did business with them.

Leighton explained that it had been the order of wise governors long before his time to forbid anyone to go on a foreign ship without his licence. The object was twofold : to protect the islanders from pirates and wreckers, and to prevent them from robbing wrecks. He had never refused a licence in reasonable cases, and had only once imprisoned anyone for disobeying this rule. It may be noted that the Commissioners of 1607, who favoured the islanders whenever possible, upheld the Governor in this.[26] He had never seized the goods of foreign merchants ; on the contrary he had used his authority to protect them from being defrauded by the islanders. The Royal Court were too partial to their own people to do this properly.

Finally there was a very curious complaint that Leighton had sold corn (i.e. the queen's wheat rent) out of the island and thereby caused a scarcity ; and it was claimed that the queen's corn could not be sold out of the island without the consent of the Royal Court. Of course the Crown like all other landowners had been accustomed to export its wheat as it pleased, and no authority was produced for the alleged right to restrict the governor's liberty in this respect : it was not suggested apparently that the restriction should apply to any-one else's corn. He had no difficulty in showing that if this claim were admitted the financial position would become impossible ; for he had to sell the corn, which was a large part of the revenue, to get ready money to pay the soldier's wages, and if he were compelled to sell it in the island at the price fixed by the Royal Court he would never get a proper price for it.[27]

While the complaints against Leighton for the most part broke down, it is clear there must have been some substantial causes at work to account for the disturbances of these years. Apparently distress caused by the falling off of trade had a good deal to do with them : Leighton said that the sailors had complained to him of great loss of trade and of Guernsey ships lying up because merchants freighted in foreign vessels, which compelled them to go abroad to earn their living. The Wars of Religion in France must have done much harm to trade ; but in addition there are indications that foreigners had in some way been unfairly treated in Guernsey, which made them reluctant to do business with the islanders. Article 22 is summarised by the law officers thus :—" By reason of sundry wrongs done to strangers the inhabitants grew odious so as trafficking to other places they were enforced to say they are of Jersey or some other country " ; and it appears from the same summary that the bailiff and jurats could not deny this, but merely said that the captain had several times been asked to consider it and some remedy ought to be found. It is reasonable to connect this with Leighton's remark in his answer to Article 7 that he had never seized merchant's goods, but had exercised his authority to defend them from being defrauded by the islanders, the Royal Court being too partial to their own people to do this properly : and it is likewise reasonable to suppose that the curious attitude of the islanders towards

A Prospect of the Bay Towne of St Hillary, Castle of Elizabeth, and Towne of St Aubin.

View of St. Aubin's Bay, Jersey, in the Seventeenth Century.

To face page 80

pirates had something to do with it. They made it a grievance that they were called on to embark against pirates even when the pirates were within a mile of the harbour, and Leighton hints that they did an illegitimate trade with the pirates. It would certainly not encourage foreign merchants to frequent Guernsey if the inhabitants had so good an understanding with pirates as to let them ride at anchor off the town with impunity.

There is also the obvious fact that Leighton was a strict and careful administrator who looked closely after the queen's revenues, getting in everything that he could claim and reviving rights which had been overlooked. A rigorous financial administration naturally increased the sense of hardship caused by bad trade. A further element in the popular discontent was a feeling of dissatisfaction with the Royal Court caused by the indefinite and fluid state of the law, and a belief that the jurats sometimes took advantage of this to give partial judgments. Saravia said in 1565, " they have no laws ; they boast of their ancestral customs, but these are changed from day to day at the caprice of the jurats " : and the report of the Royal Commission of 1579 and the Order in Council of October 1580 based on it refer to complaints of " want of due administration of justice through the liberty which the bailiff and jurats do take upon themselves to direct their judgments by precedents wherein there is neither certainty nor rule of justice, forsaking the customary of Normandy whereto they should hold themselves ". Council attempted to meet these complaints by ordering the Royal Court to follow the customary of Normandy in all points except where it was varied by the two ancient authorities (the Précepte d'Assize and the Extent of 1331) or by Order in Council. They recognised however that some customs had grown up differing from the Norman custumal, and gave instructions that these should be collected and submitted to Council. This was done and the resulting compilation as approved by the Queen in 1582 forms the well-known *Approbation des Lois*.[28] It was intended to form a code of law for Guernsey, but the intention never took effect.[29] The Royal Court persisted in deciding cases according to what they thought right without regard to the letter of the code, and law in Guernsey remained as uncertain after the *Approbation des Lois* as it had been before. The opinion of the Royal Commission of 1848 is a 19th century paraphrase of Saravia's words :—" It is sufficient to state that we found scarcely a single instance in which the law could be traced to a higher source than the discretion of the Court, or in which that discretion was itself secured from continual variation in practice ".[30]

After this decisive victory and the dismissal of his three chief adversaries from their office it is not surprising that Leighton had no more trouble with the bailiff and jurats for the next few years. The decision of the Council did however give rise to fresh difficulties in an unexpected quarter. Leighton was so zealous a Presbyterian and had done so much to establish the doctrine and discipline of Geneva in the island that he might reasonably have counted on the good-will and support of the Church. But on the contrary he now found himself involved in a quarrel with the ministers, or at least the majority of them.[31] Among the complaints which came before the Council in 1579 were some as to the way in which probate cases and the execution of wills had been dealt with (we do not know the details) ; and the Order in Council contained a provision that probate of wills and certain ecclesiastical business such as the administration of the revenues of benefices while they were vacant should be " ordered by the Bishop of Winchester and such as shall be appointed by the captain and the Royal Court to confer with him ". This was a very natural decision : such business had been dealt with in England by the Bishop's Court from time immemorial : in Guernsey the Dean's Court had done the work until the Reformation, since when it had been divided—without any express authority—between various civil authorities. The Bishop of Winchester carried out the direction of Council by appointing as his commissary to deal with wills and other ecclesiastical business the queen's procureur, Louis de Vic, an energetic and loyal official, and the right-hand man of the Governor, who describes him as " a very honest and sufficient man and the best servant to Her Majesty that ever I found in the isle ".

The ministers were greatly annoyed at the intrusion of a bishop's officer into their Presbyterian establishment. Immediately on his appointment (August 1581) they openly proclaimed that either the commissary would drive them out or they him ; and by June 1582 there had already been " great stress between them " which the governor vainly attempted to quiet, and he was reporting to Walsingham that " our free ministers here are greatly grieved and offended by the placing of a Bishop's Court in this isle, notwithstanding that the bishop's official neither hath nor doth attempt anything either upon their ministry or discipline, but only dealeth with the judgment of civil cases. . . . .By your order without my knowledge it was appointed to be re-established, but for that I will not oppose myself against your Lordship's orders. I am among them condemned as if I were a backslider ; but I have learned not to disobey my superiors, and for so slight a cause as this controversy, which is nothing but whether all ministers should be on an egality or that a bishop shall be a superintendent over them, which point whether the one or the other be, I am indifferent, for it is a thing that toucheth not salvation, I mean to us of the laity ".

Shortly after this report was written the dispute came to a head. The ministers applied to the Council with a formal accusation against de Vic, and the governor was ordered to report upon the charges. He had them investigated by the Royal Court and forwarded the result together with a report of his own to the Council (Sept. 1582).

The charges against de Vic were an extraordinary medley of old scandal and recent political animus. His adversaries raked up (and misrepresented) an incident of 15 years before, when de Vic, in his capacity as constable of his parish, had broken the head of an insubordinate parishioner at a general muster, and two charges of adultery, one 12 years old on which he had been tried and acquitted by the Church Courts. The concluding article was a vague accusation of being " a troubler of the ministry and the Church ". The chief facts alleged in support of this were that de Vic had refused to obey a summons before the consistory, and struck the elder who brought it—he admitted doing this under strong provocation—and that he had taken a minister by the gown and said that he preached a factious and seditious sermon and would have to answer for it, to which he replied that the sermon *was* seditious.

It is perfectly obvious that it was theological and political hostility and not any desire to protect the Church from moral contagion that was at the bottom of this affair, and that Leighton hit the mark when he told Walsingham that the quarrel of the ministers with de Vic was due to " the office of Commissary that he holdeth under the Bishop rather than the vices of the man or his troubling of the Church or ministers ". This attitude is intelligible enough in the case of ardent Presbyterians, but it is surprising to find them flagrantly abusing church discipline for a political object, and still more surprising that they should have ventured to send up such a case to the Council. Their heads must have been badly turned by their past success, or they would have realised that the queen and her advisers would not openly support them in establishing a Presbyterian theocracy in Guernsey, and that their best chance of keeping the position they had won was not to parade their differences from the Church of England. Leighton, as we have seen, was as good a Presbyterian as any of them ; and for 12 years past had been working hand in hand with the ministers to set up and maintain the Geneva system of doctrine and discipline ; but this was too much for him. When his efforts to keep the peace failed he naturally made up his mind to stand by de Vic : as a loyal servant of the queen he felt bound to carry out the Council's orders and to support the bishop's commissary appointed under those orders, and when that commissary was the queen's procureur and his own right hand man (" the best servant to Her Majesty whom I have or hope to find ") he had every motive to support him vigorously. He had satisfied himself, as we have seen, that the point at issue was not a matter of conscience ; and he was genuinely shocked at the proceedings of the ministers, and afraid of the scandal and mischief that would be caused if they became known in England. His report to the secretary of state ends with an earnest request that Walsingham will deal with the case himself, for if it should come before the whole Council " then do I doubt that such disordered dealings by certain of our ministers will be manifested, as their ill-doings may be hurtful to the state of religion and a great cause of renversing of that good foundation which by God's grace and my travail has here been planted ".

Walsingham appears to have complied with this request, and the matter ended with a triumph for the governor and de Vic. The latter remained procureur until he was appointed bailiff a few years later, and his chief adversaries among the ministers were compelled to leave Guernsey. Nicholas Baudouin, the leading minister and the chief mover in the attack on de Vic, went to London in 1583, professing to fear for his safety in Guernsey. Walsingham advised him to resign his benefice in the interests of the peace of the island, and gave him a handsome testimonial, armed with which he had no difficulty in getting a living in Jersey (1584). In June 1585 the lieutenant governor arrested four other ministers and searched their houses, evidently thinking that he had grounds for a charge of sedition. They were released after 24 hours detention, and left the island : three of them also obtained livings in Jersey and the governor at once replaced them by refugees from France. This caused a violent quarrel between the colloques of the two islands. Guernsey held that the offer of charges to the expelled ministers was a criticism of their action and a breach of the union between the two colloques, while Jersey insisted that their new colleagues had been improperly deprived of their charges, and that the ministers who replaced them were intruders. This led to a complete breach, and the two colloques refused to meet in synod until 1597. In Guernsey the victory of the civil power was final and decisive. Leighton had no more trouble over ecclesiastical questions, and for the rest of his long government Church and State worked in harmony.

84

But it was not long before Leighton again had trouble with a hostile party in the Royal Court. He had made his own nephew, Thomas Wigmore, bailiff, but the relationship did not prevent him from siding with the malcontents, and in 1587 the bailiff and three jurats, Nicholas Carey, John Le Fevre, and Thomas Effard were summoned to London to answer complaints made by Leighton. The queen's procureur, Louis de Vic, also came up to present the case for the governor, and the accused hired two men to murder de Vic : he was attacked with clubs in the open street at Westminister and left for dead, but afterwards recovered. The quarrel arose out of the governor's action in seizing certain French ships which had put into Guernsey (1587), which the islanders alleged to be a violation of their privilege of neutrality. It has been stated above in the chapter on Neutrality that the Council found in favour of the islanders on the question of principle. But the substance of Leighton's complaint was that the bailiff and jurats had taken advantage of their legitimate difference of opinion with him over the seizure of the French ships to make improper and groundless general charges of tyranny ("in truth the scope thereof reacheth to none other end than to slander and take away the good name of the Governor, yea, his very life, if the slanders therin contained were provable against him ").[32]

The Council found entirely in Leighton's favour. A committee of lawyers, to whom they had referred the case advised after hearing the parties, that Leighton "did not otherwise than orderly behave himself and according to letters of your Lordships unto him for his direction if the goods fell out to belong to Spaniards, whereof he had then some probable suspicions ". They were satisfied on the other hand that the more serious part of Leighton's charges were proved. The order set out that the accused bailiff and jurats had procured Louis Savarte (the Frenchman who applied to the Admiralty Court in the case of Le Levrier) to exhibit to the jurats " certain articles containing sundry unreverent and reproachful words against the Governor ", and had signed and sealed with the island seal documents accusing the governor of " seeking the overthrow of the estate of the isle by tyrannies, oppression, violence and imprisonment " ; they had levied a tax (i.e. to pay the expenses of a representative sent to London) " under colour of maintenance of their privileges but principally to deprave and defame the Governor " without the consent of the inhabitants ; and they had conspired with the bailiff's brother to hire men to attack de Vic.

Wigmore, Carey, and Le Fevre were dismissed from office

85

and sent to the Marshalsea during the pleasure of the Council, and the governor was directed to appoint a new bailiff. Rousewell (de Vic's assailant) was to be set in the pillory in Guernsey, and such persons as de Vic had named in his depositions to be bound over to keep the peace ; the representative sent up by the accused was to recover his costs from those who had employed him, not from the inhabitants.

This should have been a sharp lesson to the malcontents, and the appointment of the faithful Louis de Vic as bailiff must have strengthened Leighton's position. It is not surprising therefore that several years passed without serious trouble ; it was not till 1597 that Leighton and the jurats came into active collision again. Leighton's old enemy, Nicholas Carey, furnished the occasion for the trouble this time. On 28 August, 1597, Leighton reported to Cecil " the disloyal dealings of the Jurats of this isle seeking to smother up traitorous speeches uttered by Nicholas Carey. These Jurats ought to be punished so as to learn them to take a greater regard in matters that concern Her Majesty ". From the Act of Court[33] it appears that on 8 August the governor reported to the Court that two years before Nicholas Carey had said that on the approaching death of Her Majesty he would be one of the first to pull the governor by the ears out of the castle. After three sittings the Court decided on 27 August that Carey was not guilty. As the evidence appears to have been that the lieutenant governor had heard from Eleazar le Marchant that he had heard from James de Beauvoir that Carey had made this disloyal remark to him (de Beauvoir) it is not surprising to the modern reader that Carey was acquitted. But both Leighton and the Council took the matter very seriously.

In September 1597 orders were given for nine of the jurats to be sent up to London. Most of them were discharged in January, but William de Beauvoir, Nicholas Martin (both old adversaries) and John Effard were sent to the Marshalsea. They retaliated by accusing Leighton of violating insular privileges and oppressing the people, and were ordered to set out their grievances in full and to produce evidence. A petition in which they attempted to do this together with an answer by Leighton was referred to a small committee, consisting of Julius Caesar, the judge of the Admiralty Court, and Robert Beale, one of the clerks of the Council, who examined the documents and heard the parties. The complainants told a lamentable story of oppression and victimisation : " they are abated and curbed even to the ground ; partly by poverty and partly by terror of Leighton's vehement proceedings ; they are brought so low that what extremities soever they endure they have no means of redress ". Leighton had beaten and imprisoned jurats at his pleasure, had seized foreigners' ships and goods, had assumed the jurisdiction of the Royal Court and prevented criminal proceedings in a case of murder. Strangers were discouraged from coming to the island by his taking occasion to make report that if they came either ships and goods might be seized, or their wills might be disregarded, or they might be killed with impunity—with the result that the island which was formerly flourishing and rich by the observances of its privileges, particularly that of neutrality, was now as poor as may be owing to the breach of the same.

Leighton retorted that their complaints were not due to the good affection they bore to their country or maintenance of their privileges, but of mere malice and desire of revenge against himself, because they had been summoned to answer their undue proceedings, and because he had informed the Council of their partial dealings in Her Majesty's causes, and got a Commission which disclosed their encroachments on Her Majesty's rights and dignities. He added with obvious feeling that his adversaries had given a great deal of trouble by refusing to attend the Royal Court and otherwise neglecting their duty, " but if I, at any time in respect of Her Majesty's service, the maintenance of her honour and estimation, the preservation of her rights and privileges, do, when such abuses are undutifully offered, commit for a night or day's space any such offenders, then do they exclaim that their privileges are broken and the country is undone ".

The report of the sub-committee shows that there was much force in this. Careful examination established that the talk in the petition about breach of privileges and injury to the prosperity of the island was so much rhetoric which the complainants could not substantiate when they were asked to produce facts. The seizure of ships and goods which they referred to was the old case of 1586 which had been satisfactorily settled at the time. What they said about strangers being scared away by fear of murder, or their wills being disregarded, was loose talk which was in no way justified by the two recent cases which they quoted ; but these are of sufficient interest to call for a few words of description.

As to the first, it was quite true that a foreigner had been killed. The governor in his military capacity had given orders that strangers should land only at St. Peter Port, and that a watch should be kept at less frequented landing-places. A ship from Roscoff had been observed hanging about the island for several days, anchoring and landing men at daybreak in various small harbours, and the governor ordered the watch not to let them land. On their attempting again to land men at twilight, the watch challenged them, and, after several warnings had been disregarded, fired and hit a man, who died two days later. The governor with the captains of parishes held an inquiry as a matter of martial discipline, and asked the jurats to attend. They refused to do so, and the governor held the inquiry without them (this is the encroachment on the jurisdiction of the Royal Court complained of), and found that it was justifiable homicide.

The will case was equally clear. A French resident named Henry Tesser left his property by will to the poor. The governor refused to recognise the will, and compelled the executor to surrender the property to the Crown. This was perfectly right : the Crown was entitled by ancient custom (*droit d'aubaine*) to goods of foreigners dying in the island without direct heirs. The complainants were confronted with a clear statement of the law in the compilation of the island law recently drawn up and signed by the Bailiff and Jurats (the *Approbation des Lois*), and could only say that they thought it had been fraudulently inserted by Louis de Vic (the then procureur). The Committee naturally found that the governor was in the right on both points.

They were equally clear as to the charges of illegal imprisonment and violation of insular privileges. Four specific cases of imprisonment were alleged : the committee disregarded two of these on the double ground that the petitioners had no authority to represent the alleged victims, and that the latter had not presented the complaint themselves, although they had been recently in London, and could easily have done so. In the other two cases they thought that the imprisonment was within the governor's authority, and that the persons imprisoned had deserved it for their insubordination and insolence. One of them, William de Beauvoir, when called upon to give security for £100 to appear in London in pursuance of Council's orders " answered most contemptuously that he would not for a hundred pounds nor for a hundred pence " ; and when charged on his allegiance to give bonds to appear in six weeks said " he could not in six weeks nor yet in six months ". This was not conduct likely to be approved by Elizabeth's Council, and in fact Leighton was sharply reprimanded for not imprisoning de Beauvoir at once instead of merely reporting him to the secretary of state.

The committee further found that no infringement of the privilege of neutrality had been proved, and that the complainants, though claiming to act in the name of the inhabitants generally, could produce no public authority and admitted they had none. On the contrary the bailiff and other jurats had written to deny that the complainants had any commission " from them or the generality ", and a number of the leading inhabitants had sent up a memorial to the same effect. The general conclusion of the Committee was :—" we do not in our consciences find proved that any such breach of privileges or injustice hath been by the Governor committed as may give cause of so heinous a complaint against him ". The Council adopted their report and made an Order (24 April, 1598) :—

" Theire Lordships consideringe the clamorous and malicious proceedinge of thes men, tendinge to the defamacion of theire Governor, whose dyscreete and worthie behaviour ys well knowne to theire Lordships and acknowledged by all the inhabitaunts, and that they were not able to prove anie of the articles exhibited against him, have ordered (besides theire imprysonment), that the foresaid Nicholas Martin, William Beauvoir and John Efford shall severally and in submyssive sorte confesse and acknowledge theire false and malycious accusacions of theire Governour " in writing before the Council and in public assembly in the island. They were deposed from office and not to be re-appointed without the governor's consent.[34]

In their letter notifying this decision to the bailiff and jurats, the Council added that if the generality have any complaint against the governor, it should be dealt with as provided by the Order in Council of 1586 ; and if this fails they should send procureurs properly appointed and instructed to appear before the Council and " show their grievances in more modest and seemly terms ", where they shall receive such favour and justice as the goodness of their case may deserve. It is notable that Carey's case, which was the original cause of all the trouble, seems to have disappeared from notice in the wider issues raised by the complaints of the jurats. Carey was before the Council on 23 December, 1597, and was ordered not to depart without permission ; on 17 January, 1598, he was discharged from further attendance.

After this decisive success it is not surprising to find that Leighton had no serious trouble during the rest of Elizabeth's reign.

CHAPTER IX.

JERSEY UNDER ELIZABETH.

We have seen that on Elizabeth's accession Jersey accepted Protestantism without any trouble and settled down quietly under the new regime. During the whole of Elizabeth's reign we hear very little of Jersey : unlike Guernsey there seems to have been an almost complete absence of controversies between the governor and the people. This no doubt was partly due to the fact that for fifty years the governorship was continuously in the hands of one powerful family, the Paulets. Hugh Paulet was governor from 1550 to 1572 : his son, Amias, was his lieutenant-governor from 1559 to 1571, and governor from 1572 to 1588 : Amias's son, Anthony, was his father's lieutenant from 1581 to 1588, and in turn governor from 1588 to 1600 : finally George Paulet, brother of Amias, was lieutenant and bailiff for many years. Clearly the Paulets were in a very strong position. From 1570 onwards the governor himself was usually serving out of the island (Amias Paulet was the famous gaoler of Mary Queen of Scots), but he had had many years of experience in the island as lieutenant, and he had left his son to represent him. During these years therefore the governor was entirely free from the main difficulty of governors sent from England to administer outlying dependencies, ignorant of local conditions and local personalities. The Paulet family being strong Puritans were entirely in sympathy with the Geneva Protestantism of the leading Jersey families, and they had connected themselves with some of the most influential of them. They were on excellent terms with the de Carterets of St. Ouen : the second son of the Seigneur of St. Ouen was godson of Amias Paulet, and the heir to the seignory married the daughter of the lieutenant, George Paulet, who had himself married a Perin of Rozel. They were well secured on the English side likewise, being trusted servants of the queen, and belonging to one of the most influential of the new families : the Marquis of Winchester, Lord High Treasurer, was Hugh Paulet's half-brother. It was not surprising therefore that Jersey was quiet under Paulet rule and that the successive governors of the family had singularly little trouble in the way of disputes with the island notables or complaints to the Council. The current idea that the rule of the Paulets was tyrannical and repressive seems to derive mainly from Le Geyt, but, as will be seen below, Le Geyt's theory to this effect rests on conjectures and insinuations, and there is no positive evidence in support of it.

The island deputation to the Council in 1565, which was the only incident of any importance in the island history during the first twenty five years of the reign, was in no sense directed against the governor. It had two objects—to get sanction for the establishment of the French and Geneva church system in the island, and to regulate the question of appeals from the insular courts. Hugh Paulet was in sympathy with the petitioners on both points. He was a Protestant himself, and had served under Lord Russell in the suppression of the Western Catholics in 1549, and it must have been obvious to anyone on the spot that the choice in Jersey was between the Protestantism of Geneva and full Catholicism. The other complaint was that a practice was growing up of applying from the island to courts in England such as the Court of Chancery and the Court of Requests, and that these Courts issued processes in the island contrary to the insular charters. The case was quite clear under the charter of 1562, and after consulting the two chief justices and the governor, the Council made an order (22 June, 1565)[1] laying down very precisely that all insular suits should be decided in the islands and not in England, and that no appeal should be made from any decision of an insular court except to the King in Council, and directing that a special warning should be sent to the courts at Westminster not to award any process against inhabitants of the islands. It is clear from the words of the order that Hugh Paulet entirely agreed with this decision ; obviously it was not to his interest as governor that English courts should interfere in island matters : he would much prefer to have them dealt with by the Royal Court and the Privy Council on either or both of which he might exercise some influence if he had any reason for wishing to do so.

The quiet of Jersey was however disturbed in 1587 by a quarrel which broke out between a section of the jurats on one side and the bailiff and lieutenant-governor on the other. It began with a quite unimportant personal squabble but speedily developed, as such things were apt to do in the islands, into a constitutional question which is interesting for the light it throws upon the political ideas of the time.

Helier Dumaresq, a jurat, had a lawsuit before the Royal Court, and in the course of the proceedings the bailiff, George Paulet, made some remark which offended Dumaresq, who said " qu'il lui faisait une injure vilaine ". Such a reply addressed to the bailiff in full court and in the presence of the lieutenant-governor was considered highly unbecoming and offensive, and the bailiff determined to report it to the Council. Two other jurats, John de Carteret and Philip Journiaux, sided with Dumaresq ; they apparently had a feud with the bailiff. The lieutenant governor, who was the bailiff's nephew, imprisoned them for a day or two, and on their release they hit on the idea of getting up a petition to the Council for the abolition of the Cour Extraordinaire. It is clear that the object was simply to annoy the bailiff, and in particular to strike at his pocket because he received fees for suits in the Cour Extraordinaire ; and one cannot help suspecting that the petitioners were trading on the supposed ignorance of the Council—some of the applications of this period suggest that the islanders really thought that the people in London would believe anything—and hoped that the name of the court would make them think that it was a new and irregular device of the bailiff's. It was certainly not a considered movement for the reform of abuses, as genuine reformers would never have asked for the abolition of an existing court without providing for anything to do its work. De Carteret took the lead in the proceedings, and by private canvassing they got some signatures to their petition. The lieutenant governor considering this to be " factious and dangerous to the estate and government of the isle ", brought the whole matter before the Royal Court and the States, who resolved that the Extraordinary Court was a usual and necessary part of the judicature ; that the three prisoners deserved to be fined, and that their imprisonment was right and proper,[2] and suspended them from their office. They appealed to Council, but it was de Carteret alone who prosecuted the appeal, as Dumaresq submitted to the Royal Court and Journiaux withdrew. Council, after consulting the law officers, decided, on their report,[3] that the sentence was just and the appeal without cause, and committed de Carteret to the Marshalsea " as well for his unjust soliciting of the said cause and procuring hands and seals to overthrow an ancient court of justice, and his factious proceedings in that behalf, as for appealing without cause from a sentence justly given ", to remain in prison until he submitted himself to the Royal Court and acknowledged his fault and misbehaviour (March 1588).

The idea of sending people to prison for getting up a perfectly respectful petition for a change in the existing legal system is so extraordinary to us that it is difficult to understand how it could have been anything but a piece of sheer tyranny.

The fact that the proposal was ill-considered, or that it was intended " to procure disliking and hatred to the bailiff upon a rooted malice unjustly conceived against him " would to our ideas be good reasons for ignoring the petition, but not for imprisoning the author. But the sixteenth century looked at the matter quite differently ; and we get an interesting light on the political conceptions of the time from the opinion of the law officers and from a report on the case drawn up—evidently by one of Walsingham's secretaries or a clerk of the Council—for the use of the Council. It becomes perfectly clear that Elizabeth's Council had no desire to prevent private people from petitioning about their personal grievances or even for the reform of political abuses—it is made a great point throughout against de Carteret that his petition was not for reform but for the total abolition of the Court—nor did they wish to uphold arbitrary or oppressive action by the governor. The offence of the petitioners consisted in this, that they had privately and without bringing the matter before the States of Jersey got up a movement for the abolition of one of the ancient courts of the island. This took their action entirely out of the category of lawful petitioning, and made it " sedition and privy conspiracy ". The report concluded " that it is not lawful for any particular men not assembled in a body of state to demand the abolishing of a court of justice established and continued many ages by the approbation and consent of the estates of the country no more than it may seem lawful in England that some twenty private persons should require the abolition of any ordinary court of justice ". It would be a mistake to regard de Carteret as simply a champion of island liberties against an oppressive governor ; as we have seen, his action was due to a personal feud and a private lawsuit, and it was not till he had got into trouble over this that he became concerned about " the weal public of the isle ". The Royal Court and the States condemned his petition no less than the governor. They may no doubt have been influenced, consciously or unconsciously, by the feeling that their constitutional position would be endangered if people were allowed to go to the Council behind their backs with proposals for radical changes in the established order ; and from this point of view it was to some extent a safeguard for insular liberties to forbid private petitions on political questions. In any case the governor, the States, the law officers, and the Council all agreed in drawing the line between legitimate reform movements and criminal sedition at a point which is altogether shocking to nineteenth century ideas of political agitation and constitutional reform ; and three years later the Royal Commissioners who visited

Jersey included in their findings an ordinance (no. 6) making it a penal offence for anyone in the island to obtain the subscription or any marks or signs for the reformation of any affair public or private without the command of the captain, bailiff and jurats. This is unexpectedly drastic even for the sixteenth century, but Council had taken much the same line in Guernsey a few years before when they gave directions that no collections or contributions for the expense of deputations to London should be made " without the governor's privity ". The fact is that Council had for years past been much harassed by petitioners who came up claiming to be authorised representatives of the whole island or some parish or parishes, when they really only represented a scratch collection of people whom they had induced to sign a petition ; and they were determined, on the practical ground of saving their own time and labour as well as in the interests of public order in the islands to discourage all representations except such as were brought by duly accredited delegations from some public body.

De Carteret was in no way impressed by the authority of the Council : on the contrary their decision appears to have confirmed him in a bitter personal feud with the Paulets, and as a consequence a disposition to discover attacks on the insular liberties in almost everything they did officially. Amias Paulet died in 1588, and was succeeded by his son Antony, the lieutenant governor ; de Carteret renewed his attacks on the deceased Amias and his son, and in May 1589 he was once more before the Council " upon certain slanderous and injurious articles which he had framed against Antony Paulet and George Paulet, for as much as he took upon himself to complain in the behalf of the commonalty of the isle without commission, warrant, or other direction from them, and called things in question again which had already been ordered by their Lordships ". He failed to produce any proof of his charges, and the lieutenant governor submitted a formal document from the States certifying to " the good carriage of the said Amias Paulet in his charge ", from which Council concluded that de Carteret's " reproachful articles proceeded rather from some other evil cause and former spleen than upon just cause and reason ", and committed him to the Marshalsea,[4] until he submitted to their Lordships and Antony Paulet. They evidently thought this unlikely, as they added that if he brought up any new matter the Royal Court should examine and report on it. They were quite right in their judgment of de Carteret ; within a fortnight he produced new articles and offered to prove them by local witnesses. A small local committee (three jurats, the procureur and another) was appointed,

94

but evidently without result,[5] for by the end of the year it was decided to appoint a Royal Commission to go into these and other local disputes on the spot ;[6] and on the 7 March, 1591, Dr. Tertullian Pyne and Robert Napper were appointed commissioners accordingly. Attached to the commission were two sets of articles embodying respectively the complaints of de Carteret and John Perin, who acted with him in this stage of the controversy, and the points which the bailiff wished to bring before the commissioners. De Carteret's grievances for the most part related to specific acts of misgovernment such as are common form in the petitions of discontented islanders at this period : Antony Paulet had improperly requisitioned goods and services, he had sold guns out of the castle, had assaulted and wrongfully imprisoned people, dismissed jurats, and so forth. One or two of the articles are of more general interest : there is a suggestion that the Courts had not sat as regularly as they ought, and that the Extraordinary Court had taken work which did not properly belong to it : the complainants wanted " the behaviours and conditions of all Her Majesty's Officers to be examined and certified without respect of persons . . . not upon any generality . . . but upon particular informations to be delivered " unto the Commission : and they raised the point that under Henry VII's ordinances the bailiff and other offices should be appointed by the king direct. The bailiff in his articles asked generally that de Carteret's complaints should be examined, that appeals to Council which were then pending should be cleared off, and (vaguely) that the commissioners with the advice of the governor and States should institute necessary reforms. He added further that de Carteret had publicly given the lie to the governor, and that he had contemptuously refused to obey the governor's orders in matters concerning the queen's service, and generally that de Carteret " and his confederate have procured and as much as in them lies doth nourish a great faction and division among the inhabitants ".

The commissioners wasted no time. They had obviously done their work or most of it by 3 April, as on that date they issued a series of ordinances for the future government of the island. Their report on the articles submitted by de Carteret and the bailiff is not preserved in the Record Office, but it is given, with a full account of the dispute, in *Les Manuscrits de Philippe le Geyt*.[7] They found uncompromisingly for the Paulets and against de Carteret on practically all points : the alleged complaints of misconduct were untrue or could not be substantiated, and on the other hand de Carteret had been insolent to the governor " in calling him ' Gaoler of the Castle ' and giving him other unfit speeches ", and had disobeyed military orders (to attend a muster). The most interesting part of this report is the finding of the commissioners " that a dangerous faction was bred in the said isle by the said de Carteret " and the facts put forward in support of it. It appears that on the governor's death the Royal Court and States sent a representative to ask for the appointment of Antony Paulet, the lieutenant governor to succeed him, "which was crossed by the said Carteret and his confederates, who combined themselves into a new league, and to that purpose solicited from house to house, and one Philip Messervy having but the sign of a few of his confederacy, did neverthelesse, as if it had been in the name of the whole inhabitants of the Isle, seeke by a petition to advance and follow for some other to be Captain there. During the time of which unsettled estate, what insolent behaviour, riding, assembling, and practising, to alienate the subjects' mind from their due obedience to Her Majestie's Lieutenant there for the time, how they made themselves patrons of the lewed and unruly people within the Isle ; that Her Majestie's Lieutenant was forced to keep his Guards about him . . . ."[8]

We see here, as in the case of the petition about the Extra-ordinary Court above, how sixteenth century ideas about faction and sedition differed from ours : a respectful represen-tation from a public body like the States was harmless enough, but a popular agitation to put pressure on the queen and her Council in the matter of the appointment of Her Majesty's representative was unmistakeably on the wrong side of the line. De Carteret made his position worse by continuing his agitation after the new appointment was made, alienating the minds of his confederates from Antony Paulet, " giving out that he was established there but for a year and therefore if they would join with him he would be displaced ".

De Carteret, who evidently played the game on the " win, tie or wrangle " principle, did not give way even when he found that the commissioners were against him. A letter from the Council, dated 30 June, 1591, informs the governor, bailiff and jurats that de Carteret had " taken exceptions against the Commissioners and their proceedings, whereof their Lord-shipps find cause to mislike, and meaning to preserve and maintaine their doing as just and upright in the execution of their charge ". De Carteret was therefore sent to prison once more until he made submission and acknowledged his fault to the governor and the commissioners and paid (jointly with Perin) the costs of the Commission. The Royal Court were to call Perin before them to acknowledge his offence and pay his

A Prospect of Fermain Bay.

The East Coast of Guernsey from Fermain Bay, looking North in the Seventeenth Century.

To face page 96

half of the costs, and if he refused to bind him over to appear before Council.[9]

De Carteret had kept up his opposition long and obstinately, but he evidently felt that he could not defy the Council any longer, and on 29 July he made his submission and presumably paid his half of the costs (£83).

Le Geyt discusses the history of this affair at length and in a very critical spirit.[10] He evidently disliked some of the findings of the commissioners which he regarded as infringing insular liberties, and he tries to explain away the fact that they found for the lieutenant governor and bailiff on all points by suggesting that the Paulet influence overawed witnesses and complainants, and that some of the findings were deliberately equivocal, and so concealed the irregularities that had been committed.

As to the first point Le Geyt admits that it is pure conjecture with no actual facts to support it ; as to the second it seems hypercritical to complain that the commissioners, in reply to articles alleging improper exactions, simply said that there had been no such thing without specifying whether they meant that there had been no exactions at all or none but what were justified by law—it is at least as likely that they merely thought the charges too frivolous to be worth discussing in detail as that they were concealing the governor's misconduct. In the same way the inconsistencies and misstatements which Le Geyt criticises in the findings as to de Carteret's imprisonment seem to me to be due merely to the confusion of Englishmen unfamiliar with the law of Jersey when dealing with an intricate set of proceedings rather than to any deliberate attempt to whitewash anyone. Precisely the same confusion appears in the opinion of the law officers and in the English memorandum on the case, which were certainly not written under the influence of the Paulets. We cannot get behind the plain fact that the English commissioners after careful inquiry in the island found in favour of the Paulets on all points, and in spite of Le Geyt's insinuations and conjectures we have nothing to suggest that their conclusions were not substantially right.

In addition to their findings on the articles referred to them, Pyne and Napper also issued a body of " Orders, laws, and ordinances concerning the isle of Jersey "[11] of a general nature. Many of them relate to methods of procedure in the courts and to specific points of local law, but the first nine appear to be an attempt to bring Henry VII's ordinances up to date by redefining the constitutional powers of the Royal Court, the States, and the governor. No. 6 is the regulation already mentioned which forbids the procuring of signatures to a petition without the consent of the governor and Royal Court.

There has always been some mystery about these Ordinances ;[12] and the general opinion of the authorities is that they are not legally binding. Although it is stated in the preamble that the commissioners are authorised to make them under the Great Seal, the Commission itself contains no direct authority to this effect. It is true that No. 8 of the bailiff's articles runs :—" To establish and confirme such good orders as by you, with the advice and councell of the Captain, Bailiff, and Jurats and States of that Isle shall be thought profitable and necessary for the common wealth of the said Isle and agreable to the ancient lawes and customes thereof, and to reforme such inconveniences and disorders as shall be any wayes repugnant thereunto " ;[13] and the Commission authorises its holders " to hear and determine the causes and matters exhibited . . . .on the behalf of the same George (Paulet) and contained and specified in certain Articles . . . . the tenours of which are annexed to this Commission ".[14] The concluding words of the finding on this 8th article suggests that they were acting under this power in making the Ordinances.[15] But this hardly seems sufficient to authorise Pyne and Napper to make, without any confirmation from higher authority, an extensive code of laws of this nature ; there is no trace of any confirmation by Order in Council ; and though the Ordinances are said to be made with the consent of the governor, the Royal Court, and States, they were not registered in the island. It may be added that they do not appear, either at the time or later, to have been recognised as law or acted upon in the island.

This was a decisive victory for the Paulets, and they seem to have had no more trouble. The death of Antony Paulet in 1600 ended the long period of Paulet rule in Jersey. He was succeeded by Sir Walter Raleigh who set about his duties with characteristic energy and originality. Although his governorship only lasted for three years he left his mark on the island. He induced the States to establish a public register of title for real property, and he abolished the castle guard required of the islanders. They had been required to find a watch of twelve men every night as an outer guard : Raleigh discharged the watch and allowed their guard-house outside the castle gate to be pulled down. This was no doubt a relief to the islanders, but it was found to be purchased at the expense of safety, and in 1618 the deputies of the island petitioned Council to reintroduce the local guard.[16] Raleigh's other reform proved to be of lasting value, and it continues to this day. He is also credited by local tradition with beginning the trade between

Jersey and Newfoundland.[17] This is not actually confirmed by the documents, which show no more than that such a trade was actually in existence a few years after Raleigh's governorship,[18] but it is very probable.

CHAPTER X

GUERNSEY UNDER JAMES I.

The accession of James I brought a new world, and the malcontents of Guernsey soon decided to try their luck again. They sent up deputies with a series of complaints to be laid before Council ; a document in the Guernsey records[1] appears to represent the complaints originally put forward, and an Order in Council of 9 June, 1605[2] gives the decision of the Council. The two sets of articles correspond generally but differ in some points : apparently when the deputies were before the Council they dropped some of their requests and expanded others in more detail.

First as usual comes the old question of the governor's power to inflict imprisonment : this must be understood to refer to a general power to imprison for sedition, disorderly conduct, and generally any behaviour which was considered to be politically undesirable : the power to imprison for military offences had been clearly laid down, and never seems to have been seriously questioned. It appears from Article 6 of the petition that the islanders did not question the general power of imprisonment as such, but thought that after 24 hours the governor ought either to release the prisoner or to bring him before the Royal Court for trial.

The Council however insisted on leaving the governor a wide discretion on this point, and ruled that " the Governor shall not be restrained to commit any islander to prison upon such cause as he may think justly to have deserved the same '.

Certain limitations and precautions were added. It was provided that no one should be imprisoned for more than twenty four hours, put in irons or kept in a dungeon, unless his offence were a political one of a serious nature (" something higher than a private offence and which may concern him and his loyalty to his Majesty and the State "). In that case the bailiff and jurats were to be informed of the cause of the imprisonment " unless it be for some great cause concerning His Majesty and the State ", in which case the governor was given discretion as to whether he should inform the Royal Court and if so, when and how.

Akin to this as dealing with the arbitrary powers of the

governor but from the opposite side, is a request that the Royal Court might not lose its jurisdiction against offenders who were resident in the castle. The Council ordered that any offender against insular law who " belonged to the governor " might be prosecuted before the Royal Court in the ordinary way if he lived outside the castle ; if he lived in the castle in the governor's charge the Royal Court might demand the offender, and if he were not given up they might appeal to the Council, forty days being allowed for conference and agreement before the appeal was instituted.

Next came a long series of articles relating to the defence of the island especially so far as it involved charges upon the inhabitants and questions of purveyance. The governor was given discretion in regard to taxes for the provision of armour and munition, subject to the consent of the bailiff and jurats ; the nomination of gunners for the different parishes, provided the usual rate of pay was not increased ; and the selection of men to be in readiness for defence, the burden of attendance to be fairly shared among the community. He was also authorised to require such service of carriage for fortification of the castle as had been usual or might be necessary for defence ; it was intimated that the Council would consider any complaint of excessive requirements.

As to purveyance, it was ordered that the governor might take not more than 100 sheep a year at market rate or at a price fixed by assessors ; that he was not to take imported goods at less than the rate agreed with the sellers, but might have the right of preemption at that rate ; and that he might have 200 qrs. of the king's wheat rent (or 400 in time of necessity) delivered at the castle, the rest to be delivered at the grange in St. Peter Port.

Provision was made for further codification of the law. The Royal Court was directed to appoint a committee to correct and complete " the book of laws drawn up in 1582 " (i.e. the *Approbation des Lois*) and submit the result for the approval of the Council, and a commission was to be appointed to examine the Book of Extent (alleged to be imperfect and erroneous) and the true state of the revenues.

Akin to these legal points was a complaint about the expense and trouble caused by the prosecution of appeals (i.e. to Council), which was met by an order forbidding appeals in the case of real property worth less than forty shillings a year and personal property worth less than £40.

There remain certain articles which are notable because they relate to what may be fairly called political questions, and seem to indicate the beginnings of a movement towards political reform which was not apparent in the earlier applications to Council. This impression is confirmed by Leighton's reports referred to above, which indicate that the petitioners had gone beyond mere requests for removal of specific abuses, and had ventured to criticise some of the basic arrangements of the system of government.

The articles in question were a request that the bailiff and the king's officers might be nominated by the king and not by the governor,[3] that " the ancient use and authority of assembling the States for ordering the principal affairs of the island " might be re-established ; and that the Royal Court might be allowed their ancient right of inspecting the castle (i.e. to see if it was in a proper state of defence).[4] These requests taken together and compared with a similar movement in Jersey a few years later point to a growth in the islands of a conscious desire to give the bailiff and jurats a more important position relatively to the governor in the administration of the island.

The Council refused the first request, saying that the bailiff always had been nominated by the governor and there was no cause to mistrust his impartiality ; and they ignored the reference to the other king's officers. They added that the Royal Court might inform His Majesty if the governor " took any indirect course ". They allowed the second, but it does not appear exactly what the " restitution of the States " amounted to ; Leighton said in reference to this or a similar request that they already had this " in as much convenience as may be ", and the States had certainly met on some occasions during his term of office for purposes of taxation. Probably the petitioners wanted them to meet oftener and discuss a wider range of business.[5] As to the third point the Council avoided a direct ruling on the question of right, and simply said that they did not doubt that if request were made the governor would admit the islanders from time to time as had always been accustomed.

These findings were far from satisfactory to the islanders, and they lost very little time in returning to the charge. Their first step was the unusual and surprising one of attempting to organise common action with Jersey to procure reforms of general interest to both islands. It appears from a document in the Guernsey records[6] that in June 1606 deputies from the States of both islands met at St. Peter Port, and agreed upon a set of proposals to be presented jointly to the king. This programme included suggestions that the two islands as the remnant of the king's duchy of Normandy should once more have provincial States General " in order that better and more

102

legitimate provision might be made for the king's special rights of service and for the general laws of the country, for the regulation of justice and police administration, that the islands being thus reunited in one and the same body might by this means recover the ancient, lawful and natural right and dignity of their state ", and that appeals should no longer go to Council but should be settled in the islands by a Court of Appeal appointed by the States (" gens capables, deputés des avant dits Estats ").

These proposals may have been suggested by the ecclesiastical arrangements in force at the time, by which the colloques of the two islands met every other year in a synod, but I know of no parallel to this in seculars affairs. Nothing seems to have come of this attempt at common action ; certainly the impressive suggestions about States General and a common Appeal Court for the islands do not appear in the articles on which the Commission reported ; but considered as a movement affecting each island separately, the fact that such proposals were seriously considered is a striking indication of the growth of a sense of national identity and a desire for some measure of self-government in the islands. It comes much nearer to a political programme in the modern sense than any of the earlier proceedings against governors whose actions were disliked.

The Council was evidently impressed by the strength of the feeling in the island and felt that something must be done to satisfy it. In 1607 another Commission was appointed[7] consisting of two lawyers, Sir R. Gardiner and Dr. Hussey, with Jean Hérault of Jersey as local expert. The report of the Commission is remarkable in several respects. To begin with, the findings of the Commission are with very few exceptions put in the form of positive orders : one or two points are expressly reserved for the decision of the Council, and in some cases they say that as the matter concerns His Majesty's prerogative their order shall only be in force until His Majesty's pleasure to the contrary is signified. Evidently they regarded themselves as having plenary power to settle disputed points on the spot. Their Commission however only authorised them " to make and settle a good and firm agreement " between the governor and the bailiff and jurats in the matters in dispute between them, and to report to the Council on such matters as they could not " compound, and make a firm agreement "; and they certainly interpreted it very liberally when they made a series of peremptory orders which in some cases were flat refusals of the requests put to them.

However Council clearly agreed with the commissioners'

view of their powers, as the Order in Council of 30 June, 1608—" containing a note of such orders as we have thought fit to alter and correct . . . . amongst the orders set down by Sir Robert Gardner . . . . and James Hussey, ..., His Majesty's late Commissioners " confirms by plain implication the general body of these orders.[8]

The second point of note is the extraordinary width of range both in subject and time of the matters dealt with by the Commission. The Guernsey people seem to have brought up again almost every grievance they had ever had against Leighton from his first appearance thirty six years before, including points which had been expressly decided by the Council ; it took more than one or even several refusals to discourage a Guernseyman.

Thirdly the findings of these Commissioners are almost in every point far more favourable to the islanders and more restrictive of the governor's powers than any of the long series of previous decisions.

As usual a large proportion of the complaints refer to fiscal matters, either in the way of taxation in money or the requisition of goods and services for the castle and garrison. Taxation in kind of this sort is inevitably a source of friction but it is a little surprising to find that the complaints about supply of sheep, beer, and fuel, the delivery of rent corn at the castle and the service of carriages for the castle, which were settled by the Order of 1605, should reappear after so short an interval. Naturally the commissioners referred the complainants to the recent ruling, but it is notable that in more than one point they qualify the 1605 decisions in the islanders' favour. Thus they provide (Art. 4) for fixing by arbitration the price of the 100 sheep to be supplied each year ; and while they uphold the governor's right to enforce carriage for fortifications in case of need, they require payment to be made, and add significantly that as they do not see any defect in the fortifications there will not be any need of such carriages for " a good time hereafter " (Art. 24). Their Lordships however were less sympathetic, and decided that the custom should continue, but that the amount charged should not exceed the rate laid down in the Extent.

A remarkable point in the petitions is the request that the payment of campart should either be discontinued altogether or commuted for " some easy yearly rent ". There could of course be no question about the king's right to campart, and the suggestion that a substantial part of the king's revenue should be given up without any consideration in return is amazingly audacious. But the commissioners recorded their opinion that if the campart " were exchanged with a reasonable yearly rent it might be much more beneficial both to His Majesty and the islanders". Council ruled firmly that payment of campart should continue as formerly, adding significantly that if any composition were made for the king's camparts it should apply equally to those of private owners.

A small point, but significant as to the general attitude of the commissioners, is the complaint that the governor appointed such gunners as he liked, and required the people to pay them what he liked. Now the Order of 1605 had expressly laid down that the nomination of gunners rested with the governor, but that their pay should be as anciently accustomed or as the islanders should see fit. The commissioners naturally referred to this recent decision, but they added that in case of difference as to the rate of pay the Royal Court should decide.

As usual there is a series of complaints about arbitrary or oppressive action by the governor. As to the old question of the governor's power of imprisonment, the representations originally made to the commissioners contain an indignant protest against the wide terms of the Order of 1605 which enabled the governor to imprison for an indefinite period without informing the Royal Court, if he thought that reasons of state required it. The islanders asked that " the Governor may not hereafter assume to himself alone such an unlimited kind of power as well to accuse of disloyalty, and thereby vex at his own pleasure whom he listeth of His Majesty's best and truest subjects, as also discredit so far His Highness's Chief Judge of the Royal Court with the other Justices as to hold it dangerous to impart the same unto them, without at least such a pregnant reason and cause be rendered thereof as may evidently appear in Justice (and for such to be limited and recorded) ". But this protest, unanswerable according to modern ideas, was less acceptable to seventeenth century theories of government ; no article about imprisonment appears in the general report as having been put forward by the islanders and the commissioners made no reference to the general question, but in two complaints of specific cases of imprisonment brought before them by individual parishes, they ruled emphatically that the Order of 1605 should be strictly observed.[9] Clearly when the islanders appeared in person the commissioners must have impressed on them that there was no chance of any modification of the recent order, and that it would be better for them if general complaints about imprisonment, which might be taken as a criticism of the Council's decision, did not appear on the record.

In most of the articles of this class however, as in fiscal questions, the commissioners showed a marked disposition to restrict the governor's authority. Thus they forbade him to require the islanders to obtain his licence before going abroad except in time of war (2), or to prevent them from marrying foreign wives without his permission (for which he charged fines or yearly rents). To this Council cautiously added a proviso that the foreigners must " quietly and willingly conform themselves to the ecclesiastical disciplines and the laws and customs of the isle ".

An interesting article is No. 23, complaining that the governor forbade all the inhabitants, " of what quality soever they be, throughout all the isle, to shoot with their pieces and calivers at the fowl ; whereby shooting groweth much out of practice and the people less expert in the use of the same ; a thing dangerous in this frontier place near a foreign Prince ".[10] The force of this patriotic argument is however sadly weakened by the practical conclusion drawn from it, which is a request that shooting may be permitted " to such as are of good quality, for their exercise and pleasure ; craftsmen, and other base persons, being barred from the same, that they may not, by such pleasure, be drawn from their occupations ". The commissioners left this to the Council, who decided that anyone might be allowed to shoot game if he had a licence from the governor, the bailiff, or two jurats, with the consent of the governor if he was in at the time of the grant. This sounds less invidious than the article but probably came to the same thing in practice : " base persons " would not stand a very good chance of getting licences.

It is a very notable feature of this agitation that the complaints constantly go back to incidents of many years past : the Guernsey people evidently had a very long memory for grievances and clung tenaciously to anything which they conceived to be their right. Thus they complained that Leighton had erected a martial jurisdiction to the prejudice of the ordinary jurisdiction given by charter to the Royal Court—obviously a reference to the twenty year old case of the Breton who was shot by the watch.[11] The commissioners gave the somewhat indecisive ruling that the governor should not exercise any martial jurisdiction to the impeaching of the ordinary course of justice, except in time of war or hostility, or for suppressing robbers or pirates, or for avoiding any imminent danger. They added however that this should not be done without advice taken with the bailiff and jurats. In the same spirit the complainants charged the governor with depriving ministers of their living without any lawful charge proved against them, and the bailiff with refusing to pronounce sentence if he disapproved of the opinions of the jurats. The first of these was obviously aimed at Leighton's dealings with the ministers in 1584 ; the second admittedly referred only to the late bailiff, Louis de Vic, and was probably based on a case of 1595 in which the jurats had given an obviously partial decision against the Crown and the bailiff " stayed to pronounce a sentence so corrupt and prejudicial to the Queen's royal prerogative ". The Guernsey people were evidently bent on getting rid of any precedent which they thought might be dangerous for the future.

The note of political agitation and constitutional reform which appeared in the petition of 1604 is still plainer in 1607. The articles which have just been discussed clearly represent a considered attempt to stop every loophole for arbitrary action by the executive which past experience had brought to light. In addition there is a series of articles which can only be regarded as a direct attack on the governor's position by depriving him of powers which he had hitherto exercised without question. Thus Article 11 is a complaint that the governor appoints the same man to be bailiff and lieutenant governor ; and No. 12 says that the governor appoints and dismisses officers at his pleasure, " the danger whereof is that men preferred thus to offices, and holding the same but at the will and pleasure of the Governor, be too much at his devotion, to the prejudice of the due administration of their charges ".[12] No. 20 is a direct request that no lieutenant governor shall be appointed unless he is expressly approved by the king by letters patent, on the ground that " the now Governor hath, in very dangerous times, been away from the Isle, and placed for his lieutenant, men altogether unmeet for the place ".[13] With these we may class the request (18) that the governor shall not require any new fortifications to be built without the consent of the States, because he has in the past " commanded very chargeable fortifications in the Isle, which prove idle and needless ".

This misguided attack upon the governor's position was too much; even this sympathetic Commission was not prepared to go so far in transferring control from the king's representative to the insular aristocracy. They did indeed direct that no chargeable fortifications should be built without either consultation with the Royal Court or orders from the Council ; this was on the ground that the island was already so well fortified that they hoped there would never be need of new fortifications. They also directed that the governor should not dismiss the bailiff without the king's command or an order from the Council. On all other points they firmly declined to interfere with the discretion of the governor in exercising the powers entrusted to him by His Majesty.

The general result of this set of findings was to restrict the powers of the governor and to enhance the position and dignity of the Royal Court and the States. The governor was absolutely forbidden for the future to do a number of things : it is true that in several cases the Commission found that he had not in fact done them, or had only done them occasionally. In a number of other cases he was required to consult the Royal Court before doing things which he had been accustomed to do on his own authority. This was an obvious circumscription of the governor's undefined prerogative, and to some extent a recognition of the bailiff and jurats as a coequal authority instead of subordinates of the governor.

This was a very different result from that of earlier complaints, and we naturally ask why the commissioners should decide so many points in favour of the islanders, and why the Council, which had hitherto upheld the governor's authority at all points, should change its attitude now. The fact that Leighton was away from the island at the time of inquiry may have had something to do with the line taken by the commissioners ; his lieutenant probably did not put his case as forcibly as he would have done himself. But no doubt the character and views of their assessor had a great deal to do with the line which they took. Jean Hérault was a man of great force of character, and had original ideas on the constitutional question. As bailiff of Jersey a few years later he fought long and strenuously for the theory—previously unheard of—that the governor was merely a military officer and that the bailiff was the king's representative and the real head of the insular government. The disposition, which is manifest throughout the report, to fetter the independent action of the governor and exalt the powers of the bailiff and jurats is entirely in keeping with Hérault's policy in Jersey.

As to the Council, one obvious reason for their change is that the times had changed. Peace with Spain had been signed in 1604 ; the French wars of religion had ceased ; and now that the Spaniards no longer occupied Breton ports, and there was no need of more Armadas, the Channel Islands ceased to be so important as frontier fortresses; and a pacifically minded government felt less interest in making the governor of Guernsey supreme over the local civil authorities, and less disposition to go to the trouble of coercing the islanders for that purpose.

CHAPTER XI.

JERSEY UNDER JAMES I.

The accession of James I produced an immediate change in Jersey. James came to England with a strong prejudice against Raleigh, who he had been told was bitterly opposed to his claim to the throne, and ready to do anything to keep him out ; consequently he very soon deprived Raleigh of his office. His successor was Sir John Peyton, Lieutenant of the Tower, a man of fifty-nine who had fought with distinction in Ireland under Sir Henry Sidney forty years before and had later served with Leicester in Holland. He applied for a transfer to Jersey because he preferred a less difficult and invidious post than the Lieutenancy of the Tower, which he described to Cecil as a " place of service only composed of trouble, danger, charge, and vexation ".[1] But if he was looking for a quiet life he did not find it in Jersey.

His term of office was a time of acute controversy in the island. Two important issues were under discussion over a period of several years, the question of Church government and the relative positions of the governor and bailiff. The first of these quarrels was forced on the islanders by Peyton and the English Government ; the second started in the island and was largely, if not entirely, the work of the bailiff, Jean Hérault. The two threads crossed and were interwoven with each other as the controversies went on, and personal feuds also came in to complicate matters.

Heylyn has a story that Peyton was sent out by the Government with express orders to bring the island into conformity with the Anglican Church. This can hardly be true. Peyton was certainly Anglican in his sympathies, and soon showed that he had no love for the Presbyterian order and discipline and had no intention of supporting it ; but only two or three days after his appointment the king formally confirmed the ecclesiastical arrangements in force in Jersey : very likely he did not understand the real situation, but obviously he could not at that time have had any fixed purpose of altering it. And in 1605, when Peyton drew attention to the unsatisfactoriness of the Presbyterian system, the report of the Royal Commission made no recommendation on his complaints, and the Government took no action. It is not until 1611 that we find any clear indication that the Government were seriously thinking of introducing Anglicanism into Jersey.

On the political side he found the bailiff and jurats inclined to question the governor's authority in some points, and in particular to claim a position of greater power and independence for the States ; and there was also a tendency to differences between the governor and the islanders on questions of taxation and royal dues ; but there is no evidence of any tyranny or misgovernment on Peyton's part such as would provoke a movement against him. On the contrary Hérault himself says in his letter of 1607 to Lord Salisbury that though the financial arrangements were bad and would be a temptation to an unscrupulous governor, the present governor was a worthy man and this did not apply to him. Ten years later, the Royal Commissioners sent down to settle the controversy between Peyton and Hérault expressly found that there were no serious charges of extortion or exactions, and that the points at issue were purely political ones as to the relative positions of the governor and bailiff.

In addition to the pretensions of the States, Peyton's two law officers were centres of disturbance. Philip de Carteret, the procureur, was a son of John de Carteret the opposition leader of 1587-91, and carried on his father's feud with the bailiff with zeal and acrimony : the advocate Philip Marett, was overbearing and unscrupulous in temper, was suspected of Popish leanings, and was certainly not a sound Presbyterian. This brought him into bad favour with the ministers and also with the chief laymen of the Presbyterian party. It was in any case the duty of the law officers to maintain the king's—i.e. in practice the governor's—rights in financial and other matters, and their personal quarrels with the bailiff and some of the jurats lent additional energy to their discharge of this duty. The governor naturally stood by his officers, particularly as the bailiff, George Paulet, was not his relative and had not been appointed by him. Finally the law officers took proceedings to recover arrears due for the wardship of the young seigneur of St. Ouen during his minority. This brought the de Carterets of St. Ouen and the bailiff, who was grandfather of the young seigneur and had bought the wardship when his nephew was governor, into the field ; and there was a state of friction between the governor and his officers on one side, and the bailiff, most of the jurats, the ministers and the powerful family of St. Ouen on the other.

We do not know precisely how the matter developed, but by the middle of July 1605 Council had decided to appoint a

Royal Commission. As we have seen, trouble was on foot in Guernsey also, and Council evidently hoped to clear up the whole position in the islands once for all. On 23 July they sent instructions to both islands to prepare their evidence for the Commission,[2] and when the Commission was actually appointed, which was not until 25 July, 1607, the same commissioners, Sir Robert Gardiner, Dr. Hussey, and Jean Hérault of Jersey, were sent to inquire into the affairs of both islands under identical terms of reference.

The Commissioners according to the practice of that time framed their report[3] as a series of findings on articles embodying specific complaints, but the want—according to modern ideas—of a good review of the whole situation is to some extent met by a semi-official letter to Lord Salisbury from the local member of the Commission, Jean Hérault, written when the Commission had just finished its work in Jersey and moved on to Guernsey.[4] He sums up the problems with which they had to deal under four heads, (1) a mass of appeals on individual law-suits, mostly frivolous ; (2) a quarrel between the bailiff and the procureur " proceeding from an inveterate family hatred, which has caused most of the differences in this island, to the great hindrance of justice among the poor " ; (3) differences between the governor and the jurats as to their respective powers ; and (4) differences between the governor and the people on questions of taxation and royal dues.

The commissioners had authority to settle the various appeals, and Hérault says—somewhat optimistically, perhaps— that they had reconciled the bailiff and the procureur : it is the third and fourth heads which are of general interest. Hérault was undoubtedly right when he said that the governor's possession of the royal revenues brought him into many differences with the subjects ; as in previous inquiries in both islands, so in this instance, a great part of the articles of complaint and the commissioners' findings is taken up with points of detail relating to taxes, dues, and purveyance—whether tenants must pay their wheat rents at the Castle or only at the king's grange, as to the currency in which taxes ought to be paid, the rate of payment for workmen impressed to work at the castle, the requisitioning of meat, firewood, etc., for the garrison, and many other questions of the same kind. Hérault expressly says that the governor cannot be charged with avarice or dishonesty, and that the difficulty is inevitable as long as the governor is simply put in possession of the king's revenues and left to carry on the government out of them, and take the balance for himself. His idea is that all revenues should be collected and payments made by an independent official, and the governor given a fixed salary ; but here he is in advance of his period.

With the third point—differences between the governor and the jurats—we come to political controversies proper. In this respect there is a notable difference between the two islands : the Jersey people make no such complaints of arbitrary conduct and infringement of privileges by their governor as were common form in every petition from Guernsey. On the contrary the articles put in by the Royal Court and the inhabitants are limited to revenue matters and points of law, and it is the governor who complains of encroachment on his powers and raises constitutional issues. Apparently the jurats or some of them had already hit upon the line of policy afterwards employed by Hérault in his contest with the governor—of simply exercising the powers which they thought they ought to have and leaving the governor to protest if he liked. In the present case the governor asked that the privileges and jurisdictions of the isle might be explained, distinguished, and reduced to a certain form " they being now confounded by misprisons, uncertain interpretations, and innovations lately crept into practice ". In particular he wants the position and authority of the States clearly defined, " for that the body of this assembly doth for want of true understanding of monarchial obedience somewhat incline to a popular government, which may prove dangerous if they should not be in time enjoined to contain themselves under order and known limits ". There was evidently a general tendency on the part of the States to assert themselves, but it appears from the report that the special points at issue were whether the power of assembling the States rested with the governor or the Royal Court, whether his approval was required to the election of a jurat, and whether he could disallow ordinances of the States. The Commissioners found that the States had never been summoned without the consent of the governor or his lieutenant, but added that he should not refuse to allow a meeting on request " without he have very great reason or urgent occasion to the same ". They said nothing however about the other two points.

It was natural that any complaints on the ecclesiastical question should come from the governor. The Presbyterian system of church discipline and worship was firmly established in Jersey, and no appreciable number of people desired any radical alteration in it, although some might be inclined to grumble at the strictness of the Church Courts, and the lofty claims of some of the ministers. The governor however was an Anglican, and by 1607 the king and Council were openly committed to an anti-Puritan policy ; so in the governor's memorial we find a request (Art. 5) that the ecclesiastical

A Prospect of Mount Orgueil.

Mont Orgueil Castle, Jersey, in the Seventeenth Century.

To face page 112

estate in Jersey may be considered, and such jurisdiction established as may be thought convenient, " as well for the avoydinge the jurisdiction of a presbyterial or popular jurisdiction in the Church, as for the maintayninge of His Majesty's royal power and prerogative ".[5] What this meant is shown more precisely in the articles submitted by the procureur. He complains first that the king's (i.e. for practical purposes the governor's) right of presentation to benefices is ignored ; " of very late years the Ministers and Constables of the parish with the parishioners, contrary to law, pretend to put the minister into his charge and benefice without presentation or any other lawful course of proceeding, which form doth tend to a popular government " : and second that " by the sufferance of the bailiff and some of the jurats the ministers do use a jurisdiction arbitrary and without limitation, not acknowledging any ecclesiastical superior officer, and do at their pleasure make and alter ecclesiastical laws and ordinances ". (Arts. 15 and 19). This was a direct attack on the whole ecclesiastical system of the island, root and branch, and the Commissioners evidently felt that it was outside their terms of reference and left it to the King and Council as a matter of high policy, for they say nothing about it in their report.

These proceedings of 1607 plainly mark the beginning of the two great controversies which troubled Peyton's term of office. It was some years yet however before they became really serious. On the religious issue Peyton was waiting for a favourable opening : the political dispute did not come to a head until a new and energetic bailiff took the field. The existing bailiff, George Paulet, was not the man to lead a campaign in that cause. He was a very old man, and though he was connected by intermarriages with some of the leading Jersey families and had a bitter feud with the procureur, still as an Englishman and holding the post of lieutenant governor as well as bailiff, he would not wish to see the governor subordinated to the States. But in 1614 he was dismissed from his post of lieutenant governor, Peyton being compelled by Council to pay him a pension (as he was eighty it was not surprising that Peyton wanted a change), and Hérault, the greffier, who had procured from the king the reversion of the post of bailiff, induced Paulet to retire from this also on payment of a composition.

This change of bailiff very soon led to a sharp and prolonged outbreak of the political controversy. The two disputes, political and religious, went on side by side, and were to some extent connected ; but it will be convenient to treat them separately, the political, since it was settled first, in this chapter, the religious in the next. 113

I.—THE FIRST DISPUTE BETWEEN THE BAILIFF AND THE GOVERNOR.

We have seen that in 1607 it was the governor and not the bailiff or the States who raised the question of jurisdiction and powers, but the personality of the new bailiff produced an immediate change in the situation. It was no longer a matter of vague claims to greater power and dignity for the States or casual encroachments on the governor's authority as occasion offered, but a deliberate and well-thought-out scheme for reducing the governor to a cypher.

The new bailiff, Jean Hérault, was a man of strong character and a masterful and overbearing disposition ; he seems to have been honest and conscientious and anxious to do his best for the public service as he understood it ; but he had a hot temper and his violent outbursts in the Royal Court and the States frequently gave a handle to his enemies.[6] He was also a man of acute intelligence and thoroughly original ideas. He had clearly made use of his term of office as greffier to study the old records in his keeping, and as a result of this he conceived the startling theory that the bailiff was the king's representative in the island for all purposes and the responsible head of the insular government, and that the captain was merely the commandant of the garrison, and a military officer with no civil functions and subordinate to the bailiff.

This idea was evidently suggested to him by the accounts which he found in the Grand Coustumier of the powers and position of a bailiff in Normandy, reinforced possibly by the references to the office of bailiff in some of the early English documents. He supported his case by a curious series of arguments : the bailiff has the exclusive keeping of the king's seal and the duty of guarding the laws, and the power of the sword is committed to him : the captain and his men are bound to appear before the bailiff's court in all cases but one : the bailiff is bound to visit the king's castles and enjoin the captain to keep them in repair if there is any default : the bailiff administers the oath of office to the captain, and has precedence in the Royal Court and the States ; the bailiff's patent commands the captain to obey him in everything concerning the office of bailiff, but the captain's patent contains no reciprocal command to the bailiff.

All this was ingenious but not very sound. Hérault was misled by a similarity of names in reading his ancient authorities. A *bailli* in Normandy ruled a much wider area than the bailiff of Jersey or Guernsey ; and in the Plantagenet documents relating to the islands the titles bailiff or warden (*custos*) are used interchangeably for the great officer who was afterwards styled governor. Moreover there is a good deal of sophistry in his arguments : the references to the bailiff's exclusive jurisdiction and the requirement of the governor to obey him *in all that concerns his office*, merely express the undoubted fact that he was the head of the insular judiciary, and as such entitled to call on the governor for military force to execute the sentence of the Court when necessary. The oath taken by Peyton on entering office says nothing about his " obeying " the bailiff, but merely contains a clause requiring him " prêter sa force à la justice du Roi à ce qu'elle soit reverée et obéie et ses sentences et ordonnances dûment executés ". The argument that the governor is directed to obey the bailiff but not the bailiff to obey the governor is singularly audacious in view of the fact that before Hérault's time the bailiff's oath of office contained words binding him " to be loyal and faithful to our Lord the King *and to our Captain and his Lieutenant*".[7] The oath taken by Hérault omits this, but inserts a new clause (taken from the governor's oath) about defending the island against invasion and surprise by enemies, which had certainly not hitherto been considered as the bailiff's duty. It is evident that Hérault had taken advantage of his position as greffier to revise the traditional form so as to support him in his campaign to put the bailiff above the governor. In this connection it is significant that the procureur asked the Commission of 1607 (art. 18) to have the form of oath taken by the king's officers definitely settled " so that there may be no repugnancy between their sovereign oath to His Majesty and such inferior oaths as may be thought fit to be required of them by the magistrates ".

The reference to the bailiff's duty of visiting the castles and supervising them calls for some explanation. It was certainly an ancient custom in both islands for the bailiff and jurats to visit the castle on St. George's day with a view to seeing that it was properly garrisoned, equipped and maintained. This is set out with great precision in the Guernsey " Précepte D'Assize " (1441) which says that if the castle is not in good order the bailiff and jurats " have been wont, on behalf of our lord the king, to charge and give express orders to the captains and wardens and governors of the said places " to make good any defects.[8] Hérault was a member of the Royal Commission sent to Guernsey in 1607 and probably got to know the " Précepte d'Assize " then. The custom in Jersey had been the same as in Guernsey, but Hérault forgot or did not choose to mention the clause in Henry VII's Ordinance which puts the position in a very different light. " That neither the said captain nor his Deputy suffer any persons of the said Island to come to the

Castle on the day of St. George each year as they have been accustomed nor shall they also suffer any persons to come to the said Castle save in such form and in such number as they may always govern and put out of the said Castle at their pleasure ".[9]

This does not look as though the bailiff and jurats were regarded as the governor's superiors, and the idea of their " charging and giving express orders " to such personages as the Protector Somerset or Sir Walter Raleigh is grotesque. It is obvious that the officials whom the bailiff and jurats, supervised were merely the commandants of the castle garrisons; and the provision was intended as a check on the subordinate officials in charge at a time when Jersey and Guernsey were under one governor who could not be in both islands at once even if he resided in his charge at all.

The facts of island life for generations past were in complete contradiction to Hérault's theory of the constitution. From the time of Henry VII the governor of Jersey had held the position and powers of a viceroy, who dealt with the bailiff and the insular authorities generally as his subordinates. He appointed, and sometimes dismissed the bailiff at his pleasure and often appointed his lieutenant governor as bailiff ; an index of the relative positions of the two officials in the early sixteenth century may be found in a story told by the chronicler—the bailiff of the day was so full of importance at being made lieutenant governor that he took grievous offence when the wife of the seigneur of St. Ouen addressed him familiarly as ' Gossip '. The same idea still prevailed a century later. Philip de Carteret, seigneur of St. Ouen, writing to the secretary of state just after he had been appointed bailiff, spoke of the lieutenant-governorship which he already held as " an office of more consequence and far greater trust " than his new post of bailiff.[10] If these were the views of Hérault's successor in the bailiffship, it is clear that Hérault's theory of the bailiff's position was his own invention and had no support from island opinion generally.

It was therefore a startling innovation when Hérault began to proclaim in season and out of season his contention that he, as bailiff, was the true representative of the king and head of the island government, and the governor a mere military officer in the service of the civil power. The local circumstances favoured him at the moment : Sir John Peyton, the governor, seems to have been out of the island a good deal just then (possibly his health was bad, as we hear of his going to the baths) ; his lieutenant, an islander named Messervy, was evidently a weak and negligible person who was entirely managed by the procureur, Philip Maret. This did the governor's side no good, as Maret was overbearing, insolent, unscrupulous, and was strongly suspected of Popish leanings,[11] which made him unpopular with the Presbyterian party which included most of the leading men of the island. All the same it was a daring proceeding on Hérault's part to put forward such claims merely on the strength of a few old documents ;[12] it took an original mind to conceive the idea and exceptional courage and self-reliance to come forward single-handed to try and evict the king's governor from his place and power. For Hérault was not content merely to put forth abstract claims to superior dignity and precedence : he was working on a definite and well thought-out scheme for eliminating the governor from any serious part in the government of Jersey and re-placing him by the bailiff; and he pursued this aim for years with notable daring and persistence, skilfully taking advantage of every circumstance that seemed to give him an opening. His method of procedure was simple but audacious : he took advantage of the inactivity of the lieutenant governor to put himself and the States forward as the real rulers of the island, and bombarded the Secretary of State with letters in which he combined reports on island affairs, complaints of the negligence and misconduct of the governor, lieutenant governor, and procureur, with suggestions for reforms in the government of the island and assertions of his own position and rights.[13] The effect of the whole was to parade himself before the government in London as the responsible authority in the island and representative of the king not merely *de jure* but *de facto*, as zealous and efficient in discharging the duties of the post as the governor and his staff were negligent.

The affair opened with a dispute as to Hérault's appointment. He got a grant from the king of the reversion of the office of bailiff (28 July, 1611) and in 1614 paid a large sum to the existing holder (George Paulet, a very old man) to retire. The governor refused to recognise the appointment on the ground that his letters patent gave him the power of nominating the bailiff. Hérault was quick to see his advantage here : Henry VII's Ordinance had expressly laid down that the nomination of the bailiff and procureur belonged to the king, and forbade the captain to interfere in it.[14] This had been consistently disregarded in practice ; in fact it had been usual when appointing a governor to include in his patent the power of appointing the bailiff. Council took legal advice as to the inconsistency between the two patents, but reserved " the matter of State " to themselves. Considering King James's lofty ideas of the prerogative it is not surprising that the

Order in Council embodying the final decision (August 9, 1615) ruled that to " constitute a magistrate, or public officer of justice, is one of the essential and principal marks of our supreme power and authority, and an act merely royal and altogether inseparable from our royal person".[15] It explained that the clause had been inserted in Peyton's letters patent contrary to the king's intention, and laid down that henceforth the Ordinance of Henry VII should be strictly followed in this respect. The same order gave the bailiff a salary of 100 marks a year to be paid him by the governor out of the island revenues.

Peyton complained at the same time that Hérault had " usurped upon the office and charge of the governor " ; the details are not preserved, but it is obvious that this was the first appearance of his claim to be the supreme civil authority in the island. The difference was heard by the Council, who acquitted " the said bailly of any undutifulness to the king's majesty, or any injustice in the civil government ; but not from heat of words which have unfitly fallen from him, for which we thought fit to give him a sharp reprehension ".[16] Evidently Hérault as usual could not keep his temper when he met with opposition even before the Council, but it seems to have done his case no harm, as the Council ordered the governor to pay him £60 for his expenses, and ruled (in ambiguous and unfortunate words) " that the charge of the military forces be wholly in the governor, and the care of justice and civil affairs in the bailiff ".[17]

This was a decided victory for Hérault and a corresponding blow to the governor. Under modern conditions the question whether the right of appointment rested in the Crown or the governor would be entirely academic : if the governor had the power he would take the instructions of the secretary of state before exercising it, and in the other alternative the secretary of state would consult the governor as to the suitability of the local candidate before making any appointment. But in the seventeenth century governors were left much more to themselves : the machinery for continuous day to day control did not exist ; and the Council only interfered with the governor if someone complained of him, or their attention was somehow attracted to the spot. It was therefore a serious matter for Peyton to lose the power of appointment : he could no longer make certain that the posts of bailiff and law officers were in safe and friendly hands, and he had lost the influence attaching to the possession of valuable pieces of patronage. But the change did nothing to protect the liberties of the islanders, except in the general and negative way that it reduced the governor's powers. Appointment by the king was no guarantee that the local candidate would be appointed, or that faithful service in a lower rank would be rewarded. The bailiff was just as likely to be some place-hunting courtier who had managed to beg or buy the reversion of the office.

Hérault having won this preliminary victory at once proceeded to follow it up. He selected as his main line of attack the alleged weakness of the castles and their garrisons and the neglect of the governor and his subordinates. He reported to the secretary of state that there were only four men " pauvres et faibles de corps et d'esprit " actually living in each of the castles,[18] that the superior officers were not men of military training or experience (he complained that Sir John Peyton had appointed his butler to be porter of Mont Orgueil),[19] and he professed great alarm for the safety of the castles and the island if better precautions were not taken against surprise. How far there was any real substance in Hérault's expressed fears, and how far he merely seized on the question of safety as a useful stick to beat the governor with, it is difficult to be certain. At the time England was at peace with both France and Spain, and there was no likelihood of any war ; and the only ground for fearing a surprise attack which he could specify was that " Normandy and Brittany have been, and still are at present full of soldiers, the greater part of them rogues, who are only seeking the means to seize some strong places in order to be able under favour thereof to get better means of exercising their brigandage ".[20] It appears from one of Hérault's letters that the weakness of the guard at Elizabeth Castle had recently been proclaimed to all the world ; one market day there was only one soldier left in the castle, and he very foolishly sent round to all the taverns to hunt up his companions, so that the true state of affairs got all about the island.[21] It is impossible to avoid a suspicion that it was the unexpected present of so splendid and dramatic an example of careless guard that gave Hérault the idea of exploiting the dangers of invasion and the weakness of the defence. This line offered other advantages for the pursuit of Hérault's aims, and he made skilful use of them. He called a meeting of the States to discuss the question of defence against invasion or surprise,[22] thus at one and the same time setting off the zeal of the bailiff and States for the king's service against the slackness of the governor's people, making a practical assertion of their claim to be responsible for the whole government of the island, and giving an opportunity for establishing their case that it was the bailiff and not the governor or lieutenant governor who had the right to call the States together.

Having begun the game Hérault played it with skill and

obvious relish. The States adjourned and requested the lieutenant governor to attend. Naturally he refused ; and the States then resolved (17 February, 1616) that, until His Majesty's directions could be obtained, considering the necessity of speed in such cases, the weak guard kept in the Castle, and that all delays are dangerous, deputies should be sent to the lieutenant governor charging him in the name of the assembly to live in Mont Orgueil as captains have been used, to reinforce the garrison up to the old number and supply them with stores and munitions, and to meet the States and captains and constables of parishes in order to inspect their cannon and smallarms and drill their militia.[23]

This was a formal claim to the right of governing the Island and of controlling the military officers, and Hérault followed it up with a series of letters to the secretary of state and the king in the same spirit. He takes up throughout the attitude of a conscientious official distressed at the unsatisfactory state of the government for which he is responsible, and making recommendations to the central authority for the necessary measures of reform.

He asked for orders to be given that the captain should not leave the castles without appointing a competent lieutenant who was to be bound to reside in one of them ; that the porters and gunners should be experienced soldiers ; that a garrison of forty men should be kept in actual residence at Mont Orgueil and twenty in Elizabeth Castle ; and that the bailiff and jurats should be instructed to visit the castles at least once a year and report to the king any defects they might find. He went on to suggest that the States should be authorised to levy a tax of one sou on every pot of wine, the proceeds to go to build a pier and to buy arms and munitions (an ingenious device for providing the States with a revenue under their own control, independent of the royal domain which was administered by the king's officers) ; and he made recommendations about Church affairs—a dean should be appointed and the royal arms ought to be put up in the churches. His crowning audacity was the submission of a scheme worked out in detail, by which the king should resume the royal revenues hitherto granted to the governor and instruct his receiver to pay the expenses of government under the supervision of the bailiff. The calculation includes a salary of £500 to the captain as military commandant, and shows a balance of £541 a year remaining to the king after all charges are paid : this was no doubt expected to commend the proposal to a king who was always in want of money.[24]

Hérault's proceedings naturally met with strong opposition

from the procureur. As he was the leading king's officer in the island, the governor being absent and the lieutenant governor a nonentity, this was of course his duty ; but he did not discharge it with any prudence or tact, and Hérault skilfully outman-œuvred and defeated him. Maret was insolent and over-bearing by disposition. Hérault calls him "hautain, proterve et présumptueux ",[25] and his behaviour certainly justified the description. He treated the Royal Court with gross rudeness and refused to apologise, whereupon he was bound over to appear before the Council and suspended from office. A petition had already been sent to the king asking for the appoint-ment of a de Carteret as procureur omitting to mention that there was already a procureur in existence, Maret's appoint-ment being treated as void on the ground that by the Ordi-nance of Henry VII, reaffirmed by the recent Order in Council, only the king could appoint a procureur. The post was given to de Carteret, and he was formally installed during Maret's absence in England.

Battle was now (May 1616) fairly joined all along the line. The governor, an elderly man and apparently in poor health as he was taking a course of baths this summer, complained to the king of the " exorbitant proceedings " of the bailiff, and Hérault was ordered to appear before Council in November.[26] The result was the appointment of a Royal Commission to survey the castles and garrisons, to examine the martial and civil government, to inquire into all extortions, oppressions, and usurpations, to inquire into the controversy between Maret and the bailiff, and to deal with any other complaints that might be brought before it. The commissioners, Sir Edward Conway, and Sir William Bird, Master in Chancery, were appointed on 25 March, 1617 : they conducted their inquiries in Jersey from 29 April to 21 May and reported in July.[27]

On the question of defence they found that the garrisons (five officers and fifteen soldiers in Elizabeth Castle, three officers and sixteen soldiers in Mont Orgueil, about half living within the Castle in each case) were no worse than in Raleigh's time and the latter part of Sir Amias Paulet's (" for order much like and for number rather more than less ") : there was a watch of two men at night and four by day. Formerly an outer guard of islanders had been mounted in front of the gate at night ; but Sir Walter Raleigh had discontinued this and pulled down the guard house. The island could produce about 3,000 men for defence purposes : they were loyal and willing enough, but untrained and very badly provided with arms. This report did not bear out Hérault's alarming stories of gross negligence and imminent danger, but it did show that during the years of peace a certain amount of slackness had crept into the arrangements for defence. The Commissioners recognised that the garrisons could not be kept permanently on a war footing, and they admitted that unless this were done neither the castles nor the islands were " free from surprise, spoil, invasion, or conquest " ; but this could be provided for. They could easily be made safe against any sudden attack : if the people were well armed, exercised, and commanded, they could prevent any " spoil or invasion " of 2000 or 3000 men ; and a larger force with guns could not be moved without some warning being given to the central government if not to Jersey, in which case the islanders could retreat into Elizabeth Castle and hold out till help was sent from England.[28]

Council adopted the views of the Commissioners—that no drastic change of system was necessary but that the existing arrangements should be brought into a state of efficiency. They ordered (15 June, 1618) that Mont Orgueil should be garrisoned with thirty men, and Elizabeth Castle with twenty, besides a porter and master gunner in each castle ; that a man of experience fit to command on occasion should always be resident in Elizabeth Castle, that the local guard abolished by Raleigh should be restored ; that the porters and gunners should be ex-soldiers ; and that the militia should be mustered and their arms inspected twice a year by officers of the castle.

It was further ordered that the governor should take an inventory of his stores and send it to the Council and that at every change of governor the lieutenant, bailiff and two jurats should make an inventory and certify it to the Council, giving a copy to the incoming governor. As there had been complaints of Castle stores being sold to the inhabitants and used for ships going to Newfoundland, it was laid down that stores might only be supplied to the inhabitants in time of danger when they could not be otherwise furnished, provided they paid for them and the money was used to replace them.

On the civil side the commissioners found that the only real question they had to deal with was the controversy between the bailiff and the governor as to their position and powers : they expressly said that there were no serious complaints of extortion or misgovernment. On examination, the bailiff's sweeping claims could not be maintained ; they were entirely contrary to history and common sense ; and, on the report of the Commission, Council ordered that, " as the governor is trusted by His Majesty with the charge and government of the Island as may best suit with the safety of the place and His Majesty's service otherwise ", he should henceforth be styled governor and not captain, no meeting of the States should be called without his consent, or his lieutenant's in his absence (there was a proviso that, if the bailiff or Royal Court demanded a meeting, the governor was not to delay it for more than fifteen days except for grave reasons which he must make good before the Council), and the governor was to have a veto on any proceeding of the States prejudicial to His Majesty's interests.

This completely disposed of the bailiff's claim to be the king's representative and head of the island government : The commissioners gave as their reason for upholding the governor's power of calling the States that " that power did keep up the lustre of the governor in the eyes of the people, who did by the governor see a principal mark of the king's sovereignty ". But, subject to their decision on the main issue, Council were obviously anxious to do what they could for the bailiff, whom they recognised as an upright and conscientious officer even if he had an excessive idea of his own importance. He was given precedence of the governor in the Royal Court and the States, though nowhere else ; a dispute between him and the governor as to the amount of salary payable to the bailiff was decided in his favour, and his request that all records relating to the king's revenue should be kept in the Greffe and be open to the jurats was granted.

Hérault's quarrel with the procureur ended in a notable victory. The commissioners found unhesitatingly that Maret had been grossly insolent to the Court[29] and had been justly punished ; and further that his successor was properly in office having been validly appointed by His Majesty's letters patent. The Council peremptorily ordered Maret on pain of banishment to go back to the island and " make public submission and satisfaction for the wrong that he had done to our justice ".

Council also granted a series of petitions which the States had submitted through the commissioners.[30] They related to fiscal questions, some of which had a direct political bearing : for instance the States wished to levy a small tax on wine to provide arms for the militia and to cover the expense of fortifications, and a customs duty to build a pier ; they asked permission to import English commodities on licence to be granted by the Royal Court, and for exemption from custom for island products sent to England to be dressed and brought back again; they wanted scholarships for islanders at the English universities, and the benefits in respect of wardships recently granted in England. These were straightforward requests—several of them indeed were merely for things which had already been granted to Guernsey, which suggests that Hérault's visit to Guernsey with the Royal Commission of 1607 had borne fruit—and there was no reason to think that the States put them forward for the purpose of supporting Hérault's campaign against the governor or with any ulterior motive whatever. But though the grant of these requests might make no serious difference for the present, some of them contained the germs of future changes. The new taxes provided the States and the Royal Court with what they had never had before, a permanent source of revenue under their own control ; hitherto they had only levied occasional direct taxes to pay the expenses of deputations to the Council, and had usually made themselves very unpopular by so doing.

It was a new thing also, and on a small scale a diminution of the governor's authority, that the issue and control of import licences should be put in the hands of the Royal Court.

But for the time being the victory was decidedly with Peyton. The bailiff's audacious attempt to oust him from his position had been repelled ; an express order of the Council had established the governor beyond question as the king's representative and head of the insular government. He had lost the power of appointing the bailiff and law officers direct, his powers had been slightly limited in one or two matters of detail, and he had had a warning that his job of governing the island called for a certain amount of tact and consideration ; but for practical purposes his supremacy was substantially unimpaired.

The dispute seems to have been entirely a personal matter between Hérault and Peyton. The alleged supremacy of the bailiff was an original idea of Hérault's, not the programme of a party. He carried the States a certain distance with him in the earlier stages : they were probably willing to bait a weak lieutenant governor and an unpopular procureur, and they may have been genuinely concerned about the weakness of the defences ; no doubt also they were swept away by his masterful leading ; but there was apparently no general interest in the cause which Hérault maintained. He was left to fight it out alone before the Council when Peyton took up the challenge, and the decision was accepted without question and apparently with indifference.

2. PEYTON'S RETURN MATCH WITH HERAULT.

One result of the religious controversy in Jersey[31] was that it gave Peyton his chance of revenging himself on Hérault. It is not surprising that he took advantage of it. Hérault had made a deliberate attempt to usurp the position and duties of the governor and to degrade him to the position of a mere commandant of the castle garrison. His main attack had failed, but he had caused Peyton much worry and expense,[32] had got his procureur dismissed and a friend of Hérault's put in his place, and had deprived him of the right of appointing the bailiff and the law officers which all previous governors had enjoyed. Even when the controversy had been settled by the Order in Council of 1618, Hérault did not cease to give trouble. At the important meeting of the States (15 April, 1620) to receive the dean's appointment he had made a series of unpleasant scenes.[33] He began by protesting repeatedly against the governor's action in assembling the States, and claiming that this could only be done by the bailiff. Peyton kept his head and his temper and declined to be drawn into a discussion, simply saying that he had sufficient authority for what he did and quietly insisting that the States were called together to take notice of His Majesty's pleasure concerning the dean. Hérault next flew into a rage because the dean's patent of appointment was directed first to the governor and delivered by the dean to the governor : he snatched the patent out of Peyton's hands, saying " C'est à moi à qui elles doivent être premièrement addressées, car c'est moi qui représente la personne du Roi en cette chaire ici ", slapping his hand on the chair. He ended by picking a quarrel with the dean over his precedence and his right to sit with his hat on. No wonder that Philip de Carteret reported a few days later that " the Governor and the Bailiff stand on ill terms ", and that his attempts to reconcile them had failed.[34]

Shortly after this Hérault made a mistake which gave his enemies their opportunity. The dean got to work promptly to establish the Anglican system, and one of his chief duties in this respect was to substitute churchwardens for elders and deacons of the Presbyterian model. The bailiff suddenly stepped in and ordered the appointment of the churchwardens to cease. The real reason was a dispute as to jurisdiction : the church-wardens were to take the oath before the Dean's Court, but since the discontinuance of the dean's office the bailiff had assumed the power of administering oaths in ecclesiastical as well as civil matters.[35] Hérault was not a man to part with an atom of his customary jurisdiction or with the fees involved, and he stopped the proceedings accordingly. He seems to have realised his mistake before long and withdrew his pro-hibition, but the mischief was done. He had gained a reputa-tion in high quarters of being Presbyterian in his sympathies and disposed to obstruct the king's Anglican policy,[36] and this had evidently not been removed by his professions of active support in procuring the appointment of a dean. Now he had committed an act of open insubordination; his adversaries seized on the opening he had given them, and in June 1620 he was summoned to appear before Council. The case was not heard till November, when Peyton exhibited a set of articles against him. Hérault said that he succeeded in defending his conduct: " Lord Verulam said that I had shown my affection to His Majesty by the performance of His Majesty's pleasure, so no act was entered on the Council Book against me ". But his hot temper and overbearing disposition were too much for him, and he was sent to the Marshalsea for insolence—" in respect I was too vehement in my answers to the Lord Chancellor, who asked me whether I thought to be in Jersey ! " " But when I was gone the Lords were told that by opposition to Peyton I had done the King disservice, so the King was moved to give my place to Sir W. Parkhurst and recompense me ". He was released from the Marshalsea the same evening (22 November, 1620) on signing a bond not to go to Jersey without leave.[37]

Hérault seems to have been regarded as suspended from office rather than actually dismissed. Apparently the Council considered that not having been guilty of any actual misconduct he could not be dismissed, and, as he held his office under royal letters patent, his resignation was necessary to create a formal vacancy ; but they felt that in view of his difficult temper and his perpetual friction with the governor, he ought in the interests of the public service to be decently got rid of. An order was drafted (probably in March 1621)[38] giving him a pension of £100 a year payable out of island revenues in consideration of his resigning his office of bailiff, " His Majesty having occasion to use his services near his person "—a polite fiction, apparently. Hérault however would not resign : he wanted a public hearing of the charges against him and to have his pension secured.[39] The Council then applied pressure : in June 1621[40] the governor was directed to appoint a judge delegate to do the bailiff's work until His Majesty should otherwise dispose of the office ; and in April 1622[41] Peyton was notified that His Majesty, meaning that the post should be properly filled and not executed any longer by a substitute, had appointed Parkhurst " as provisionally chosen to execute that charge until further order be given ", and was directed to pass a grant of the office (by virtue of his commission) under the island seal.

This was a very curious method of procedure, especially considering the king's recent and emphatic decision that the appointment of a bailiff was for the king alone and not for any lesser authority. Hérault believed that this was a design of

Peyton's to recover his lost power of appointing bailiffs, but he was mistaken here.[42]   Parkhurst was not a friend of Peyton's (Peyton said that he had never seen him before his appointment), and the reason for adopting this course of procedure undoubtedly was that the Council were uncertain (as the wording of their letter shows) about the validity of Parkhurst's appointment, and meant to make it plain that he must look to Peyton for his salary and would have no claim on the king if payment from island revenues proved to be illegal.

Hérault however was stubborn, and, though excluded from Jersey and deprived of his salary, he steadily refused to resign and continued to petition to be given copies of the charges against him and a hearing to clear his name.   Finally in 1622 a small committee (the Duke of Lennox, Lord Arundel, and Calvert, the secretary of state) was appointed to consider the case.   They found in his favour so far as misconduct was concerned but clearly thought him better out of office in Jersey. Hérault says they recommended him for a pension of £100 a year and to be continued His Majesty's servant, and given a place worth £700 or £800 " if I could find anything in the king's gift of that value, so it might not come directly out of His Majesty's coffers "[43]—a proviso which speaks volumes for King James's financial position.   At last in August 1624 a letter from Council, after setting out first that " His Majesty found it not suitable to remove an officer without sufficient cause ", and second that there was no means of relieving Hérault but either by paying the pension of £100 a year or restoring him to office, proceeded to order that he should be restored to the office with arrears since the date of his sequestration.[44]   The bailiff's salary being paid out of insular revenue, did not come " directly out of His Majesty's coffers ", but out of the pocket of the governor, who received the surplus after the costs of administration had been paid ; and it is evident that it was this consideration which determined the choice of the alternative adopted.

This was a victory for Hérault at last, though a very costly one.   But even so his troubles were not quite at an end. Peyton, on receiving the order to pay arrears, pointed out with unanswerable logic that Parkhurst had been pointed bailiff and paid as such by express order from the king, and that he (Peyton) could not be expected to pay twice over.[45]   So all Hérault got by way of arrears was so much of the bailiff's emoluments for the period of his suspension as had not actually been paid to Parkhurst.   He had however the satisfaction on his return of receiving a public welcome from the States, who sent a deputation to meet him and reconduct him to his presidential chair.[46]   He died within two years of his restoration.

127

CHAPTER XII.

THE FATE OF PRESBYTERIANISM IN JERSEY AND GUERNSEY.

About the time of Hérault's first quarrel with Peyton the ecclesiastical controversy which had been simmering for years came to boiling point. For the last forty years of Elizabeth's reign the Presbyterian system of church government had been established in both islands and was actively supported by the secular power. Immediately on James's accession the islanders petitioned[1] to be allowed to retain their ecclesiastical discipline, saying that Elizabeth had permitted and allowed them, as part of the Duchy of Normandy, " the use of the Government of the reformed Churches in the said dutchy ". This was misleading. Presbyterianism had been set up in the islands with the consent and help of the governors, who were themselves Puritan in sympathy, but had never been formally recognised by the queen or the Council except for the two town churches of St. Helier and St. Peter Port, and then with the express stipulation that the country parishes should follow the Anglican order—a limitation which was entirely disregarded. How far the English government knew and connived at the state of affairs is not clear. Walsingham, when secretary of state, certainly knew of it and—being himself a Puritan in sympathy—approved, but it is quite likely that he did not tell all the members of Council. In any case the true facts were evidently not realised in Whitehall at this time, and James granted the petition (August 1603). But the situation soon changed. Sir John Peyton, who succeeded Raleigh as governor, was an Anglican with no liking for Presbyterianism ; he also had a strong practical motive for taking the other side. His patent gave him the right of appointing to vacant livings, but this lost much of its value under the *Discipline* of the insular church, which made the appointment of a minister dependent on the approval of the Colloque. This was not given unless the Colloque had satisfactory reports of the candidate's life and doctrine, and unless he subscribed to the *Discipline*.[2] Peyton was not a man to give up any of his rights, and it is not surprising that he was soon asking the Council to put a stop to the working of the Presbyterian assemblies and to uphold the king's rights and prerogatives. The Council did nothing at the time, which throws a good deal of doubt on Heylyn's story that Peyton was sent to Jersey with express instructions to put down Presbyterianism there ;[3] but after the Hampton Court Conference of 1604 the policy of the Government became definitely anti-Puritan, and Peyton and his superiors were soon in complete agreement on ecclesiastical policy in Jersey. A report by Dr. Hussey, one of the Royal Commissioners of 1607, to the treasurer shows that before 1611 the government had already decided to introduce the Anglican system of church government in Jersey, and had taken some preliminary steps in that direction.[4]

It was necessary however to proceed cautiously. The Government evidently did not wish to issue an order *proprio motu* for the establishment of the Anglican liturgy and church discipline in Jersey. They preferred to wait till they had some plausible excuse for interference and some show of a desire for change in the island itself. It is not difficult to see their reasons. The King had quite lately given his formal consent to the continuance of the Presbyterian system in Jersey ; the official explanation was that he had been misled by false representations, but all the same it would not look well suddenly to reverse his action. Possibly also the old argument that the islands being part of Normandy must be governed by Norman law and custom, coupled with the undoubted fact that the only Protestant Church existing in Normandy was the French Presbyterian one to which the island Church was affiliated, carried some weight. Further, there were the practical considerations that the islands were important frontier fortresses, the defence of which against foreign attack depended on the good-will of the islanders ; and that in case of any general disaffection the governor could not control the people unless the garrison were brought up to war strength of at least 300 men—a most unpleasant prospect for James's impecunious administration.

Within a few years of James's accession therefore the position was that Peyton, with the full sympathy of his superiors, was watching his opportunity to strike a blow at the Presbyterian system. He began by persistently refusing to give the church courts the backing which they had hitherto had from the civil power, and by allowing the law officers to bring ecclesiastical cases before the Royal Court. Then in 1609 he appointed an Englishman in Anglican orders as chaplain of the castle : the Colloque refused to receive him failing satisfactory evidence of his calling to the ministry, and directed the minister

of St. Helier to take charge of the castle services.   It is unlikely
that either the chaplain or his English flock took any notice of
this, and the governor replied by sending his chaplain to represent him at the meetings of the Colloque : for though the
members had refused him the right hand of fellowship as a
brother minister, they could not refuse to receive the governor's
delegate.[5]

It should now have been obvious to the ministers that
Peyton was " looking for trouble ", but a little later (December
1609) they decided to try the effect of a set appeal to him.
The Colloque wrote him a letter setting out that the people
generally were imbued with the idea that the church courts
had no jurisdiction, but that all jurisdiction spiritual as well as
temporal belonged to the Royal Court : in consequence the
church assemblies had fallen into contempt, many people
refused to obey when summoned to appear before them and
vexed the ministers by publicly denying their authority ; unless
a remedy were soon provided it was to be feared that Papists
and evil livers would find a door open for the overthrow of the
Church of God.[6]

So far from shewing any sympathy for their troubles
Peyton joyfully seized the opportunity to deal the ministers a
stinging rebuff.[7]   He replied at once that he was informed by
jurats and others that the church courts had seriously en-
croached on the authority of the magistrates ; he could not
therefore make any direct reply to their request for help until
he had details of the particular cases they had in mind.   As to
their ecclesiastical discipline, he would do what he could to
uphold it " so far forth as it may be rightly understood to be
granted from his majesty . . . . ; but my advice to every
one of you is, that you should walk humbly before your lay
brethren, and bestow two parts of your time in study of divine
things, and then to preach and write, so as you may be re-
verenced in the present and memorable in future times ".
This was a plain advertisement to the people at large that the
church courts could be defied with impunity, and it is not
surprising that a year or two later (March 1613), out of seven
offenders cited before the Colloque, none appeared ; and the
assembly was powerless.   Some of the black sheep of the
Church went further ; one Clement Maçon, who had good
reason to dislike the church courts, collected signatures on
Sacrament Day to a petition " au préjudice de l'ordre ecclésiastique établi en ces iles ", told the Colloque that he had
done it by the authority of the lieutenant governor, and refused
to do penance saying that the governor had promised to protect him.   Maçon was finally induced to express regret and

was received into the peace of the Church ; but the Church continued to be gravely troubled by the attitude of the civil power. In 1612 the lieutenant governor alarmed the Colloque by sending orders that no strange minister should be allowed to preach in any island church without his consent—an obvious blow at the connection with the French Protestant Churches— and asked the ominous question what power the governor or his lieutenant had in church assemblies. Nothing seems to have come of this, but in June 1613 the storm broke. Peyton had at length found the opening which he had long been looking for.

He appointed to a vacant living a young islander named Elie Messervy, who had studied at Oxford and taken orders in the Church of England. The Colloque refused to recognise his episcopal ordination or to admit Messervy unless he would subscribe to their *Discipline*. They soon found that Peyton had manœuvred them into a completely untenable position. They could not dispute his right to nominate to the living : if they recognised his nominee it meant a breach in their Presbyterian system which was certain to be followed by others as livings fell vacant ; if they refused to recognise Messervy on the grounds of his Anglican orders, this was a defiance of the governor's authority and an open declaration of hostility to the Church of England which would have the worst possible effect on the minds of the king and the Council. They wanted to refer their difficulties to a synod of both islands, obviously with a view to making common cause against episcopacy ; but Peyton refused to allow the synod to meet ; and on 2 November, 1613, Council letters were sent to both islands announcing the king's resolution to establish religious uniformity in all his dominions, and consequently to introduce Anglicanism into the islands as opportunity offered. Jersey was directed to send representatives of both parties, " as well of them that embrace the present ecclesiastical government as of those that dislike it " to state their case before the Council ", that some course might be ordered as should seem expedient and answerable to the uniformity of ecclesiastical government in other parts of His Majesty's dominions ". The Colloque sent four ministers—Effard, Olivier, de la Place, and Bandinell. The other party was represented (naturally) by Messervy and by Maret, the procureur, who was said by his enemies to be a concealed Papist and by himself to be persecuted for his attachment to the Church of England. These brought with them a petition (possibly the one which had got Maçon into trouble with the Colloque) signed by people who professed to dislike the *Discipline* and to wish to be re-united to the Church of England. The matter was referred to a committee, consisting of the Archbishop of Canterbury, Lord Zouch and Sir John Herbert, the secretary of state. The decision was to revive the office of dean " for the restoration of peace and good order in the island ", the post to be given to an islander. The Anglican liturgy in a French translation was to be used, but with a dispensation for the time being from the use of the surplice, the sign of the Cross in baptism, and kneeling communion (three points specially obnoxious to Presbyterians) ; and a body of canons was to be drawn up by the insular church " as near in conformity with the Church of England as their laws and usages (from which His Majesty had no intention to derogate) would bear ".[8]

The attitude of the government was now perfectly clear, they meant to put down Presbyterianism and reduce the islands to conformity with the Church of England, but they did not wish to do so—or rather did not wish to appear to do so—arbitrarily and against the will of the islanders. The letter of 1613 announcing the king's decision was a very astute and cautious document ; James had evidently learned useful lessons from his struggles to set up episcopacy in Scotland. It made the king's wishes and ultimate intentions very plain, but the only direct order contained in it was that the islanders should send representatives to state their case. Only after hearing both sides would the king decide on any action, and there were artful suggestions that he would in any case be prepared to allow modifications of detail to suit local customs, provided the main principles of the Anglican system were not affected ; and even that he might dispense with uniformity altogether if sufficient ground were shown. The direction that " those who dislike the present ecclesiastical government " should be represented was of course a plain invitation to malcontents, but there was nothing in the letter that could be held up as an attempted infringement of insular privilege.

The reasons for this cautious approach are obvious. The Presbyterian system had been officially established in Elizabeth's time with the active co-operation of the queen's representatives and the tacit connivance of the English government, and James had formally sanctioned its continuance. It was the accepted view that the constitution of the islands required them to be governed according to Norman law and custom, and there was no Anglican church established in Normandy ; the choice there was between the Roman Catholic Church and the French Reformed Churches of the Geneva model. And finally the Government were for practical reasons unwilling to create too much discontent among the islanders since they had to rely on their loyalty for the defence of the islands. No wonder therefore that they decided to proceed cautiously and to wait for an opening before they made a move.

Agreeably to this line of policy, nothing was done immediately to put in force the decisions of the Government on the general question. But the particular dispute which was the occasion of the general controversy was settled by an express order that Elie Messervy should be admitted with all convenient expedition into his benefice " there peaceably and quietly to exercise the forme used in the Church of England ".[9] The Colloque received Messervy on his undertaking to make no changes in his church unless he received further orders from king or Council (July 1614).[10]

At this point there was a lull in the ecclesiastical conflict, and for four years no further action was taken to carry out the policy of the Government. No doubt their attention was chiefly occupied by the furious controversy between the bailiff and the governor which broke out early in 1616, and was not finally settled until the Order in Council of June 1618. But they kept the church question in mind, and when the Royal Commission of 1617 had sent in its report and they had come to a decision as to the lines on which the secular quarrel was to be settled, they took up once more the task of bringing Jersey into conformity with the Church of England. The point of attack which they selected was the appointment of a dean, and the choice was a masterpiece of tactics. It was the key to the whole position. The existence of a dean was intensely repugnant to Presbyterian sentiment, it being an essential point in their theory of church government that all ministers were equal, and that all ecclesiastical authority was derived from the church assemblies and not from appointment by a hierarchical superior or a secular sovereign. It also had the practical advantage that the king could control the island church through a dean of his own appointing, whereas a Colloque was independent of him—an example on a small scale of James's well-known aphorism ' No bishop, no king '. It could not be denied that the office of dean was part of the ancient constitution, or that under Henry VII's Ordinances the king had the right of appointing him.[11] This was especially effective against Hérault and his supporters, who had just been appealing to this very clause to deprive the governor of his power of appointing the bailiff and law officers. And a deanery was a piece of patronage the hope of obtaining which could be used with effect to bring over ambitious ministers to the Government side. Apparently it was so used. Heylyn, who visited the island in 1628, has preserved a story[12] that when the four ministers were sent to London in 1613 to represent the Presbyterian case, one of them, de la Place, was induced by hopes of the promotion to report to the other side what line the deputation intended to take and what arguments they would use. The official papers do not confirm this, so far as de la Place is concerned, but they put it beyond doubt that the Government took full advantage of their opportunity to win over some of the delegates. In February 1618 Bandinell (who was later made dean) was publicly advocating in the island—with more zeal than tact—that a dean should be appointed;[13] and about the same time another of the delegates, Olivier, sent the secretary of state a long paper containing practical suggestions as to the best way of carrying out the king's wishes in church matters. It was significantly accompanied by a covering letter asking that " such competent maintenance be allowed unto us (i.e. the ministers) that is required, both for to encourage us to do the work of the Lord faithfully, and also to procure to us that due respect which of right belongeth to the holy ministry ".[14] Clearly the government had succeeded in dividing their chief opponents ; other ministers besides Messervy were ready to accept episcopacy ; and the two recent Commissioners, Conway and Bird, who were consulted by Council on the church question, could report with some show of plausibility that " it will stand with the desire of the ministers, the liking of the people and the honour and use of the church discipline if there be a dean nominated only by the King ".[15]

On 14 June, 1618, orders were sent to the States to nominate three ministers from whom the king would choose the dean. This direction was not obeyed until March 1619, but it appears that Bandinell had in fact been chosen before the end of 1618,[16] and he was appointed and took up office early in 1620. The delay in carrying out the king's order was due to negotiations over details : the States of Jersey realised that opposition on the main question was useless, that the Government was determined to have its way, and that all that they could do was to try and save something from the wreck of the Presbyterian cause. Their efforts were chiefly directed to two points : to restrict the jurisdiction of the Dean's Court as much as possible, and to get the widest discretion they could in the use of the Anglican liturgy and ritual.

The first of these points is sometimes expressed negatively by saying that the Dean's Court should not have power to deal with " contentious causes ", sometimes positively by saying that its jurisdiction should be limited to " spiritual causes concerning preaching and sacraments ", and such matters as marriage, bastardy and probate. What this meant was that the laymen did not want the dean to have any power to decide questions relating to property such as tithe, or the legal validity of a will (as distinguished from the question whether it had been duly executed by the testator) ; and they wished the Royal Court to retain the power, which it had assumed when the dean ceased to exist at the Reformation, of punishing spiritual offences such as heresy, blasphemy, sabbath-breaking, and immorality generally. In the heyday of Presbyterianism the Royal Court had been guided by the church courts in dealing with such offences ; in fact their work in this respect largely consisted in punishing offenders who were denounced to them by the Consistory or the Colloque, but technically the jurisdiction rested with the lay court, and as long as the local gentry who composed the Royal Court and the States were also as a rule elders in their parishes, the secular and the spiritual powers worked for the most part in harmony. Now that the governor's neglect and active hostility had broken the power of the church courts the civil magistrates had no desire to surrender any part of their criminal jurisdiction to the dean.

The position is well summed up in a letter of Hérault's to the secretary of state[17] towards the end of the controversy in which he says that the choosing of the Dean has been much hindered by " the idle and indiscreet threats and boasts about the powers that the dean would have over the people's rights and liberties ", uttered by Elie Messervy, and reports that he had persuaded the ministers and jurats to come to an agreement as to the limits of the dean's jurisdiction.

The articles are :—

(1) The dean to give judgment according to the opinion of the majority of the ministers sitting with him.

(2) Nothing to be settled about ordination or ecclesiastical censures without the assent of at least seven ministers.

(3) The king's subjects not to be required to plead except before the ordinary judges.

(4) The existing authority of the Royal Court not to be diminished.[18]

The first two articles are obviously intended to placate the ministers by reducing the dean as nearly as possible to the position of a moderator of the Colloque. They recall the curious argument which Hérault used to reconcile the States to receiving the dean when appointed : " there had always been a dean in the island, and whosoever did moderate the Colloque on proposition day had the place and office of a dean ". It was the second two articles that chiefly interested the lay members of the States ; and it is plain throughout that the leading laymen as a body were not really very much attached to the Presbyterian church courts and their discipline, or much concerned about the question whether the insular church was governed by a dean or a Colloque ; and they certainly were not ready to defy the king's declared will in such a cause. What they wanted was to protect the jurisdiction of the civil court from any kind of ecclesiastical encroachment. They were entirely in agreement with the views expressed some thirty years earlier by Sir Thomas Leighton, a stronger Presbyterian than any of them :—" I have learned not to disobey my superiors and for so slight a cause as this controversy, which is nothing but whether all ministers shall be on an egality or that a bishop shall be superintendant over them, which point whether the one or the other be I am indifferent, for it is a thing that toucheth not salvation, I mean to us of the laity, for *vos non sic* was spoken to John and James and their fellows ".[19]

The second point stood on quite another footing. It is perfectly clear that the islanders as a body were sincerely attached to the Presbyterian form of service in which the sermon was the central feature and did not wish to see it replaced by the Anglican Prayer Book, especially as in their eyes some of the Anglican ritual savoured of Popery. It is significant that an anonymous paper entitled " Proposals for the Establishment of a Dean ",[20] and obviously prepared in the island as a compromise designed to save as much as possible of the Presbyterian system, ends with the appeal : " It is also humbly desired that a special care be taken that the ministry and preaching of God's word which hath long flourished in the island may not now by any alteration come to be an only dumb and reading ministry ". In the same spirit Hérault's report (quoted above) on the scheme which he had induced the ministers and jurats to accept, stipulates that His Majesty should agree to the Liturgy being left to the discretion of the ministers.

But even on this point the islanders were not prepared to oppose the king's will. The last effort in the cause of Presbyterianism was a resolution passed by the States on 9 November, 1618[21] in which they thanked His Majesty for his special care of them, and humbly requested to be upheld if they proceeded no further (in the nomination of ministers for choice of a dean) because it did not appear to them that the brief by which he was pleased to confirm their ecclesiastical government had been revoked by him. They submitted themselves with all humility to his wise and gracious prudence and discretion. This was not the kind of protest which would alarm any government, and as a matter of fact it was not really addressed to the Government at all. Hérault explained to the English authorities that it was passed because Elie Messervy's wild talk about the power of the dean had frightened people,[22] and the States had to make a show of doing something in order to pacify them. He apologised to Conway for signing the resolution on the ground that it was the best course possible in the circumstances. It got His Majesty's wishes carried out with the good will of the people, whereas " if compulsion had been used to make them obey, and the matter pressed on before their feelings were prepared for it, there would have been nothing but grumbling and discontent ".[23]

Accordingly on 18 March, 1619 the States formally submitted to the king's decision and nominated three ministers for the selection of a dean. In fact it had already been decided to appoint Bandinell, but it was a year before the actual appointment was made.

This was not because of further opposition in the island, but because the Bishop of Winchester stood up for the rights of his see. The original idea was that in virtue of Henry VII's Ordinance an appointment by the king was all that was required. But the Bishop found a record that after this Ordinance Henry himself had presented a dean to the Bishop of Coutances to be admitted by him. So a revised patent was issued setting out that the right of nomination and presentation belonged to the King and that of admission to the Bishop.[24] The result was that Bandinell was detained in London nearly six months " to his insupportable charge " and had to pay fees first for the royal patent of appointment, then for a presentation to the bishop, also under the Great Seal, then for an institution by the bishop under the episcopal seal, and finally for a commission from the bishop to exercise jurisdiction (according to instructions to be issued by his Majesty under the Signet). Sir William Bird sums up the position somewhat caustically :—
" So that poor Mr. Bandinell hath almost as many seals and instruments for his poor deanery as any Bishop hath for a good bishopric in England, and instead of what Bishops have— writs of restitution of temporalities—he hath a letter in the King's name to the Governor for such proportion of allowance due to the place as heretofore belonged thereto ".[25] In the circumstances it was lucky for Bandinell that the governor was anxious for the appointment of a dean and willing to pay his salary.

Finally Bandinell returned to Jersey " loaded with patents ",[26] and was sworn in as dean at a meeting of the States on 15 April, 1620, not without some unpleasantness.[27]

Hérault, the bailiff, was in a very fractious temper : he opened the proceedings by making himself offensive to the governor because the States' meeting had been summoned in his name, and because the royal letters were addressed to the governor first and the bailiff second, and went on to be disagreeable to the new dean about the precedence to be assigned to him in the States. Two ministers (de la Place and Daniel Brevin) protested formally against the oath to be taken by the dean, saying that they would not acknowledge him to be their dean or their superior in anything and that they had signed and sworn another Discipline ; but only one or two lay members supported them and some of their own ministerial brethren reproved their rashness and presumption. It was noted that the bailiff, so far from censuring those objectors, checked the dean and the other ministers who answered them.[28]

The dean at once settled down to his double task of substituting his own court for the Consistories and the Colloques, and churchwardens on the English model for Presbyterian elders and deacons, and of inducing the ministers to use the Anglican Prayer Book. This was not an easy or pleasant job. Philip de Carteret wrote anxiously to the archbishop that when he got back to Jersey on 19 May he found " great discontent in many of the people and much dissension between the bailiff and the dean " : he was doing his best to get things quieted down " as shall make it appear how much I affect the accomplishment of His Majesty's pleasure ". Meanwhile he was afraid that a bad account of the position might reach London and annoy the king, and he begged the archbishop to " free us therein until I can effect that whereby His Majesty shall receive all contentment ".[29]

The question of church government seems to have been settled fairly soon in spite of some difficulty with the bailiff (as to which see below). In July 1620 Peyton reported to the Council[30] that he had got churchwardens appointed and did not blame the ministers for the delay. But he says " I wish I could as easily clear most of them of excusing the practice of the Liturgy, by His Majesty equally commanded ". It is evident that the change in the form of service was greatly disliked, and that the dean had to go very cautiously and gradually in enforcing the use of the Prayer Book (by " mild proceedings and, at their earnest suit, discreet delation " as the governor says). But though he " endeavoured by all peaceable and plausible means to advance " the Liturgy, with the active support of the governor, he was " enforced to suspend one of the brethren[31] from the exercise of his ministry as well for unreverend speeches against the Book of Common Prayer, as

138

for that he pleaded pretence of conscience, and yet would not (for the satisfaction of himself and others) accept the Dean's proffer of rectifying his scruples by argument ".

The next step was the preparation of canons to take the place of the temporary instructions for the exercise of the Dean's jurisdiction issued by the king on the appointment of Bandinell. A draft was prepared by the dean and ministers and submitted to a Committee of Council, consisting of the archbishop of Canterbury (Abbott) and the bishops of Lincoln (who was lord keeper), and Winchester : after they had heard objections from the Royal Court and revised the draft, the Canons were issued by the king under his Sign Manual and Signet on the 30 June, 1623.[32]

They were uncompromisingly Anglican in substance. Anyone who impeaches the king's supremacy or declares that the Church of England as it is now established under the King's Majesty is not a true and apostolic church purely teaching the doctrine of the prophets and apostles is declared to be *ipso facto* excommunicated ; all persons are required to submit to the Prayer Book service and all ministers to observe it with uniformity and without addition or alteration (3) ; no minister is to be admitted to any benefice without episcopal ordination (13).

Some concessions were made to insular feeling. The control of the Church in the island is vested by the Canons in the dean, who for all disciplinary purposes exercises the power of a bishop ; and the Bishop of Winchester, though nominally the Ordinary, is left with nothing but an appellate jurisdiction over cases heard in the Dean's Court. This Court was given full power to censure and punish offences against religion and morality according to ecclesiastical law, to deal with subtraction of tithes, and to suspend and deprive ministers. The wish of the laity that the dean should have no " contentious jurisdiction " was therefore not met ; but to conciliate the Royal Court a proviso was added that the powers of the Dean's Court should be without prejudice to the power of the civil magistrate in regard of bodily punishment for the said crimes." An attempt to compromise with Presbyterian principles appears in Canon 21, which requires the dean in cases handled in Court " to ask the advice and opinion of the ministers then present ". This contemplates that the ministers shall sit as assessors with the dean, and is intended to mask the objectionable features of hierarchical jurisdiction by giving the Court the appearance of a Presbyterian Colloque. It will be noted however that the dean, though bound to ask the advice of the ministers, is not bound to take it ; except that in the case of offences committed by ministers he is required by Canon 50 to have the advice and consent of two ministers before proceeding to suspension and sequestration, and the consent of the majority of the ministers present in the island before pronouncing sentence of deprivation.

The effect of the Canons, which still remain in force, is to give the insular church a curious position of semi-independence relative to the diocese of Winchester of which it forms a part, and to preserve, in the constitution of the Dean's Court, a fossil relic of that 17th century movement which aimed at bringing Episcopalians and Presbyterians into one church establishment on the basis of a compromise between the powers of a bishop and those of a Presbyterian synod.

This was the end of Presbyterianism in Jersey, except for a temporary revival under the Commonwealth. In Guernsey the course of events was quite different. The Privy Council letters of November 1613 were sent to both islands, and made it plain, as the States realised as soon as they were read, that the Government meant to introduce Anglicanism into the island if they were given any opening. No opening however was given : the laity of Guernsey held firmly with the ministers, and opposed a steady but respectful resistance to all attempts to make a breach in their Presbyterian system. They were so intent on fighting their own battle that they refused repeated appeals from the brethren in Jersey to meet in Synod with a view to organising a common resistance to the danger.[33] This was a selfish policy ; they said frankly that they refused " à cette fin que nous ne fassions chose aucune qui puisse préjudicier à nos églises ", the calculation evidently being that they needed all their strength to fight their own battle and had none to spare for propping a failing cause in Jersey ; but though not magnanimous it was successful. They were more fortunate than Jersey inasmuch as their governor, Lord Carew, was an absentee and apparently took no interest in the cause of episcopacy, and the lieutenant governor and bailiff, Amias de Carteret, belonged to a family of Presbyterian sympathies : they had therefore no enemies to fear inside the insular administration, and therefore attacks from outside were much less difficult to deal with.

Such an attack was not long in coming. A man named Le Page, who had been excommunicated by his parish minister, appealed to the Court of Arches, which summoned the minister to appear before it. The Colloque and the States at once united to oppose this as an infringement of their constitutional rights. The minister went to London furnished with instructions from the States not to recognise the jurisdiction of the Court. He could not apparently obey these instructions literally because the king himself took cognisance of the case, and he could only obtain leave to return to Guernsey temporarily on condition that he went back to London. He reported this to the States, and they directed him not to go back as he was needed in his parish. The Court of Arches then excommunicated him and added point to this proceeding by sending the plaintiff, Le Page himself, to notify the excommunication to the Colloque. Church and State united in resistance : the Colloque authorised the minister to continue in his charge, and the States protested formally that the island had a church establishment of its own established by royal authority, and was not subject to any other ecclesiastical jurisdiction. The Colloque followed this up by sending one of their number to appeal directly to the King. Their choice turned out to be a good one ; they sent de la Marche,[34] a young man of ability and force of character, who came back entirely successful after two interviews with the king himself. Although the secretary of state pressed hard for the appointment of a dean and the introduction of the Anglican service in Guernsey, the king decided that the existing state of affairs should continue. The reasons for this decision were obviously those set out in the memorandum which Lord Danby, the governor of the islands, wrote on the question in 1637.[35] The essential point was simply that the islanders were united in a strong attachment to the Presbyterian Church, and that it would be folly to alienate them by insisting on a change when their loyalty was necessary for the defence of the island. These motives were of course greatly strengthened when war with France broke out, and Buckingham's expedition went to the Ile de Ré : the importance of the islands as frontier fortresses automatically increased, and at the same time the war was being fought in alliance with the French Protestants with whom the Church of Guernsey was closely connected.

Later Archbishop Laud, who did his best to make the Protestant refugee churches in England abandon their Presbyterian order and conform to the Anglican Church, certainly had his eye on Guernsey.[36] Heylyn says that he would have proceeded to reform the Church in Guernsey, and had actually selected a person with knowledge of the islands[37] to conduct a visitation, on the report of which he would have taken action, but was prevented by the outbreak of the troubles in Scotland. This is borne out by a letter of 5 November, 1636, from Laud's secretary,[38] William Dell, to Lord Danby, setting out that the king understands that Jersey had been reduced to " some reasonable conformity " with the Church of England, but Guernsey had not, and that His Majesty was of opinion that " as great if not greater care of conformity ought to be had of this island as of Jersey ", and conveying the king's instructions that Danby should take this business into his present consideration, that both islands may go alike and that Guernsey as well as the other may conform to the Church of England.

Danby replied with the memorandum referred to above (it is endorsed in Laud's hand)[39] deprecating on political grounds any attempt to change the existing church system in Guernsey. This was written in April 1637. Three months later the famous Prayer Book Riots in Edinburgh broke out, and, as Heylyn says, the king and Laud had no time to think about the Church in Guernsey.

To do Laud justice he did not propose to depend entirely on coercion to produce uniformity ; as a former President of St. John's and Vice-Chancellor of Oxford he thoroughly understood the importance of education, and in 1635 he established fellowships at Oxford for Channel Islanders who were preparing for the ministry.[40] The object of course was to encourage them to study in an Anglican atmosphere instead of in the Presbyterian surroundings of Saumur and Geneva. The ideas of the Government went even further, for it appears that about this time they had schemes of substituting English influence for French in the life of the islands generally. A note in Secretary Windebank's hand of " Council business undispatched " on 18 October, 1633, contains the item :— " Mr. Attorney to be advised with concerning the laws of the isles of Jersey and Guernsey. The subjects there are governed by the edicts of France. In the time of Henry III of France they received many of his edicts. That their children may be bred in England. This was moved 4th June 1633".[41] Another note of Windebank's dated 15 November is endorsed with a list of business to be attended to by Council which includes " Laws of the islands of Jersey and Guernsey and breeding of their children ".[42]

It is not fanciful to suppose that Laud was the moving spirit in this scheme for Anglicising the islands through education and the use of the royal right if wardship. It was exactly in keeping with his doctrinaire temperament to contemplate such an attack on the ancient institutions and privileges of the islands on pure grounds of abstract theory and without the slightest regard to the furious opposition it would arouse. The Council took no action however, and before long they and the king had more immediately pressing matters to occupy them.

The difference between the fortunes of the Presbyterian cause in the two islands is very striking, and it is interesting to consider the reasons for it. They resolve themselves into two : in Guernsey laity and clergy were unanimous in resisting the change, and in Jersey they were not ; in Guernsey the governor took no steps to bring about any alteration in the Presbyterian order—as we have seen Lord Danby[43] reported to the Government that any attempt to do so would be unwise—whereas Peyton in Jersey showed himself from the first hostile to the Presbyterian order and anxious to take any opportunity of attacking it. He succeeded in driving a wedge between the clergy and the leading laymen. He had steadily refused to give any backing to the church courts or to let the lay magistrates enforce their sentences, and had in fact encouraged delinquents to defy spiritual censures. This was the weak point in the Presbyterian system : many people, not all of them notorious evil livers, disliked the inquisitorial proceedings of the church authorities and the high line which ministers and elders took ; and members of the Royal Court were jealous of spiritual courts which tended to encroach on their jurisdiction. Conway " had observed that the islanders have ever endeavoured to draw all ecclesiastical power into the hands of their jurats",[44] and Heylyn says that one of the constables actually accused the ministers in the States of hypocrisy and tyrannical government.[45] It is clear that there was a genuine feeling against the church courts already in existence for Peyton to work on ; and it has already appeared that while the States and the Royal Court were sincerely attached to the Presbyterian form of service and reluctant to give any judicial power to a dean, they were not at all inclined to embark on a crusade against the English government for the church courts or the Presbyterian equality of ministers.

It is at first sight a surprising feature of this ecclesiastical controversy that Hérault does not appear as a defender of the island church. His sympathies were certainly Presbyterian or at any rate not in the least Anglican ; and from his past record we should naturally expect to find him foremost in championing the rights of the island in ecclesiastical as well as in civil matters, and delighted to carry on his quarrel with the governor on this new ground. But on the contrary he was on the Anglican side throughout, at least after the royal letters of 1613 had made the king's wishes plain : as his own letters show he was anxious to get some modifications in point of detail to suit local circumstances, but on the main question he was actively working for uniformity with the Church of England.[46]

There can be no doubt that it was his attitude in the civil controversy which determined the line he took here. Throughout his contest with the governor he had protested loudly and repeatedly that he was the civil government of the island and the king's representative, and it was obviously impossible for the king's representative to come out as a leader of the opposition to the king's declared policy in church affairs. If he wanted to defend the church he must either resign his post as bailiff, or publicly recant his cherished theory that the bailiff was the king's representative in Jersey. He evidently saw the dilemma, and having made up his mind, like the Politiques in France a generation earlier, that the political issue was more important than the religious one, adopted the line of supporting the king's policy (subject to restriction of the powers of the dean and indulgence in enforcing the Liturgy). He quotes the chancellor (Bacon) as saying in Council that he (Hérault) had sufficiently expressed his desire " to run His Majesty's courses ".[47] His letters to the secretary of state show that as early as 1616 he was recommending the appointment of a dean and parading his zeal for the Royal Supremacy by complaining that the lieutenant governor would not put up the Royal Arms in the churches, and that throughout the ecclesiastical controversy of 1618—9 he was reporting to the Government as to the steps taken to carry out the king's ins-structions, and professing to be doing his best to smooth away difficulties. When Hérault, the champion of insular rights, took this line it is not surprising that the other lay notables were not disposed to run any risks for the Presbyterian cause. A good idea of their attitude is given in a letter of de Carteret to Sir William Conway :—" I had advertisement from London how these things were managed, whereby I judged it would prove a fruitful labour to insist on that establishment past, and to have consented to any thing derogating from it I thought I should have done you wrong. I chose to lay aloof and not meddle in it. . . . . . .I know not in this business how I may avoid either the ill will of my country or the distaste of the State here ".[48] When the Seigneur of St. Ouen, a man of undoubted Presbyterian sympathies, candidly avowed that that he did not think it worth while to make himself unpopular in high quarters for the sake of Presbyterianism, it is clear that the material for a Presbyterian crusade did not exist in Jersey.

But Peyton not only succeeded in separating the ministers from the laity : he also managed to drive a wedge into the ministry itself by appointing the Anglican priest Messervy to a living and, still more effectually, by holding out hopes of preferment to the ministers delegated by the church to represent it. A house divided against itself—doubly divided in fact—could not stand against the wishes of the English Government and the steady persistence of Peyton. In Guernsey on the other hand clergy and laity held together and carefully refrained from giving any opening, while the governor did nothing to make one. The result was that Presbyterianism remained the established religion of Guernsey until the Restoration. For as long as the English Government kept to their cautious policy of waiting for an opportunity before acting, they necessarily depended on the zeal and intelligence of the governor to create or make use of an opening. It was not until Laud came to power that there was any likelihood of this caution being abandoned. Laud was logical to the point of pedantry, always ready to enforce authority in small things as well as great with all the doctrinaire's recklessness of practical considerations.[49] He was apparently ready to take the initiative and order an episcopal visitation, an intensely provocative step which the islanders would have regarded as an attack on their political independence as well as an outrage on their religious convictions, and they would have been unanimous in resisting.

CHAPTER XIII.

THE CHANNEL ISLANDS IN WAR-TIME (1626-1630).

On Hérault's death the governor and the majority of the Royal Court agreed in recommending the appointment of Philip de Carteret, Seigneur of St. Ouen, as his successor, and the Government acted on this suggestion, greatly to the advantage of the administration of the island. De Carteret was a man of high character and a strong sense of public duty ; as the head of the richest and most powerful family in Jersey he had great influence in the island and an intimate knowledge of local affairs and local feeling ; and, since the de Carterets had repeatedly intermarried with English families of rank and—as the correspondence shows— de Carteret was on friendly terms with leading members of the Council, he was less insular in his ideas and had a better appreciation of the problems and difficulties of the English Government than most of the notables of the islands. He was therefore invaluable as a mediator and interpreter between London and the island authorities, and all parties found the advantage of having a bailiff who worked harmoniously with the governor in the public interest and who at the same time was ready to protect insular privileges when necessary.

This was particularly fortunate because for a few years the islands came into the limelight when war, first with Spain and then with France, made their affairs of some political importance. The war with Spain did not affect them so much, but early in 1626 the Council realised that they were " exposed to invasions or raids from the ships of Spain or Dunkirk or from pirates ", and sent strict orders to Peyton to carry out the ordinances laid down by the Commissioners of 1618, and to put Jersey in a state of defence by repairing and increasing the fortifications, strengthening the guard at the castle, and making all arrangements for arming and mobilising the inhabitants in case of need.[1] When Charles I went to war with France as well (June 1627) the position of the islands became much more serious. The French Government refused to recognise their ancient privilege of neutrality, as has been explained above, and in addition to their losses of trade they were in constant fear of invasion. Richelieu was believed to be set on conquering the islands for France, and throughout these years the governors of the islands were constantly reporting threatening concentrations of troops and ships in various Norman and Breton ports. The Government evidently thought there was grave danger : in 1627 the Royal Court of Guernsey were formally assured in answer to their representations that the king would " in all tymes and all occasions, continue his protection unto you in such sort as shall give you security, and shew how much he esteemes that portion of his inheritance, and the unspotted faith and duety of those his subjects of those Islands ";[2] and at the end of 1628 Lord Danby, the governor of Guernsey, was made responsible for the defence of both islands on the ground that " it being given out that a Peere of that Kingdome undertaketh the attempt, that he may be encountered by another Peere of ours ".[3] There was also the practical reason that Peyton, the governor of Jersey, was a very old man and not living in the island.

As was usual in war-time, the garrisons of the islands were reinforced from England, a company of 200 men drawn from the county train-bands being sent over to each island, and billeted on the inhabitants. This at once led to a variety of controversies. In Jersey the defence of the castle gave rise to difficulty : Peyton wanted an additional guard of 20 men mounted at the castle every night : the inhabitants refused to supply the men themselves, and even objected to their being taken from the English company. They argued that the soldiers were sent over to resist an enemy's landing, not to defend the castles : Peyton who knew that the castle required a garrison of at least 100 men to be reasonably safe was afraid that if the soldiers lost heavily in trying to oppose a landing in force he would not have enough men left to defend the castle. This curious difficulty did not arise in Guernsey because the governor was made captain of the company sent there, and it was universally admitted that, this being so, he could post his own men where he liked.

There was also trouble over the billeting : during the defence controversy some of the Jersey people enforced their arguments by turning out the soldiers whom they were billeting ; and even when this had quieted down they " continued in their refusal of billeting the soldiers or using them basely in their diet and injuriously in their persons ".[4]

The situation was not improved by the fact that Charles I's impecunious government provided the soldiers with pay very irregularly or not at all, and the men could not of course pay for their keep out of their own pockets. No wonder the people began " to murmur and grudge against the soldiers, thinking them a burden, especially wanting money to relieve them "; and to avoid really serious trouble large sums were advanced locally to pay the soldiers. De Carteret, who was paymaster of the Jersey company, paid out far more than he received from the Government : in Guernsey the States found the money for pay and by September 1629 had advanced nearly £1400 for this purpose, and were pressing for payment on the ground that there was great distress in the island owing to loss of trade, the capture of their shipping, and taxes for fortification as well as for the soldiers' pay.[5]

Not unnaturally there were quarrels between the soldiers and the inhabitants. The Cornwall and Devon men sent to Jersey contained a substantial proportion of bad characters, who broke into houses and robbed and assaulted people in the streets. On the other side some of the soldiers were attacked and badly hurt by the inhabitants, one even by a jurat. This put the governor and bailiff in an awkward position, and they applied for a commission giving them power to try the soldiers by martial law : they agreed that such offences ought not to come before the civil court which would be prejudiced and unduly severe (" if put to the justices they will hang them ", said Peyton), and meanwhile the accused soldiers had to be kept in the castle. On the other side the Royal Court could not be trusted to do justice when soldiers were the complainants: the bailiff himself reported that in such cases " the testimony of any of the soldiers is refused, that only of the inhabitants is taken, who are sure to lay the fault upon the soldiers as beginners of the quarrel ".[6] No commission seems to have been granted: probably the difficulties which arose out of the establishment of martial law in Guernsey made the Council hesitate about extending it to Jersey.

The garrison of Guernsey does not appear to have given any serious trouble. This was probably because the men were drawn from a better class : they were taken from London and Middlesex, and the lord mayor and lord lieutenant were expressly told to levy skilled artisans " of the better and more staid sort " taken from specified trades : the idea apparently was that they could be used to complete the fortifications of the castle. Also Lord Danby's rank would give him greater authority both with his own men and the islanders, and he succeeded, as was indicated above, in getting a commission of martial law. This at any rate enabled him to deal with offences committed by the soldiers without troubling the local courts, although the wide terms of the commission had raised a grave constitutional question. Danby asked for and obtained a commission " according to the example of the Provincial

148

governments in Ireland", empowering him "to punish, by fine or imprisonment all such, either inhabitantes or soldiers as upon theyr appoynted guards or any other way shall neglect their duetyes, or miscary themselves to the disturbance of the peace and that union which ought to be maintayned" between the islanders and the garrison. He wanted it, he said, "the better to conforme some perverse spiritts amongst that people, whoe conceive themselves litle lesse than a free state, and are rather pevish in their oppynions then sensible of their owne daungers". The Guernsey people took alarm at this as an infringement of their liberties, and made formal remonstrances to the Council, who assured them that the king's intention was that martial law should only apply to soldiers, and withdrew the commission pending further instructions. This brought Lord Danby and his lieutenant governor into the field, protesting that these letters of the Council would "work ill effects amongst that people, apt enough to be misled" and "reflect upon my Lord Danby in point of honor", and that the commission had in fact been very little used in practice but was absolutely necessary in time of war. The recent Council letters were recalled, but the island deputies stuck to their point and finally obtained a decision that the application of martial law should be limited to soldiers of the garrison.[7]

The necessities of war-time were always liable to stir up constitutional questions in the islands unless the governor exercised extreme tact and judgment, and a few months later there was trouble in Jersey. The war with Spain still dragged on in an inactive way after peace had been made with France (April 1629), and in the summer of 1630 Biscayan privateers were hanging about Jersey, landing raiding parties from time to time, and threatening to cut out ships from under St. Aubins fort. The lieutenant governor, a soldier named Rainsford, decided that a guard at St. Aubins fort was necessary until the privateers were got rid of, and ordered one to be mounted every night drawn from the two watches furnished by St. Brelade and St. Lawrence parishes. Rainsford had express orders to see to the safety of the fort, and it was universally admitted that the guard was needed for this, but his method of providing it brought him into collision with parochial privileges and parochial patriotism, and he found himself plunged into a first-rate political crisis. No guard appeared on the first night, and the constable of St. Lawrence, when called to account for disobeying orders, insisted that he was bound to maintain the privileges of his parish and that they were not obliged to do any duty at St. Aubins Tower and would not begin it. Rainsford imprisoned the constable, only to find

149

that he was regarded as a martyr in the cause of the liberties of the island and, as such, was visited in prison by " most of the parish, all the constables, and some of the jurats ". Rainsford was compelled much against his will to lay the matter before the States—" where though many of them were parties I was forced to make them my judges ". The States could not deny that the watch was necessary, but showed a strong disposition to maintain that it ought to be provided and paid by the governor. De Carteret and some other leading men did their best for Rainsford, and finally the States consented to provide the watch provisionally and to petition the Council on the question of right. But they insisted that the watch must be found by all the parishes of the island in turn, with the natural result that the more distant parishes complied with the order very unwillingly and sometimes not at all and the poorer people complained bitterly of the hardship of having to do this night duty when they were busy with harvest work.

Rainsford however paid no regard whatever to popular feeling. He was very angry that his orders had been questioned at all and still more because the States did not recognise his right to imprison without the consent of the Royal Court. " By the grace of God ", he told the Council, " I will assume this power as belonging to my place in martial cause to commit the defendants. And if any of the constables and people continue in this stubbornness of so high nature and dangerous a consequence, I will keep the leaders of the mutiny in prison until I understand His Majesty's and your Lordships' pleasure ".[8]

His insistence on his prerogative and his high and mighty temper led him into the incredible folly of forcing a quarrel upon de Carteret, the bailiff, although he had stood by him vigorously in the dispute over the watch and his local influence was Rainsford's best hope of getting what he wanted done by the people. It arose out of the same question of the governor's power to imprison, but in this case Rainsford certainly put a very strained interpretation on his rights. A Jersey man named Pallott was arrested in Guernsey on suspicion of having acted as pilot to a French privateer in the war : the charge broke down, but the lieutenant governor was not satisfied about him and sent him to Jersey in case there was any charge against him there. Pallott's consistent bad luck in the matter of falling in with enemy ships might reasonably make the authorities suspicious : it appears that since the French business he had also been—as a prisoner, he said—on board a Biscayan privateer for some time. The lieutenant governor and the bailiff both issued warrants for his arrest : the constables executed the bailiff's warrant and de Carteret put the man on bail; then, as a matter of courtesy, he told his officers to take him to the lieutenant governor. Rainsford was very angry that his warrant had not been executed first, imprisoned Pallott in spite of his being on bail, and stormed at de Carteret when he tried to explain his position in a friendly way. De Carteret naturally told him that " if he did take upon himself to imprison by force the king's subjects he must look to answer it " : he was anxious to support the Government whenever he could, but he felt bound to stand up for the rights of the civil power which Rainsford habitually treated with contempt—" he doth so slight the Justice (i.e. la Justice, the Royal Court) that he hath told two constables that if they did talk any more to him of the Justice he would lay them by the heels ".[9]

Rainsford was now at odds with practically everyone on the island, and the position of affairs must have been impossible. Peyton wrote to de Carteret in an attempt— apparently unsuccessful—to reconcile him with Rainsford, and the whole quarrel went up to Council. They referred it to Conway, who was regarded as an expert in Jersey affairs ever since he had served on the Commission of 1617 on the Hérault- Peyton controversy. His report[10] (5 August, 1630) is a very verbose and inconclusive document which can have given Council very little help on the practical issues which had to be settled. It did not get anybody very far to say " I cannot collect any difficulty for the Lords to put a happy end to the present question by setting down instructions with the consent of the inhabitants when and in what classes they shall be called upon to serve with their persons and arms for the defence of the island, how long the same shall be continued, and at whose cost ".

One or two points however emerge clearly. Conway had no doubt that Pallott's case was entirely a civil matter, and therefore for the bailiff and Royal Court alone : he thought that the people of Jersey had shown great loyalty in the war in spite of heavy losses from the stoppage of their trade, and hinted very plainly that it was not a time for pressing them too hard (" respecting the conjuncture of the time whether it be proper to despair the people or attempt to bring novelties upon them ") ; and it is plain from this passage and the reference to settling the disputed questions of service with the consent of the people, that Conway had no idea of upholding Rainsford in his claim " to command and order it (i.e. matters of defence) as I see cause ", and generally to ride roughshod over the States and Royal Court.

Council never seems to have come to any formal decision. A little later (November 1630) peace was signed with Spain, and problems of insular defence would naturally cease to be urgent or important. When this cause of friction was removed there was nothing in the islands to raise any constitutional questions ; and, as we have seen, Laud's project of enforcing conformity on the Church in Guernsey never got to the stage of overt action.

From this time onwards the islands disappear from the view of the historian until the Civil War brought them once more into the picture.

CHAPTER XIV.

CHARACTERISTICS OF THE PERIOD.

A number of general considerations on the history of the period suggest themselves. The records show repeated controversies between the islanders and the governors sent them from England, and it is possible to draw conclusions of some interest as to the relations between the islanders and the central government, the problems which the administration of these dependencies presented, and the way in which the Privy Council dealt with them.

The most striking feature of the case is that from the accession of Henry VII until the death of Elizabeth the various disputes contain nothing which can be called a political element. The petitions of 1605 and 1607, as we have seen, show signs of a change in this respect, but for more than a hundred years no person or party in the islands attributed any of the evils which they complained of to defects in their political system, or dreamed of any kind of political reform ; nor did any governor of the central government itself show any desire to introduce constitutional changes. All parties concerned accepted the ancient constitutional arrangements as fundamental and unchangeable : their controversies were not about the validity or the application of the principles involved, but about pure questions of administration which raised no point of principle. An excellent illustration of this attitude is afforded by de Carteret's action of 1587 in Jersey, when the Privy Council, the governor and the Royal Court and States were all agreed that for a private person to get up a petition for the abolition of an ancient court of justice was sedition and deserved to be punished as such.

This same case is interesting also as an example of another characteristic feature of these controversies—the appeal to local privileges. The islanders were naturally and reasonably very tenacious of their peculiar constitution and liberties, and very much on their guard against any encroachment on them. The various Guernsey complaints against Leighton are full of charges about his attempts to overthrow the estate and liberties of the island. Actually these are little more than rhetorical flourishes : there is no evidence that any governor (later than Hugh Vaughan) really attempted to infringe any island privileges, and certainly the Council was always scrupulously careful not to encroach on anything that could be shown to be an ancient liberty of the islands. It would be unkind and unfair to apply Dr. Johnson's definition of patriotism as " the last refuge of a scoundrel " to the insular complainants : most of them were not in any sense scoundrels ; but it is an unquestionable fact that in very many cases their grievances began with a private law-suit or with some personal squabble with the governor or bailiff, and it was only after they had been defeated in this that they discovered that the liberties of the island were in danger.

There was one class of case however in which the island privileges were genuinely involved : in time of war there was apt to be a real clash between the military necessities of defence and the terms of the island charters, and unless the governor showed quite exceptional tact and self-control, he was likely to find a serious constitutional question on his hands. When Leighton in 1587 obeyed the Council's orders to seize Spanish goods he was at once in difficulties over the island privilege of neutrality ; and in 1630 Rainsford in Jersey discovered that his orders for a night watch at St. Aubins Tower—reasonable and indeed essential from a military point of view—conflicted with the ideas of the parishes as to their local rights and obligations. The islanders, though perfectly loyal, knew and cared little about foreign politics, and were not eager to assume additional burdens because the king had seen fit to go to war with France or Spain.

A brief examination of the complaints submitted to the Council makes it clear that, where more than mere personal quarrels were involved, the questions at issue fall into two main classes, viz. revenue matters—including under that head Crown dues of all kinds, taxes such as customs, purveyance (for supplies for the garrison), and customary *corvees* such as the obligation to provide work or cartage for the fortifications— and alleged arbitrary or oppressive acts by the governor (e.g. imprisonment on his own authority, compelling the people to serve against pirates, etc.). The allegations in this second class vary considerably in degree, from the full-blooded tyranny exercised by Hugh Vaughan in Jersey to the few and comparatively minor acts of arbitrary power ascribed to Leighton ; but the point which is common to all the complaints is that they are directed against simple misgovernment, and do not involve any difference of opinion on constitutional issues. It is the same with the revenue disputes : no political theories about the right of taxation or the boundaries of the prerogative enter into the case, the question is simply whether the governor has collected customs at a higher rate than the old charters allow, whether the tenants of Fief St. Michel are or are not liable to pay campart, or some other similar matter of detail. Friction between the governor and the people on fiscal questions was inevitable with the system of government in force, under which the governor took the Crown revenues of every kind, paid the ordinary expenses of government, and kept the balance as his salary. This was an obvious temptation to a greedy and unscrupulous man ; and if the governor was merely an honest and efficient servant of the queen, the islanders were bound to suspect personal motives in his financial strictness. In any case they knew that the island was poor, and saw, or thought they saw, that the governor was rich—in 1607 the Guernsey people objected to doing unpaid guard duty at the castle on the ground that " His Majesty meaneth not that the Governor shall alone reap all the profit and commodities of the said Government (which are very great for so little a country) unless he stand to all that is requisite for the safe keeping of the said Castle to the end the people be not charged of so burdenous a service ":[1] in these conditions paying taxes struck them as a personal matter, and therefore annoyed them much more than the collection of income tax by an impersonal and disinterested revenue authority. Jean Hérault undoubtedly hit the mark when he told Lord Salisbury that the governor's possession of the royal revenues brought him into many differences with the subjects, and suggested the appointment of an independent finance officer to receive the revenue and pay all salaries and expenses.[2] But Hérault was ahead of his time : no such system was practicable in the early seventeenth century because there was no source, in the islands at any rate, from which the necessary supply of trained permanent officials could be drawn.

The " islanders " meant, for the practical purposes of government, the local aristocracy of landowners and merchants who, as jurats, parish constables, and so forth, controlled the judicial and administrative machinery of the islands. The common people never dreamed of questioning their authority : the foreign scholar, Saravia, who was schoolmaster in Guernsey, observes with surprise that the jurats " lord it over them like dumb cattle ", and that the people so far from objecting are quite contented with the position.[3] Every movement against the governor was in fact headed by jurats or members of the jurats' families : even in 1578, the only occasion on which we hear of a popular disturbance directed against the jurats,[4] the opposition party in the Royal Court speedily got control of the agitation and turned it against the governor.

The island aristocracies, like most such bodies, were torn by bitter personal and family feuds; but they agreed in a common desire to be left to perpetrate occasional jobs or legalised raids on the royal domain without interference from the governor, and a common dislike of being stirred up by outsiders in the name of loyalty and efficiency ; and, being a body of high-spirited and tenacious Norman gentry, they could be formidable adversaries for a governor from England. The position was made much more difficult by the absence of any really impartial or professionally competent court of law in the island. Any dispute whether of law or fact affecting Crown rights had to come before the Royal Court, which consisted entirely of local notables, all landowners or merchants, who had very often a strong interest, as a class if not individually, in deciding against the Crown, and not being trained lawyers had not the restraint of a professional conscience.

As an instance of how this might work in practice, an experience of Leighton's in Guernsey is illuminating.[5] An island seigneur claimed to collect treizièmes and camparts from his tenants, these being royal dues which belonged to the Crown. The Royal Court found in his favour, the governor thought because " the greater part of them having the like petty feages do persuade themselves that by carrying of this pretended title of Beauvoir's feage against Her Majesty, thereby each of them may challenge all kind of royalties on their fiefs, as well as he ". On the governor appealing to Council the law officers reported that the proceedings in the case were very partial, the bailiff being excluded from the sentence without just cause, and the sentence being given by two brothers-in-law of Beauvoir and another jurat affected to his cause ; and Council ordered the governor to have the case retried in his presence by impartial jurats. He did his best, but he reported that " to find a competent number that should not be partial, it is a thing un-possible ", and the new court justified his foreboding by insisting on finding against the Crown once more, refusing " to hear or weigh anything that could be produced for the confirmation of Her Majesty's right " ; and the bailiff refused to pronounce " a sentence so corrupt and prejudicial to her right and royal prerogative " until the Council had been notified—a proceeding which was not strictly constitutional, and which was remembered and brought up as a grievance years afterwards.

The extraordinary fluidity of the island system of law and legal procedure was an important factor of the situation. The Royal Court was supposed to enforce the ancient customary law of Normandy as laid down in certain recognised text-books. In practice it did what it saw fit in the individual case before it. As the Royal Commission of 1846 discovered, the Court considered itself competent not merely to deal according to its discretion with any case not covered by the text-books, but also to vary the rules laid down in the books as it thought necessary. Down to the nineteenth century the jurats of the Royal Courts were much more like a circle of kings of the Homeric Age declaring the dooms which they received from Zeus than the judges of a modern state administering an organised system of statute or customary law.[6]

The consequence was that no governor could form any rational opinion from lawbooks, precedents, or anything else as to what the decision of the Court on any disputed point was likely to be,[7] or even what startling developments an ordinary lawsuit might produce. When Chamberlain in Guernsey began an apparently straightforward suit against the dean about their respective rights to tithes, he suddenly found himself in the midst of a first-class constitutional struggle : the Royal Court had picked a quarrel with the procureur, sentenced him for contempt of court, and claimed that this had the effect of suspending him from office, and that the governor must appoint a new procureur.

A civil suit between private persons might have results almost equally surprising to an Englishman. We might take as an instance a case which gave the Privy Council a good deal of trouble about 1580. Nicholas Carey, of a leading family in Guernsey, sued a jurat named James Guille for a debt of £40 : the Court found for Guille, and Carey then " broke out in very injurious and infamous words against Guille in Court, calling him ' larron ' ". The Court at once proceeded to try this allegation of theft and when Carey failed to establish it to their satisfaction (all he could say was that Guille was improperly in possession of a wheat rent that belonged to the queen) first sent him to prison and then fined him 20 nobles to the queen and 20 to Guille.[8]

To an Englishman accustomed to courts which administered a well-defined system of law and tried carefully limited issues according to strict rules of procedure, such proceedings must have had a nightmare quality suggestive of the game of croquet in ' Alice in Wonderland ', where the balls turned out to be hedgehogs and the mallets flamingoes and acted accordingly. In an island court apparently any kind of lawsuit might suddenly turn into anything else.

Of course this made the position of the governor more difficult and correspondingly strengthened the hands of the local aristocracy when they wished to give trouble. There can be no doubt that the latter quite realised their advantage in this respect. Throughout this period we find the Council making repeated efforts first to extract from the islanders a clear statement of the customary law by which they claimed to be governed and second to make them keep to it when it was drawn up, but they were met with a steady passive resistance which completely defeated their efforts.[9]

It was not the mere fact that they had to deal with an insular aristocracy that made trouble for the Council and the queen's representatives in the islands. Government by the local gentry was regarded by all parties at that time as the natural and inevitable way to run any country, and the queen and her Council found no difficulty in using them as their instruments in England. The justices of the peace who did the judicial and administrative work of an English county under the supervision of the Council were men of the same class, and exercised very similar powers to those of the island jurats : the difference lay partly in the position and ideas of the island gentry, and partly in the constitution of the islands. The island families were at least as ancient and as well-descended as their English compeers, but they were poor and their estates were small and tended to become smaller by constant subdivision. It is worth noting that suggestions for the introduction of a system of entail and primogeniture were repeatedly put forward and were favourably regarded by the Government. For instance in 1618 the law officers reported on a petition from Jersey to this effect, that it would be for " His Majesty's service, and the general good of that island and that by this means many good houses may be raised in that isle ",[10] by which they undoubtedly meant landed families able to undertake the responsibility and expense which the Government expected the leading English gentry to bear in the public service. It may be observed that the one island family which in income and outstanding position closely resembled an English county family, the de Carterets of St. Ouen, were also much less insular and more English in their general attitude than their fellow islanders. We find them in successive generations making English marriages, cultivating friendships with leading men at court, and, when they held insular offices, showing a grasp of the general political situation and a disposition to meet the reasonable requirements of the central government which was not common in the islands. The governor of Jersey could usually reckon on keeping his subjects quiet and getting the Government's orders carried out as long as he was on good terms with the de Carterets, and this was certainly one of the reasons why Jersey through most of this period gave much less trouble than Guernsey. No wonder the law officers thought that it would be good for the king's service to have more families in the position and frame of mind of the de Carterets.

The islanders generally were not in the same stage of political thought as England. They were untouched by the characteristic ideas of the Elizabethan age, and did not share in the passionate devotion to the Crown or the aggressive national sentiment of the English. They were still medieval in their ways of thinking—loyal enough but regarding the Crown as something distant and remote from them, and with few thoughts beyond their own island affairs. The medieval cosmopolitanism, or at least absence of national feeling, comes out in their attitude towards their French neighbours. They were obsessed, particularly in Guernsey, with the idea that their traditional neutrality was a sufficient defence. The Guernsey people themselves said that they " wished to be friends of all rather than subjects of any " :[11] Leighton, a typical Elizabethan Englishman, said that they were " a people impudent, still seeking to tread down your Highness' prerogative, cowardly in courage, and somewhat too kind to the French ".[12]

No doubt plenty of English country gentlemen were also thoroughly rustic and parochially minded, but the Quarter Sessions of the most remote and backward English county contained a leaven of gentlemen who had been courtiers, soldiers or sailors, or at least had been educated at one of the Inns of Court. And English J.P.'s were continuously supervised by the Queen's Government : they were periodically visited by Judges of Assize, and were constantly under the eye of the Star Chamber. The island gentry were too poor to go to Court or to the wars ; and they were protected by distance and the difference of their constitution from minute control from Whitehall. There was no authority over the jurats but the Council itself, and this was too much overloaded with business and too ignorant of local details and personalities to exercise a close and regular supervision.

The governor was of course the representative of the crown in the islands, and it is clear from the documents that Council expected him to do to some extent the work which the Star Chamber did in England.[13] But there were limits to the control which he could exercise. By the constitution of the islands the inhabitants had the right of appealing to Council against illegal or arbitrary action on the part of the governor. Council could not therefore refuse to receive and consider complaints regularly put forward by responsible persons.

And the islanders saw to it that there were plenty of complaints. They were Normans, with a full share of the high spirit, the tenacity in holding to what they believed to be their rights, and the litigiousness of the Norman character. Not all their complaints were pursued in a regular or constitutional way. Cases of sheer violence were not unknown : in 1586 the bailiff and jurats being summoned to London to answer for their conduct, hired men who set upon the queen's procureur with clubs and left him for dead in a Westminster street.[14] Even when complaints were put forward in a more correct method the Council constantly found difficulty in making up its mind whether a deputation which brought them up really represented the whole community (island or parish) or merely a casual collection of persons got together by personal canvassing. It was evidently a standing temptation for people of an adventurous disposition to persuade a few of their neighbours to appoint them as delegates, and go off to London to try their luck with the Council. If they failed they probably got a few months in the Marshalsea, besides losing their time and money : if they succeeded in persuading Council that there really was a grievance and that they were authorised to represent it, they might get a promise of redress and go home to be received as saviours of their country. The next stage almost invariably was a dispute as to whether the expenses of the delegate should be paid by a general tax, or by the particular people who had profited by their action, and in the latter case, which they were.

Council must have found the continual complaints and legal appeals from the islands a serious addition to the burden of their duties. At this period they were not merely the only authority which could decide disputes between the governors and the islanders, but also the working government of England for all purposes. They faced their task manfully, though they occasionally show signs of impatience and weariness, which is not surprising considering the mass of trifling lawsuits which came up to them ; and an examination of the records leaves one with a high opinion of the paternal rule of the Tudors, and of Elizabeth's Council as the instrument which executed it. In their dealings with island affairs they were thorough, conscientious, and to the best of their power impartial. They had no desire any more than the islanders for constitutional innovations ; on the contrary they were clearly genuinely anxious to observe faithfully the charters and privileges of the islands : there is no trace of any attempt to encroach on anything that could be shown to be an ancient liberty. They were no doubt well aware that the islands were important

160

outposts the defence or at least the economical defence, of which depended on the loyalty of the inhabitants : probably also they were influenced by the theory current at the time, that as long as the Queen held the Channel Islands *and governed them according to Norman law and custom* she retained a good title *de jure* to the whole Duchy of Normandy.[15] But there was something more than merely interested motives at work ; respect for the ancient rights of the subject was a matter of conscience as well as expediency with the Tudors and their counsellors. It is significant of the ideas of the time that Robert Beale in his " Treatise of the Office of a Counsellor and Principal Secretary of State to Her Majesty " says :— " Take heed of any letters that may be against the law and liberty of the land, whereto the Prince is sworn ; *and it is the inheritance both of the Prince and the subject*", and he expressly includes among the collections of information which the secretary of state ought to make and keep by him " a book of the privileges of Guernsey and Jersey, of the ancient customs of Normandy and the said isles ".[16]

Council were quite aware that they were dealing with an unfamiliar legal and constitutional system, and took corresponding care to see that cases were fully heard and investigated before they came to any decision. They usually referred complaints to a small committee including one or two civil lawyers of distinction, who called the parties before them and examined them personally and at length ; and when commissions of inquiry were sent to one of the islands it was the regular practice to appoint a leading man from the other island as a member ; the idea obviously being that as he would understand local conditions without being involved in local feuds or prejudices he would be a competent and safe guide for the English members.

As was natural in an authoritarian age Council firmly upheld the Governor against anything that looked like sedition or disorder, and repressed any attempt to curtail his dignity or his authority as the representative of the sovereign ; but they had no idea of having any officer uncontrolled, or of permitting oppression or tyranny (according to the ideas of the period as to what constituted tyranny). And they knew perfectly well how to distinguish between the substance of a complaint and an irregular or disorderly way of putting it forward. Thus in the Guernsey dispute of 1586 over the right of neutrality, they found for the islanders on the question of principle at the same time as they punished the complainants for their improper behaviour towards the governor ; and again in 1604 the committee of Council thought that the complainants should receive "some meet censure" for their disorderly proceedings, but that their grievances ought to be examined on representations being made in a proper way.[17]

Shortly after the accession of James I we become conscious of a certain change in the political atmosphere. It would be a mistake to attach too much importance to Hérault's' attempt to make the bailiff the supreme political authority, and reduce the governor to a mere commandant of the garrison. This was a political freak—the original idea of an ingenious and masterful man, not the programme of a party. Of course a party programme, in the modern sense of a connected list of measures which some body of men wished to see carried, did not and could not exist in 1603. But with the turn of the century there is certainly a definite and more or less conscious disposition to take any opportunity that might offer to reduce the power of the governor and to increase that of the bailiff and Royal Court. Earlier complaints had been directed against acts of simple oppression and misgovernment or what the islanders regarded as such, but the Guernsey petitions of 1605 and 1607, and to some extent Hérault's activities in Jersey a few years later, show that the island aristocracies were becoming conscious of themselves as a political force, anxious to restrict the governor's prerogative powers, and prepared to claim a larger share in the government of the island.

A change in the attitude of the central government is also perceptible. Hérault's success in depriving the governor of the power of appointing the bailiff and law officers was due largely to a skilful appeal to the king's self-importance ; it would not be difficult to persuade James I that any such appointment was "an act merely regal and altogether inseparable from Our Royal Person". But this does not stand alone ; as we have seen, the findings of the Royal Commission of 1607 and the decisions of Council on their recommendations were almost all in the direction of limiting the hitherto undefined prerogative of the governor, and giving increased power and responsibility to the bailiff and Royal Court, to some extent raising them from the position of subordinates to that of an independent and co-equal authority. There is a passage in the Report of the Commission of 1617 which is very significant in this respect :—

"And for the civil government in cases where the civil and martial may be for his majesty's service mixed, your honors may be pleased to limit the pretences. A worthy governor being a sure pillar to that estate, which lies remote from this kingdom, and a worthy bailiff being a principal support for the conservation of the estate, if their virtue and good affections be seconded with meet and due limitted commission ; for where they cease to balance one another equally the danger grows alike from either of them being left with unlimited power, if malice, ambition or desire of change possess them ".[18]

This is not merely a question of making the judiciary independent of the executive : the Tudors and early Stuarts thought that the judges and all courts of law ought to be subordinate to the king and his Council. Moreover the bailiff and Royal Court were an executive as well as a judiciary body. The idea here is rather that both executive and administrative powers should be divided between two coordinate authorities. This scheme of establishing two distinct sets of offices with equal powers to balance each other is in its essence a confession of weakness. Elizabeth's Council saw no need of any one as an equipoise to the governor, because they had no doubt of their own power to control him whenever they thought it necessary, and they would not have dreamed of parting with any of their authority to a local aristocracy. The incident is typical on its small scale of the difficulties and uncertainties of a period of transition. The seventeenth century was beginning to be unwilling to accept the unquestioned supremacy of the king and his Council, and the sovereignty of Parliament was still in the future : men had not yet learned that a system of independent and equally balanced authorities will not work.

The following abbreviations have been used in the footnotes :—

Actes des Etats ... ...
(Guernsey)

Actes des Etats de l'Ile de Guernesey, 1605 —, (Guernsey, 1851 —)

Actes des Etats ... ...
(Jersey)

Actes des Etats de l'Ile de Jersey, 1524-1800, (Jersey, La Société Jersiaise, 1897-1917, in 19 fascicules).

Cal. Patent Rolls ...

Calendar of Patent Rolls (London, Stationery Office, 1891 —).

Cal. S.P. Dom. ... ...

Calendar of State Papers, Domestic (London, Stationery Office, 1856 —).

Chroniques (Syvret) ...

George S. Syvret, *Chroniques des Iles de Jersey, Guernesey, Auregny et Serk, auquel on a ajouté un abrégé historique des dites iles* (Guernsey, 1832).

de Schickler, *Eglises du refuge ... ...*

F. de Schickler, *Les Eglises du refuge en Angleterre,* 3 vols. (Paris, 1892).

Falle (ed. Durell) ...

Philip Falle, *An Account of the Island of Jersey,* ed. E. Durell (Jersey, 1837).

Heylyn, *Survey ... ...*

Peter Heylyn, *The Second Journey, containing A Survey of the Estate of the two Ilands of Guernezey and Jarsey, with the Isles appending* (being the second part, pp. 277 ff., of *A Full Relation of Two Journeys: The one into the Main-Land of France, the other into some of the adjacent Ilands,* London, 1656).

" Historical Documents "

A series of transcripts of documents drawn from the collections in the Public Record Office, the Greffe in Guernsey, etc. These transcriptions are kept in the Bailiff's Room, Royal Court, Guernsey.

H.M.C. Salisbury ...

Historical Manuscripts Commission, *Calendar of the Manuscripts of the Marquis of Salisbury at Hatfield House.*

Jersey Prison Board

Printed papers prepared in connection with the Jersey Prison Board Case, heard before the Privy Council in 1894. These papers, containing a large collection of historical documents relating to the Channel Islands, were not published, but copies may be found in the British Museum, the Bodleian, the London Library, and in the libraries of Jersey and Guernsey.

Le Geyt ... ...

Les manuscrits de Philippe le Geyt, Ecuyer, lieutenant-bailli de l'ile de Jersey, sur la Constitution, les lois et les usages de cette ile (4 vols., Jersey, 1846-7).

Le Quesne, *Constitutional History* ...

C. Le Quesne, *A Constitutional History of Jersey* (London, 1856).

L. and P. Henry VIII   *Letters and Papers, Foreign and Domestic, Henry VIII,* 21 vols. with addenda (London, Stationery Office, 1864-1932).

S.G. Trans. ... ...   La Société Guernesiaise (formerly " Guernsey Society of Natural Science and Local Research "), *Report and Transactions,* (Guernsey, 1882 —).

S.J. Bulletin ... ...   La Société Jersiaise, *Bulletin Annuel* (Jersey, 1875 —).

NOTES TO CHAPTER I.

1. On these survivals, see A. J. Eagleston, " Parliamentary Analogies from the Channel Islands," *History*, IX (1924), pp. 103-9; but it must be remembered that the reforms of 1948 in both Jersey and Guernsey have made far-reaching changes, and many of these analogies no longer apply to current practice.

2. Syvret, *Chroniques;* A. Mourant, *Chroniques de Jersey, 1585, par un auteur inconnu*, etc., Jersey, 1858; cf. A. J. Eagleston, " The Chroniques de Jersey in the light of contemporary documents," *S.J. Bulletin*, XIII (1936), pp. 37-62.

3. See Livy, VIII, 40; Cicero, *Brutus* 16, 62; Polybus VI, 54. The fragment preserved by Suetonius (Julius 6) of the speech delivered at his aunt's funeral, setting out the greatness and antiquity of the *gens Julianus* is not at all unlike some passages in the *Chroniques* (e.g. ch. III).

NOTES TO CHAPTER II.

1. In 1513 Lord Howard reported to Wolsey, " The Normans are bringing their goods to Guernsey for fear of the King's landing there, and say that if the English come and do not burn the country, base Normandy will yield to them " *(L. and P. Henry VIII,* 1, 2, no. 1907). The lieutenant governor of Guernsey reported to the same effect in 1543, see *ibid.,* XVIII, 2, no. 23. The Wars of Religion gave new life to the old idea. At one time the Huguenot leaders offered the province to Elizabeth; see Conyers Read, *Mr. Secretary Walsingham* (Oxford, 1925), 1, p. 245.

2. On this episode, see E. T. Nicolle, " L'occupation de Jersey par les Comtes de Maulevrier," *S. J. Bulletin,* IX, pp. 168-188; R. Lemprière, " L'occupation de Jersey par le Comte de Maulevrier ", *ibid.,* X, pp. 102-111; and A. J. Eagleston, " The Chroniques de Jersey in the light of contemporary documents," *ibid.,* XIII, pp. 38-40.

3. E. T. Nicolle, " The Capture of Sark by the French in 1549 " . . . . *S. J Bulletin,* X, pp. 157-173.

4. *S. J. Bulletin,* X, p. 137.

5. *L. and P. Henry VIII,* XVIII, 1, no. 915.

6. *Cal. Patent Rolls., 1467-1477,* p. 124. The text is printed in *Jersey Prison Board,* Attorney General's Memorandum, Appendix part II, pp. 172-3.

7. Confirmation Roll, 1 Henry VII, part 1, m. 12; printed in *Jersey Prison Board,* Attorney General's Memorandum, Appendix, part II, pp. 175-6.

8. *Dictionary of National Biography,* s.v. Harliston, Sir Richard.

9. See below, pp. 7-9.

10. *Rotuli Parliamentorum,* VI, pp. 397-8, 504.

11. E. T. Nicolle, *Mont Orgueil Castle* (Jersey, 1921), p. 38; Le Quesne, *Constitutional History,* pp. 125, 567-8.

12. His patent is dated 28 February, 1486 *(Cal. Patent Rolls, 1485-1494,* p. 80; cf. *ibid.,* p. 189).

13. If the story, given above, of Harliston's treasonable designs on the islands is true, the fact that de Carteret was his son-in-law may have lent some plausibility to the accusation.

14. Presumably Le Boutillier was provided with a plan.

15. Printed, in French, from an eighteenth century copy under the seal of the bailiwick of Jersey in *Jersey Prison Board,* Attorney General's Memorandum, Appendix part II, pp. 176-9.

16. Printed, in French, from an eighteenth-century copy under the seal of the bailiwick of Jersey in Jersey Prison Board, Attorney General's Appendix, part II, pp. 183-8.

17. *Cal. S. P. Dom. Addenda, 1580—1625,* pp. 632-3.

18. See the preface to *Actes de Etats (Jersey), 1524—1596.* " La Justice " is the regular name for the Royal Court in documents of this period.

19. *Actes des Etats (Jersey), 1524—1596,* pp. 11-14.

20. *Ibid.,* p. 24.

21. *Actes des Etats (Guernsey), 1605—1651,* pp. 42-3,

22. A very interesting summary of the functions of the States will be found in a document entitled " Description des îles particulièrement de celle de Jersey " drawn up in 1618 *(Cal. S.P. Dom. Addenda, 1580—1625,* pp. 565-6. It is a brief account of the insular constitution, and as it was submitted to the Council by the bailiff and his partisans, who were then in violent controversy with the governor as to the respective powers of the two offices, it certainly would not minimise the importance of the

States. " Cette assemblée ", it says, " se fait quand il est question de pourvoir à la place vacante de quelqu'un des jurés de la cour, ou bien quand il est question d'envoyer vers le Roi pour les affaires publiques de l'île, ou quand il est question de pourvoir à la sureté du pays quand il est menacé de quelque danger, ou quand il est question de lever quelque argent pour la necessité publique ". This is a very restricted list of functions for militant insular patriots to attribute to the chief assembly of the island

23. *Approbation des Lois, Coutumes et Usages de l'Ile de Guernesey.* (Guernsey, frequently reprinted).

24. *Cal. S.P. Dom. Addenda, 1580—1625,* p. 22 (no. 56).

25. It will be noted that the paper of 1618 quoted above does not mention legislation among the functions of the States of Jersey.

26. The Royal Commission of 1607 expressly ordered that the bailiff should give sentence in accordance with the majority of votes " without gainsaying or opposing himself against any jurat's opinion ".

NOTES TO CHAPTER III.

1. Overy was governor c. 1495 to 1500. *(S.J. Bulletin*, IV, p. 373; VI, p. 87). His patent is dated 6 November, 1499 *(Cal. Patent Rolls, 1494—1509,* p. 189), but he had held the office certainly since 1496 *(ibid.,* p. 88).

2. *Rapport des Commissiares envoyés à Jersey, l'an 7 du règne de Henri VIII,* Société Jersiaise, 1878.

3. Vaughan was governor from 1502 to 1532 *(S.J. Bulletin*, VI, pp. 87-9). Between the death of Overy (1500) and Vaughan's appointment, John Lemprière was governor of Jersey for two years. *(Ibid.,* V, pp. 310-313).

4. The Chronicler says that he killed the man in a " combat à mort ou à vie " and took his arms. This is an embroidery of the truth. What happened was that Sir James Parker questioned his right to joust, on the ground apparently that he was not entitled to arms. Vaughan produced a grant of arms from Garter, and the king ruled that it was valid and Vaughan entitled to joust. He killed Parker in the course— Holinshed says by accident — but did not take his arms. See Harleian MS. 4900, p. 17.

5. On Vaughan's misgovernment see the author's article in *S. J. Bulletin*, XIII (1936), pp. 43-8. Much of this chapter is based upon the report of the Commission of Inquiry held in 1515, the petitions of the people of Jersey sent to the Council in 1529 and the report of the commission of 1531. These are discussed with reference to the original documents in the author's article *ibid.,* XIII, pp. 43-8, 305-310; cf *ibid.,* VI, pp. 87-110.

6. *L. and P. Henry VIII*, I, no. 1829.

7. *Chroniques* (Syvret), p. 43.

8. For the contest between Vaughan and Helier de Carteret, see the author's article in *S. J. Bulletin*, XIII, pp. 48-53.

9. *S.J. Bulletin*, XIII, pp. 53-4.

10. *S. J. Bulletin*, VII, pp. 198-203.

11. Patent Roll, 16, Henry VIII, part I, m.38.

12. *Chroniques* (Syvret), pp. 53 ff.; *S.J. Bulletin*, XIII, pp. 53-4.

13. The Cardinal is obviously referring to the petition from the island mentioned above, but forgot that it was not sealed with the seal of the bailiwick. De Carteret with admirable courage and readiness seized on this point.

14. It is a curious detail, and one not likely to have been invented, that the Cardinal says ' thou ' to de Carteret all through the stormy scene in the Star Chamber, but changes to the respectful ' you ' here.

15. *S.J. Bulletin*, XIII, p. 51.

16. *Chroniques* (Syvret), pp. 52-3.

17. *S.J. Bulletin*, V, p. 79.

18. *S.J. Bulletin*, VI, pp. 87-110; XIII, pp. 43-8, 305-310.

19. *S.J. Bulletin*, XIII, pp. 51-2.

20. *L. and P., Henry VIII*, vol. III, part 2, no. 2677.

21. *H.M.C. Salisbury*, VI, p. 50.

22. *Chroniques* (Syvret), p. 14; *Jersey Prison Board*, Attorney General's Memorandum, Appendix, part II, pp. 163-167.

23. *L. and P. Henry VIII*, V, p. 638 (no. 1509).

24. Sir Anthony Ughtred, governor of Jersey, 1532-34 *(S. J. Bulletin*, IV, p. 374).

25. Sir Arthur Darcy, governor of Jersey, 1534-36 (*ibid*).

26. Lord Vaux, governor of Jersey, 1536-37 *(ibid*.

27. Edward Seymour, Earl of Hertford and later Duke of Somerset, governor of Jersey, 1537—1550 (*Ibid*., p. 375).

28. *Chroniques* (Syvret), pp. 65-7.

29. *Acts of the Privy Council*, N.S., I, pp. 400-1, 458; *L. and P. Henry VIII*, vol. XXI, part 1, no. 793; *Chroniques* (Syvret), p. 67.

30. *Chroniques* (Syvret), pp. 70, 71.

31. *Acts of the Privy Council*, N.S., I, pp. 554-5.

32. *Actes des Etats (Jersey)*, *1524—1596*, pp. 9-10.

33. He was sent there in 1539 as a commissioner to fortify the town and again in 1541 to inspect the defences.

34. Sir Hugh Paulet, governor of Jersey, 1550—1574 (*S.J. Bulletin*, IV, p. 375).

NOTES TO CHAPTER IV.

1. The Acts of 1534 (the Annates Act, Submission of Clergy and Restraint of Appeals Act, the Papal Dispensations Act and the two Acts of Succession) all applied to " this realm or any other the King's dominions " or to " any person subject or resident within this realm or elsewhere within any of the King's dominions ". The acts for the dissolution of the monasteries contain no limitation of places but simply grant to the King all monasteries of certain specified classes.

2. I have never seen any evidence that this was paid in the Channel Islands (Le P.).

3. *L. and P. Henry VIII*, XII, no. 473.

4. *S. J. Bulletin*, X, p. 326.

5. *Acts of the Privy Council*, N.S., II, p. 412.

6. *Cal. Patent Rolls, 1549-1551*, pp. 347-8.

7. *Chroniques* (Syvret), pp. 75-6.

8. *Cal. S.P. Dom. Addenda, 1547-65*, pp. 484-5.

9. A copy of their submission is preserved in " Historical Documents", II, pp. 174-5 : they " submit themselves to the Queen's Most Excellent Majesty, acknowledging their erroneous judgment as well against Katherine Cauchés and Guillemine and Perrotine her two daughters and the infant of the said Perrotine executed by fire for supposed heresy."

10. *Chroniques* (Syvret), pp. 77-78; cf. the act of the Royal Court printed in Le Quesne, *Constitutional History*, pp. 570-1 and *Cal. S.P. Dom. Addenda 1547-65*, pp. 498-9.

11. *Cal. S.P. Dom. Addenda, 1547-65*, p. 487.

12. *Ibid.*, p. 526.

13. *Ibid.*, pp. 558-9.

14. *L. and P. Henry VIII*, XVIII, part 2, no. 24.

15. *Cal. S.P. Dom. Addenda, 1547-65*, p. 529.

16. *Cal. S.P. Dom. Addenda, 1566-79*, pp. 13-14.

17. *S.G. Trans.*, XII, p. 510.

18. *Cal. S.P. Dom. Addenda, 1547-65*, pp. 513-4.

19. *Ibid.*, p. 526.

20. On this incident, see the author's paper " The Dismissal of the Seven Jurats in 1565," *S.G. Trans.*, XII, pp. 508-516.

21. *Recueil d'Ordonnances de la Cour Royale de l'Isle de Guernesey*, I (1852), pp. 18-19.

NOTES TO CHAPTER V.

1. *Cal. S.P. Dom. Addenda, 1547-65*, p. 529.

2. The text of this bull is printed in *Falle* (ed. Durell), pp. 232-241.

3. E. Dupont, *Histoire du Cotentin et de ses Iles* (Caen 1870-85), III, pp. 113-6 (there are some interesting indications here that the privilege may be older than the bull); see also the cases quoted in *Falle* (ed. Durell), p. 171.

4. *Chroniques* (ed. Syvret), p. 70.

5. *L. and P. Henry VIII*, XIX, part 1, nos. 20, 65.

6. *Cal. S.P. Dom. Addenda, 1566-79*, pp. 13-14 and cf. the governor's report in 1557, *ibid.*, *1547-65*, p. 454.

7. *L. ant P. Henry VIII*, IV, no. 4440.

8. *Ibid.*, XVIII, part 1, no. 915.

9. *Cal. Patent Rolls, 1558-1560*, p. 337; text (in English translation) in W. Berry, *History of the Island of Guernsey* (1815), pp. 324-7. The original is in the Guernsey Greffe.

10. *Falle* (ed. Durell), pp. 228-232.

11. *Cal. S.P. Dom. Addenda, 1566-79*, p. 554.

12. *Cal. S.P. Dom. Adddenda, 1580-1625*, p. 42.

13. On this incident, see the author's paper "Guernsey under Sir Thomas Leighton," *S.G. Trans.*, XIII, pp. 87-8 and references there given.

14. *Cal. S.P. Dom. Addenda, 1580-1625*, pp. 210-211.

15. Council letter of 11 June, 1587, in "Historical Documents", V, pp. 213-4.

16. It should be observed that Elizabeth's wars in France were not wars between two nations in the modern sense; in 1562 and again in 1591 English troops were supporting the Huguenot party in a civil war.

17. (E. Cleirac), *Us et coutumes de la Mer* (Rouen, 1671), p. 357. It appears that this work was first published at Bordeaux in 1647.

18. *Cal. S.P. Dom. Charles I, Addenda, 1625-1649*, pp. 210, 218.

19. Falle, *An Account cf the Isle of Jersey* (1694), p. 216; in Durell's edition, p. 172.

20. *Cal. S.P. Dom., Charles I, Addenda, 1625-1649*, p. 264.

21. *Ibid.*, pp. 221-2.

22. *Cal. S.P. Dom. Charles I, Addenda, 1625-1649*, p. 259 (no. 9).

23. *Ibid.*, p. 264.

24. It is noteworthy that the Order in Council (of 8 August, 1689) speaks of this as a provisional measure and is apologetic in tone :—"His majesty in council is this day pleased to declare that (being at this time strictly obliged in his treaties with his allies and confederates to prohibit in all his dominions all trade and commerce whatsoever with France) he does not think it fit or expedient to dispense with the execution of this said order in this present and extraordinary juncture of time; yet, it is not the intention of His Majesty in any manner whatsoever to revoke or infringe upon any privileges that may have been granted by his royal predecessors to the inhabitants of the said island of Guernsey." J. Duncan, *History of Guernsey* (London, 1841), pp. 229-230.

NOTES TO CHAPTER VI.

1. " Documents concerning the transfer of Ecclesiastical Jurisdiction over the Channel Islands from the See of Coutances to those of Salisbury and Winchester," *S.J. Bulletin*, V, pp. 251-265.   The bull quotes as a precedent the transfer of Calais from the diocese of Therouanne to that of Canterbury.

2. It is noteworthy, however, that this incumbent took the precaution of getting institution from the Bishop of Coutances also.

3. *State Papers, Henry VIII*, vol. IX (1848), pp. 18, 27.

4. *Ibid.*, p. 38.

5. *Acts of the Privy Council*, N.S. I, p. 13.

6. Acts of the Privy Council, N.S., VII, p. 213; *S.J. Bulletin*, V, pp. 259-264; Dupont, *Histoire du Cotentin et de ses Iles*, III, p. 443.

7. Note that the Pope's bull is quietly ignored and Henry VII's letter *(S.J. Bulletin*, V, pp. 255-6) treated as the operative document.

8. *S.J. Bulletin*, V, pp. 264-5.

9. *Cal. S.P. Dom. Addenda, 1580-1625*, pp. 20 (no. 49), 21 (no. 52).

10. The idea may have been reinforced by the fact that the Protestants were very strong in Normandy, and at one time made a more or less formal offer of it to Elizabeth.

11. *Institutes*, part 4. ch. 70.

12. *H. M. C. Salisbury*, vol. XIII, Addenda, p. 93.

13. *Falle* (ed. Durell), p. 195.

NOTES TO CHAPTER VII.

1. *Cal. S.P. Dom. Addenda, 1547-65*, pp. 498-9.

2. As early as 1548 the Royal Court of Jersey naturalised a French minister and provided for his support; see the Act of Court in *Falle* (ed. Durell), p. 436.

3. F. de Schickler, *Eglises du Refuge*, II, p. 441.

4. *Chroniques* (ed. Syvret), p. 98.

5. Dupont, *Histoire du Cotentin et de ses Iles*, III, p. 441.

6. *Chroniques* (ed. Syvet), p. 100.

7. *Falle* (ed. Durell), p. 195; cf. the letter to Paulet, *Cal. S.P. Dcm. Addenda, 1566-79*, pp. 29-30.

8. De Schickler, *Eglises du Refuge*, II, pp. 378-9.

9. *Discipline Ecclésiastique des Iles de la Manche, 1576 et 1597*, ed. G. E. Lee (Guernsey, 1885); de Schickler, *Eglises du Refuge*, II, p. 381; Heylyn, *Survey*, pp. 338 ff.

10. Charles II's charter to Rhode Island in 1663 allows a wide religious toleration on the express ground that the colony was too remote to make any breach of "the unity and uniformity established in this nation." See D. G. Ritchie, *Natural Rights* (1903), p. 201.

11. De Schickler, *Eglises du Refuge*, II, pp. 379-81, 391-4.

12. De Schickler, *Eglises du Refuge*, II, pp. 391-4, 411.

13. The *Discipline* has a curious provision for the first establihment of a consistory in a parish which had not had one before. The minister is to call in a suitable number of dignitaries and God-fearing jurats, " car les dits magistrats serviront non seulement de guide au peuple rude et mal exercé mais aussi de bride pour leur présence et authorité reprimer les tumultes et factions populaires."

14. De la Croix, *Jersey: ses Antiquités, ses Institutions, son histoire* (1859-61), III, p. 391. In 1576 several people were imprisoned for not taking the Sacrament (having presumably failed at the catechising), and were ordered not to be released till they could say the Commandments and the Lord's Prayer.

15. De Schickler, *Eglises du Refuge*, III, pp. 406-7.

16. E.g. two people who had been married in a Catholic church produced a certificate that they had made confession of their fault in a Reformed church in Brittany and been admitted to Communion. The colloque ordered that the certificate should be publicly read in church and that they should acknowledge the truth of it and ask pardon for the scandal. See de Schickler, *Eglises du Refuge*, II, p. 417.

17. *Ibid.*, p. 418.

18. *Cal. S.P. Dom. Addenda, 1580-1625*, p. 605.

19. Readers of *The Heart of Midlothian* will remember that when Jeannie Dean's husband was presented by the Duke of Argyle to a parish the Duke's representative on the spot disposed promptly and firmly of any doubts as to the harmony of the election. "As to its being an unanimous call, I wad be glad to ken what business the carles have to call onything or onybody but what the Duke and mysell likes . . . . Scruple! Deil any of them has been bred up to scruple onything that they're bidden to do."

20. De Schickler, *Eglises du Refuge*, II, pp. 442-3; III, 362-5.

21. See the instances *ibid.*, II, pp. 413-421.

22. "Historical Documents", V, 115-6.

NOTES TO CHAPTER VIII

1. See Saravia's account — *S.P. Dom. Addenda, 1547-65,* pp. 558-9.

2. *Cal. S.P. Dom. Addenda, 1547-65,* pp.454, 529.

3. *Cal. S.P. Dom. Addenda, 1547-65,* pp. 513-4.

4. *H.M.C. Salisbury,* vol. I, p. 295.

5. On this incident, see the author's paper " The Dismissal of the Seven Jurats," in *S.G. Trans.,* XII, pp. 508-16, where the document is printed.

6. Patent Rolls, 8 Elizabeth, part 9, mm. 27-9; the patent is dated 18 February, 1566.

7. *Cal. S.P. Dom. Addenda, 1566-79,* p. 15.

8. *Ibid.,* p. 26.

9. *Cal. S.P. Dom. Addenda, 1566-79,* pp. 44-5.

10. *Ibid.,* p. 301.

11. *Ibid.,* p. 45.

12. *Cal. S.P. Dom. Addenda, 1566-79,* p. 62.

13. *Ibid.,* p. 64.

14. *Ibid.,* pp. 62-4.

15. *Second Report of the Commissioners appointed to inquire into the State of the Criminal Law in the Channel Islands, Guernsey,* (1848), pp. 311-3.

16. On Leighton's governorship, see the author's paper " Guernsey under Sir Thomas Leighton, 1570-1610," *S.G. Trans.,* XIII, pp. 72-108. The documentation of much of what follows will be found in that article.

17. This can hardly be true. A note of 36 warrants given by the captain and dean to Effard and Carey for fortifications between September 1568 and November 1569 *(Cal. S.P. Dom. Addenda, 1566-79,* p. 130) shows that they had £527 and a balance of £62 was left in Chamberlain's name.

18. On this commission see Eagleston, *op. cit.,* pp. 75 ff. For the documents see *Cal. S.P. Dom. Addenda, 1566-79,* pp. 554, 562-3, 563-8, 569-570; *Acts of the Prviy Council,* N.S. XI, pp. 200-1, 325-6, 335-6. The report is preserved in the Chancery Miscellanea, bundle 10, no. 12.

19. I.e. Hamond.

20. The text of the October order is printed in *Jersey Prison Board,* Attorney General's Memorandum, Appendix, part III, pp. 915-7; cf. *Acts of the Privy Ccuncil,* N.S., XII, pp. 174-8, 196-7, 231.

21. *Cal. S.P. Dom. Addenda, 1580-1625,* p. 28.

22. I.e. unless the garrison were permanently kept on a war footing. In time of war or danger of war it was usual to tell off 300 men from the militia of the southern counties to garrison each of the islands.

23. *Acts of the Privy Council,* N.S. XIII, pp. 19, 69.

24. The order is printed in *Jersey Prison Board,* Attorney General's Memorandum, Appendix, part III, pp. 918-20; cf. *Acts of the Privy Council,* N.S., XIII, p. 143.

25. Cf. *Documents relatifs a l'Ile de Guernesey,* I (Guernsey, 1814), p. 17 (report of 1607).

26. *Ibid.,* pp. 11-12.

27. " To offer the Queen's wheat to sell is of no purpose, for they make full account to have it again for nothing."

28. *Cal. S.P. Dom. Addenda, 1580-1625,* pp. 98-9; *Approbation de Lois, Coutumes, et Usages de l'Ile de Guernesey* (frequently reprinted in Guernsey).

29. See T. Le Marchant, *Remarques et Animadversions sur l'Approbation des Lois* .. . ., Guernsey, 1828; and *Second Report cn the State of the Criminal Law in the Channel Islands, Guernsey*, pp. viii-x.

30. *Second Report*, p. xvii.

31. On this incident, see the author's paper " The Quarrel between the Ministers and the Civil Power, 1581-5," in *S.G. Trans.*, XII, pp. 480-490.

32. On this incident, see *S.G. Trans.*, XIII, pp. 88 ff.

33. Printed in F. B. Tupper, *History of Guernsey and its Bailiwick* (1876), pp. 174-5; cf. *S.G. Trans.*, XIII, p. 92.

34. *Acts of the Privy Council*, N.S. XXVIII, p. 421.

1. *Cal. S.P. Dom. Addenda, 1547-65*, p. 566.
2. "Allouent leur emprisonnement comme pour justes et raisonnables causes".
3. *Cal. S.P. Dom. Addenda, 1580-1625*, pp. 244—5; Cf. *Acts of the Privy Council*, N.S., XV, p. 335.
4. *Acts of the Privy Council*, N.S., XVII, pp. 162-3.
5. *Acts of the Privy Council*, N.S., XIX, pp. 137, 213-4.
6. *Ibid*, XX, p. 118.
7. Le Geyt, IV, pp. 236 ff.
8. Appended to the Report are depositions from ministers in the island, produced by Paulet, that de Carteret had raised a dangerous faction; Le Geyt, IV, pp. 255-6.
9. Le Geyt, IV, pp. 314-5.
10. Le Geyt, IV, pp. 236 ff.
11. Le Geyt, IV, pp. 327 ff.
12. That is, as to their legal validity; there is no doubt, of course, that they were actually made or that they are perfectly good historical evidence.
13. Le Geyt, IV, p. 263.
14. Cf. *Acts of the Privy Council*, N.S., XX, p. 288-9. The text of the Commission is printed in *Jersey Prison Board*, Attorney General's Memorandum, Appendix, part II, Supplemental Appendix, pp. i-vi.
15. "We have allso established and confirmed divers lawes according to the effect of this eighth article, with especiall saving to her Majesty, her heires and successors, of all rights, titles, royalties, jursidictions and preheminences" (Le Geyt, IV, p. 265). Le Geyt is clearly mistaken in doubting *(ibid.*, p. 493) whether the Commission actually referred to the bailiff's articles; he had apparently not seen the text of the Commission.
16. *Cal. S.P. Dom. Addenda, 1580-1625*, p. 591.
17. See Falle (ed. Durell), p. 383; Le Quesne, *Constitutional History of Jersey*, p. 215.
18. See Falle (ed. Durell), loc. cit., and for Guernsey, *Actes des Etats (Guernsey)*, I, pp. 26-7. On Raleigh's governorship in general, see *S.J. Bulletin*, IX, pp. 96-106.

NOTES TO CHAPTER X.

1. " Historical Documents " VIII, 70 ff.

2. *Cal. S.P. Dom. Addenda, 1580-1625*, p. 463 (no. 44).

3. Direct appointment by the king would only have protected island liberties in the negative sense of preventing the governor from putting in his own man : under the conditions of the seventeenth century it would merely have meant throwing the office open to competition among place-hunting courtiers. The islanders no doubt understood this as their petition ("Historical Documents," VIII, 70 ff) asked that the Bailiff should be elected by the governor and States, and their nomination confirmed by the king. Nothing is said in the Order in Council about this part of the scheme : it was evidently too audacious a conception for James I's Council.

4. This right of visit and inspection is expressly mentioned in the Précepte d'Assize, (Sir Havilland de Sausmarez, *The Extentes of Guernsey*, La Société Guernesiaise, 1934, pp. 135-6).

5 *Actes des Etats (Guernsey)*, I, pp. 1 ff.

6. " Historical Documents," VIII, 114-6.

7. The Commission and the report of the commissioners are printed in *Documens relatifs à l'Ile de Guernesey*, in two parts, Guernsey, 1814. The report gives the complaints brought before the commissioners set out in articles, each article being followed by the finding of the commissioners on it.

8. *Documens relatifs à l'Ile de Guernesey*, part 2, p. 71.

9. *Documens relatifs à l'Ile de Guernesey*, part 1, pp. 5, 57-8. The second of these cases is noteworthy as showing that the Royal Court did not object to imprisonment by the governor as such, but only to his doing it without their knowledge and assent. In this case the douzaine of the parish had been imprisoned and kept in irons by the governor on the complaint of the Royal Court that they would not pay their contribution to the upkeep of the pier.

10. *Documens relatifs à l'Ile de Guernesey*, part 1, p. 20. Leighton was a great game preserver. In a private letter (1581) to the earl of Leicester he asked for a falcon to kill his pheasants " which are in infinite number " (*Cal. S.P. Dom. Addenda 1580-1625*, p. 41 (no. -3).

11. See above, pp. 87-8.

12. *Documens relatifs à l'Ile de Guernesey*, part 1, p. 13.

13. *Ibid.*, p. 18.

NOTES TO CHAPTER XI.

1. *H. M. C. Salisbury*, XV, p.174.

2. See above, pp. 102-3, for the remarkable effect of these letters in producing common action by the two islands.

3. The report does not appear ever to have been printed in its entirety. There are extracts printed in *Jersey Prison Board*, Attorney General's Memorandum, Appendix, part II, pp. 284-6. The commission is printed *ibid.*, pp. 281-4, and a letter from the Council (30 June, 1608) approving the Commissioners' orders (*ibid.*, pp. 286-7). Cf. *Falle* (ed. Durell), p. 358 and the full summary of the proceedings in Le Quesne, *Constitutional History of Jersey*, pp. 223-241.

4. *Cal. S.P. Dcm. Addenda, 1580-1625*, p. 499.

5. Le Quesne, *Constitutional History of Jersey*, pp. 165-6.

6. The Commissioners of 1617 said they thought " the bailiff's violences are rather in words to keep up his authority than in act to oppress justice, believing of him even by the testimony of his enemies to be very sincere in the execution of justice" (*Cal. Dom. Addenda, 1580-1625*, pp. 582-3 (no. 47).

7. See for instance the oath taken by Hostes Nicolle in 1561 (*Actes des Etats, Jersey*, 1524-1596, pp. 29-31; cf. *Cal. S.P. Dom. Addenda, 1580-1625*, p. 548.

8. Sir Havilland de Sausmarez, *The Extentes of Guernsey* . . . . . La Société Guernesiaise, 1934), pp. 136, 148.

9. *Jersey Prison Board*, Attorney General's Memorandum, Appendix, part II, pp. 183, 188.

10. *Cal. S.P. Dom, Addenda. 1625-49*, p. 119 (no. 99).

11. See Hérault's letter of 18 March, 1615 (summarized in *Cal. S.P. Dom. Addenda, 1580-1625*, pp. 550-1) — " Il a été nourri et elevé aux seminaires d'Espagne ou il a appris des maximes fort pernicieuses qu'il retient encore. A raison de quoi et pour ce qu'il avait refusé de rendre raison de sa foi aux ministres de cette ile et de retracter quelques propos qu'il avait tenus contre l'honneur de Dieu et qu'il ne recevait pas le sacrament de la Cêne, le bailli mon dernier predecesseur et les justiciers s'opposèrent formellement à son admission en la dite place et protestèrent à l'encontre ".

12. [Possibly he was doing much the same as his contemporaries, the common lawyers, were doing in England on the strength of a few old documents such as Magna Carta—Le P.]

13. *Cal. S.P. Dom. Addenda, 1580-1625*, pp. 550 ff.

14. *Jersey Prison Board*, Attorney General's Memorandum, Appendix, part II, pp. 185, 190.

15. Le Quesne, *Constitutional History of Jersey*, p. 248.

16. *Acts of the Privy Council*, N.S., *1613-14*, pp. 604-5, 621-2 ; Le Quesne, *Constitutional History*, p. 259.

17. Le Quesne, *Constitutional History*, pp. 259-60.

18. *Cal. S.P. Dom. Addenda, 1580-1625*, pp. 550-1 (text, in part, printed in *Jersey Prison Board*, Attorney General's Memorandum, Appendix part II, pp. 301-5).

19. *Cal. S.P. Dom. Addenda, 1580-1625*, p. 552 (no. 86).

20. *Ibid.*, p. 551 ; *Jersey Prison Board*, Attorney General's Memorandum, Appendix, part II, p. 303.

21. *Cal. S.P. Dom. Addenda, 1580-1625*, p. 550 ; *Jersey Prison Board*, Crown Appendix II, p. 295.

22. *Cal. S.P. Dom. Addenda, 1580-1625*, p. 546.

23. *Ibid.*, pp. 546-7.

24. *Cal. S.P. Dom. Addenda, 1580-1625,* pp. 550-1; *Jersey Prison Board,* Attorney General's Memorandum, Appendix, part II, pp. 301-5.

25. *Cal. S.P. Dom. Addenda, 1580-1625,* p. 555 (no. 92).

26. *Ibid* (no. 93); *Jersey Prison Board,* Attorney General's Memorandum, Appendix II, pp. 312-3.

27. *Cal. S.P. Dom Addenda, 1580-1625,* pp. 564-583; Le Quesne, *Constitutional History,* pp. 269 ff; *Jersey Prison Board,* Attorney General's Memorandum, Appendix, part II, pp. 331-7.

28. As Peyton said in an earlier report on the defences, " it has ever been usual for the Sovereign and Council of State, to whom intelligence of wars and dangers are first known, to signifie their pleasure to the Governors, and to order the sending thither pinnaces and soldiers, as the islanders cannot make sufficient resistance " (*Cal. S.P. Dom. Addenda, 1580-1625,* p. 531. This has a curious likeness, on a small scale, to the discussions about the liability of England to invasion before 1914.

29. Considering that Maret after his appearance before the Council went back to the island and impudently denied in the face of the secretary of state's letter to the bailiff that the Council had given any decision in his case, it is not surprising that the Royal Court sent him to prison or that Hérault described him as " hautain, proterve et présumptueux ".

30. *Jersey Prison Board,* Attorney General's Memorandum, Appendix, part II, pp. 333-7; Le Quesne, *Constitutional History,* pp. 281-3.

31. See below, chapter XII.

32. In 1624 Peyton mournfully reported :" My salary is £400 a year less than former governors had, I have sold land worth £400 year, and am still £4,000 in debt. I have nine grandchildren to provide for ": (*Cal. S.P. Dom. Addenda, 1580-1625,* p. 662.

33. *Cal. S.P. Dom. Addenda, 1580-1625,* pp. 622-3.

34. *Ibid.,* p. 625.

35. See Peyton's report to the Council, 19 July, 1620 (*Cal. S.P. Dom. Addenda, 1580-1625,* p. 626), and Hérault's own account of his action (*ibid.,* pp. 646-7).

36. See Maret's letters of 1617 (*ibid.,* pp. 580-1); *Acts of the Privy Council, 1619-21,* p. 395.

37. *Cal. S.P. Dom. Addenda, 1580-1625,* pp. 652-3, 671 (no. 81).

38. *Ibid.,* p. 635 (no. 57).

39. *Ibid.,* pp. 652-3 (no. 6). Apparently he was afraid that Peyton would refuse to pay a pension to him as well as a salary to the new bailiff. There seems to have been some negotiation over the amount, as Hérault says (ibid,, p. 671, no. 81), that he refused a pension of £40.

40. *Acts of the Privy Council,* N.S., *1619-21,* p. 395.

41. *Ibid., 1621-3,* p. 213.

42. *Cal. S.P. Dom. Addenda, 1580-1625,* p. 662 (no. 48). Probably Parkhurst was the unnamed office-seeker referred to in de Carteret's letter of 20 March, 1621 (*ibid.,* pp. 632-5). De Carteret (who wanted the post himself) warned the secretary of state against the appointment of an Englishman who could not know the language of Jersey law and procedure " hardly known to ourselves; and if he thinks to exercise it wholly by deputy, and not to make the greatest part of his residence here, it can be but a very ill precedent ".

43. *Cal. S.P. Dom. Addenda, 1580-1625,* p. 671 (no. 81).

44. *Ibid.,* p. 670 (nos. 79, 80).

45. *Ibid,* pp. 665 (no. 56), 673 (no. 91).

46. Le Geyt, IV, p. 32.

NOTES TO CHAPTER XII.

1. Heylyn, *Survey*, p. 379.

2. How this might work in practice will appear from the fact that in 1595 an English Presbyterian, one Snape, was made chaplain to the castle and was received by the Colloque on testimonials from "the churches of the province of Northamptonshire ', i.e. non-conformist bodies which were under the ban of the English government (de Schickler, *Eglises du refuge*, II, p. 447 ; cf. *ibid.*, p. 462, and Le Quesne, *Constitutional History*, p. 165.

3. P. Heylyn, *Aerius Redivivus* (1672), pp. 389-390.

4. *Cal. S.P. Dom. Addenda, 1580-1625*, p. 529 (no. 14).

5. De Schickler, *Eglises du refuge*, II, pp. 469 ff.

6. This appeal is printed in Le Quesne, *Constitutional History*, pp. 573-4.

7. *Ibid.*, pp. 574-5.

8. Le Quesne, *Constitutional History*, pp. 167-171 ; Heylyn, *Survey*, pp. 384 ff ; de Schickler, *Eglises du refuge*, II, pp. 475 ff.

9. *Acts of the Privy Council*, N.S., *1613-1614*, pp. 454-5.

10. De Schickler, *Eglises du refuge*, II, p. 479.

11. *Jersey Prison Board*, Crown Appendix II, pp. 185, 190.

12. Heylyn, *Survey*, pp. 385-6.

13. *Cal. S.P. Dom. Addenda, 1580-1625*, p. 602.

14. *Ibid*, pp. 588-9.

15. *Ibid.*, pp. 606-9.

16. See Bandinell's letter to the secretary of state, *ibid.*, p. 600.

17. *Ibid.*, pp. 609-10 (6 March, 1619).

18. *Ibid.*, p 609.

19. *Ibid.*, p 62.

20. *Ibid.*, pp. 604-6.

21. Le Geyt, IV, p. 262.

22. *Cal S.P. Dom. Addenda, 1580-1625*, pp. 609-610.

23. *Ibid.*, p. 610.

24. *Ibid.*, p. 618.

25. *Ibid.*, p. 621 (a private letter of Bird to Conway).

26. *Ibid.*, p. 624.

27. *Ibid.*, pp. 622-4.

28. See the full report of this meeting, *ibid.*, pp. 622-3, and compare Bandinell's account, *ibid.*, 623-4.

29. *Ibid.*, p. 625.

30. *Ibid.*, p. 626.

31. This was no doubt de la Place, " who much impatient (as commonly the miscarrying of our hopes much torments us, as the loss of a possession) to see himself deluded, forsook the Countrey " (Heylyn, *Survey*, p. 389). He retired to Guernsey " where he became a determined leader of Presbyterianism" (Le Quesne, *Constitutional History*, p. 172).

32. The Canons are printed in Falle (ed. Durell), pp. 245-262, and in Heylyn, *Survey*, pp. 390-411. Cf. *Cal. S.P. Dom. Addenda, 1580-1625*, pp. 654-5.

33. De Schickler, *Eglises du refuge*, II, pp. 484 ff.

34. On de la Marche, see his diary and an account of his life and of the Presbyterian system in Guernsey by T. W. M. de Guérin and W. Rolleston, in *S.G. Trans.*, XI, pp. 193-236.

35. Tupper, *History of Guernsey* (1876), pp. 226-7. *Cal. S.P. Dom. Addenda, 1625-49*, p. 556. Danby expressly says that King James "was then satisfied with these reasons and would not suffer any alteration to be made ".

36 Heylyn says the Government meant to deal with Guernsey after Jersey was settled, but were prevented by the distraction first caused by the breach with Spain and then by the French War (*Survey*, pp. 412 ff.).

37. Was this Heylyn himself?—Heylyn, *Cyprianus Anglicus* (1668), p, 357.

38. *Cal. S.P. Dom. Addenda 1625-49*, pp. 537 (no. 67).

39. Ibid., p. 556; Tupper, *History of Guernsey* (1876), pp. 226-7.

40. Schickler, *Eglises de refuge*, II, p. 497.

41. *Cal. S.P. Dom., 1633-4*, p. 262 (no. 15).

42. *Ibid.*, p. 288 (no. 60).

43. See his memorandum in Tupper, *History of Guernsey* (1876), pp. 226-7; *Cal. S.P. Dom. Addenda, 1625-49*, p. 556.

44. *Cal. S.P. Dom. Addenda, 1625-49*, p. 195.

45. Heylyn, *Survey*, p. 383.

46. E.g. *Cal. S.P. Dom. Addenda, 1580-1625*, pp. 550-1.

47. *Cal. S.P. Dom. Addenda, 1580-1625*, p. 671 (no. 81).

48. *Ibid*, pp. 624-5.

49. The Venetian ambassador, an astute and impartial observer, told his government that Laud had "desired to govern London as though it had been a college or a religious house ". Horatio Brown, *Studies in the History of Venice* (1907), II, p. 307.

NOTES TO CHAPTER XIII.

1. *Cal. S.P. Dom. Addenda,1625-49*, p. 104 (no. 41).

2. *Actes des Etats (Guernsey)*, I, pp. 94-5.

3. *Cal. S.P. Dom. Addenda, 1625-49*, p. 328. The peer of France was apparently M. de Thoiras who had defended the Ile de Rhé against Buckingham, and was made a Marshal of France. See *Actes des Etats (Guernsey)*, I, p. 139.

4. *Cal. S.P. Dom. Addenda, 1625-49*, pp. 278 (no. 67), 279 (no. 71), 285-6 (no. 92).

5. *Ibid.*, pp. 349 (no. 83), 350 (no. 88).

6. *Ibid.*, pp. 295 (no. 18), 324 (no. 130).

7. See the documents in *Actes des Etats (Guernsey)*, I, pp. 105-122.

8. *Cal. S.P. Dom. Addenda, 1625-49*, p. 375.

9. *Ibid.*, p. 377 (no. 58).

10. *Ibid.*, p. 379 (no. 63).

1. *Documens relatifs à l'Ile de Guernesey* (1814) part 1, p. 7.

2. *Cal. S.P. Dom. Addenda, 1580-1625*, p. 499 (no. 22).

3. Above, pp. 38-9.

4. *Cal. S.P. Dom. Addenda, 1580-1625*, pp. 29-30 (no. 72).

5. *H.M.C. Salisbury*, VI, p. 50; *Acts of the Privy Council,* N.S. XXI, p. 296.

6. Iliad, I, 238; IX, 99. [It might be more apt to compare the jurats with the lawmen of certain Danelaw boroughs at the time of Domesday or the *schöffen* of medieval Germany, to whom they are historically related. They were, and still are, an almost unique survival of a characteristically medieval legal institution. Cf. Le Patourel, *The Medieval Administration of the Channel Islands* (1937), p. 116.—Le P.]

7. [Compare the precisely similar complaints of Otto de Grandison in the fourteenth century, *Ancient Petitions of the Chancery and the Exchequer* (Société Jersiaise, 1902), pp. 21-3,—Le P.]

8. *Cal. S.P. Dom. Addenda, 1580-1625*, pp. 2-3, 8 (no. 20).

9. [As the justices itinerant had been defeated in the fourteenth century. But it would be interesting to know how English judges of the early seventeenth century would have reacted to a demand, from the outside, that they should codify the common law.—Le P.]

10. *Cal. S.P. Dom. Addenda, 1580-1625*, p. 596 (no. 80).

11. *Cal. S.P. Dom. Addenda,1547-65*, p. 529.

12. *H.M.C. Salisbury*, III, p. 225.

13. I append a few instances showing what sort of powers the governor exercised either on his own initiative or by order of the Council. In 1546 Lord Hertford sent a peremptory letter to the States of Jersey complaining of the neglect of some of the inhabitants to contribute to the costs of defence and ordering them to establish a guard at St. Aubin, and "together with my lieutenant" to raise the cost of the guard from the parishes : if any one refused to pay, the Royal Court was directed to imprison him until he had paid, and had also received such other punishment as might be a terror to others (*Actes des Etats, Jersey*), *1524-1596*, pp. 14-16). In 1543 the lieutenant governor of Jersey was ordered by royal letters to punish " such as shall be vant parlers and will by any means withstand or let the setting forwardness of any such things as may be to the benefit and preservations of our said isle " (*L. and P. Henry VIII*, XVIII, part 2, p. 80). Directions to the governor to supervise the action of the Royal Court are frequently to be found on the Council Register. Thus in May 1580 the governor of Guernsey was instructed to call the bailiff before him and examine him as to the complaint of one Overy about detention of tithe deeds. If the complaint proves to be true, he is to command the baili ffin their Lordships' name to restore the deeds and do justice, and to report to Council so that order may be given for the punishment of the bailiff if he has acted unjustly. On 13 June orders were sent to "the Captain, Bailiff and Jurats " for a rehearsing of Overy's case, the bailiff and those jurats who were parties to the case not to sit, but the captain to act with the other jurats. Again on 15 August of the same year, on complaint of one Elton that he could get no justice from the bailiff, the governor was ordered to call both parties before him and try to bring them to agreement, reporting to Council if they would not agree. Closely akin to this is a Jersey case in which the governor was directed to enforce arbitration, himself and three representatives of each side to be arbitrators (16 April, 1582). Finally it may be noted that the Order in Council of 28 August, 1580, as to the complaints of the Guernsey

people (*Acts of the Privy Council*, N.S., XII, pp. 174-8) contains two remarkable provisions : the captain is directed to see that the fees taken by the Royal Court are ordered according to the ' Précepte d'Assize ' (art. 9), and that all exaction of taxes extraordinarily imposed by the Royal Court is redressed (art. 14).

14. *Acts of the Privy Council*, N.S. XV, pp. 379-82. London air seems to have had an inflammatory effect on island tempers. When Nicholas Carey was up in connection with the lawsuit mentioned above he met one of the other side at Charing Cross on his way back to the Star Chamber, and according to the latter's petition Carey " after many infamous words did strike your said orator with his fist on the face and with great oaths swore that he would cut off the ears of your said poor orator, and was about to draw his dagger to execute his evil purpose had not your orator presently escaped his fury " (*Cal. S.P. Dom. Addenda, 1580-1625*, p. 8 (no 22).

15. *H.M.C. Salisbury*, vol. XIII, Addenda, p. 93.

16. Dated 1592. It is printed in Conyers Reade, *Mr. Secretary Walsingham* (1925), I, p. 426.

17. British Museum, Lansdowne, MS., 143, fo. 387.

18. *Cal. S.P. Dom. Addenda, 1580-1625*, pp. 582-3 (no. 47). This passage is quoted in Le Quesne, *Constitutional History*, p. 263.

Index

186

Episcopacy (in Scotland), 132.
Essex, Earl of, 72.
Excommunication, 43, 61, 62, 65, 140. See also Penalties.
Extente, 74, 81, 101, 104.

Falle, Philip, 47.
Fellowships (at Oxford), 142.
Flanders, 7, 44, 45, 46.
Fleet prison, 24, 33.
Fleming, Thomas, 74.
Foreign ships, 66, 79, 80.
  ,,   wives, 106.
Fortifications, 11, 28, 37, 66, 68-72, 74, 101, 104, 105, 107, 123, 146, 148, 154.
  ,,   warrants for, 175 note 17.
Foster, Richard, 27.
Fox, Richard (bishop of Bath and Wells), 8.
Foxe, John (martyrologist), 37.
Franciscans (observant), 35.
French Reformed Church, 55, 56, 59, 129, 131, 132, 141.
  ,,   landing, 39, 66.
  ,,   driven out, 5.
  ,,   forbid trade, 47.
  ,,   occupation of Sark, 5, 6, 66.
  ,,   occupation of Jersey, 5, 6, 9, 21, 22, 28, 167, note 2.
  ,,   Politiques, 143.
  ,,   Refugees, 37, 55, 60, 84.
  ,,   ministers, 174 note 2.
  ,,   ships seized, 44, 45.
Frontier fortresses, 5, 10, 11, 12, 28, 66, 68-72, 74, 101, 104, 108, 129, 141, 146, 160.

Gallais, see Le Gallais.
Gardiner, Sir R., 103, 104, 111.
Garrisons, 10, 28, 31, 33, 47, 120, 121, 129.
  ,,   billeting of, 147.
  ,,   of Castle, Guernsey, 10.
  ,,   ,,   Jersey, 28, 33, 116, 119, 120, 121, 124, 147.
  ,,   from England, 10, 12, 31, 33, 47, 147, 148, 175 note 22.
  ,,   payment of, 10, 73, 80, 147.
  ,,   quarrels with Islanders, 148, 149.
Generality, 14, 43, 89, see States.
Geneva, 38, 54-56, 58, 62, 72, 82, 83, 90, 91, 132, 142.
Gibraltar, 10.
Gosselin, Helier, 41.

Governor, of Guernsey, 1, 10-12, 16, 31, 36, 37, 39-41, 45, 46, 53, 56-60, 62, 64, 68-72, 74, 75-80, 82-6, 88, 89, 100-8, 147, 149, 153-6, 159, 160, 161, 163, 178 notes 3, 9, 180 note 28, 184 note 13. See Carew, Chamberlain, Danby, de Carteret (Amias), Leighton.
  ,,   of Jersey, 1, 6, 7, 9-13, 16, 21, 29, 30, 31, 33, 34, 36, 46, 56-60, 62, 90, 92, 93, 96-98, 109-127, 130, 133, 137, 142-4, 146-150, 153-6, 158-163, 167, note 22, 180 note 28, 184-5, note 13. See Baker, Darcy, Harliston, Overy, Paulet (Amyas), Paulet (Antony), Paulet (Hugh), Peyton, Raleigh, Somerset, Vaughan, Vaux, Ughtred.
  ,,   See Captain.
Grand Coutumier, 114.
Greffe, 123.
Greffier, 113, 114, 115.
Grindal, 57. See Canterbury.
Guille, James, 157.
Gunners, 101, 105, 120, 122.

Hamond, John, 74.
Hampton Court Conference, 129.
Harliston, Richard, 5-8, 167 note 13.
Harry Tothill, 26. See Payn.
Henry III, king of France, 142.
Henry IV, king of France, 72.
Henry V, king of England, 5, 35, 36, 66.
Henry VII, king of England, 2, 5, 6, 7, 8, 9, 15, 17, 32, 49, 51, 116, 137, 153, 173 note 7.
  ,,   ordinances of, see Ordinances.
Henry VIII, king of England, 1, 17, 36, 37, 49, 66.
Hérault, Jean, 103, 104, 108-127, 133, 135, 136, 137, 143, 144, 146, 151, 155, 161, 162, 179 notes 6, 11, 12; 180 notes 29, 39.
Herbert, Sir John, 131.
Hertford, Earl of, see Somerset.
Heylyn, Peter, 109, 129, 133, 141, 142, 143, 182 notes 36, 37.
Holland, 109.
Home, Robert, 58.
Howard, Lord, 167 note 1.

190

191